Freedom Without Responsibility

BRUCE N. WALLER

Freedom

Without

Responsibility

TEMPLE UNIVERSITY PRESS
Philadelphia

Temple University Press, Philadelphia 19122
Copyright © 1990 by Temple University. All rights reserved
Published 1990
Printed in the United States of America

The paper used in this publication meets the minimum
requirements of American National Standard for Information
Sciences—Permanence of Paper for Printed Library Materials,
ANSI Z39.48-1984 ⊗

Library of Congress Cataloging-in-Publication Data

Waller, Bruce N., 1946–
Freedom without responsibility / Bruce N. Waller.
p.   cm.
ISBN 0-87722-716-0 (alk. paper)
1. Responsibility.   2. Free will and determinism.   I. Title.
BJ1451.W28   1990
123'.5—dc20   89-48481
CIP

For
Russell Lawrence Waller
and
Adam Norris Waller

CONTENTS

ACKNOWLEDGMENTS ix

ONE
Introduction: No-Fault Naturalism 3

TWO
Two Views of Free Will 7

THREE
Individual Freedom Without Moral Responsibility 27

FOUR
The Value of Freedom Without Moral Responsibility 51

FIVE
Responsibility: The Nonmoral Varieties 63

SIX
Self-Making and Its Limits 77

SEVEN
Why the Best Efforts Cannot Support
Moral Responsibility 89

EIGHT
Nonjust Deserts 109

NINE
Racing Luck and Just Deserts 121

CONTENTS

TEN

Denying Moral Responsibility and Enhancing
Moral Behavior   129

ELEVEN

The Radical Denial of Moral Responsibility   141

TWELVE

Morality Without Moral Responsibility   151

THIRTEEN

Rejecting Responsibility, Preserving Freedom   175

FOURTEEN

No-Fault Naturalist Freedom   195

NOTES   205

BIBLIOGRAPHY   223

INDEX   233

ACKNOWLEDGMENTS

Many people shaped, challenged, and sharpened my ideas about free will and moral responsibility. My friend and colleague John G. Sullivan was a generous source of insights and encouragement. Frequent conversations with faculty and students at Elon College kept my thoughts on this subject churning and changing, and I particularly benefited from talking with Lamar Bland, Jan Boxill, James Coley, Russell Gill, Barbara Gordon, Tom Henricks, Bryan Hilliard, Jim Pace, Jim Pickens, Barbara Plumblee, Anne Ponder, Martha Smith, and Rudy Zarzar. George N. Schlesinger offered sound advice, kind encouragement, and incisive questions. George Graham helped immeasurably in exploring the psychological issues and pushed me to think harder and better about a number of related questions. E. M. Adams heightened my awareness of the profound social importance of these traditional philosophical problems. Terry Moore often showed me new and enlightening perspectives. In addition, it should be obvious that those philosophers whose work I criticize are also among those from whom I gained the most.

A number of people helped in special ways. Teresa LePors, with her wonderful powers for locating obscure sources, was invaluable. Jane Cullen, at Temple University Press, was generous with encouragement and guidance, and also found two excellent anonymous referees whose suggestions and criticisms were quite useful. In her remarkable copy-editing work Doris Braendel not only corrected numerous errors but also straightened out a number of twisted and cumbersome sentences. Richard Gilbertie, the production editor, skillfully and efficiently shepherded the manuscript through all the tricky turns leading to publication.

My new colleagues at Youngstown State University provided the encouragement that sustained me through the final stages, and their extraordinary generosity to my entire family in helping us with all the tasks of moving—finding a home, discovering new playgrounds and playmates, selecting a pediatrician—transformed the moving process from overwhelming to almost pleasant, and gave me opportunity to complete the final, time-consuming details of the book. The warm welcome we received from many people in Youngstown, in particular from Tom Shipka and Chris Bache and their families, is deeply appreciated.

Finally, thanks to my mother-in-law, Rose Newell, for her frequent and friendly encouragement, and to my wife, Mary, for the many discussions we had of this subject (especially its social implications and its relation to issues in psychology) and for her constant warm support.

Any virtues of this book are entirely the product of my fortunate social environment; however, those delightful people who make up that environment deserve no credit. The many defects of the book are the result of my intractable obstinacy, for which I deserve no blame.

Several sections of this book are based on earlier papers. Thanks to the editors of *Analysis, Behaviorism, The Journal for the Theory of Social Behaviour, Metaphilosophy, New Ideas in Psychology*, and *The Southern Journal of Philosophy* for permission to draw upon articles published in those journals.

Freedom Without Responsibility

CHAPTER ONE

Introduction:
No-Fault Naturalism

"Is DETERMINISM COMPATIBLE with free will and moral responsibility?" For centuries philosophers have argued the merits of compatibilism (determinism is compatible with free will and moral responsibility) versus incompatibilism (determinism is incompatible with free will and moral responsibility). Unfortunately, that debate has swirled around an insidiously loaded question. When debating whether determinism is "compatible with free will and moral responsibility," both compatibilists (who answer affirmatively) and incompatibilists (who answer negatively) assume that free will and moral responsibility are linked together—that if determinism is compatible with one it must also be compatible with the other. That entrenched assumption has muddled compatibilist/incompatibilist debates in two critical ways. First, arguments to prove that free will is compatible with determinism are thought to establish that moral responsibility is also compatible with determinism; and, second, arguments against the compatibility of moral responsibility with determinism (or naturalism) have been misinterpreted as denials of compatibilist free will. But in fact the question of whether determinism leaves room for free will is quite different from the ques-

3

tion of whether determinism is compatible with moral responsibility. By distinguishing those issues it is possible to preserve a notion of naturalist-determinist free will that satisfies what we actually want from free will while also insisting that moral responsibility *cannot* coexist with determinism.

THE TRADITIONAL QUESTION—"Is determinism compatible with free will and moral responsibility?"—confuses the issue at another important point. As Thomas Nagel notes in *The View from Nowhere*, the contemporary problem of free will and moral responsibility stems from naturalism rather than determinism: "The essential source of the problem is a view of persons and their actions as part of the order of nature, causally determined or not" (1986, p. 110). Thus the question is not really whether *determinism* threatens free will and/or moral responsibility; rather, the issue is: when miracles and souls and nonnatural forces are banished from the world, and we acknowledge that humans are fully products of and participants in a naturalist-mechanist world, can we still make legitimate claims and ascriptions of freedom and/or moral responsibility? Even if—as may be the case—determinism is not strictly true, and some micro-events are genuinely random, that will have no bearing on the questions here being examined: are free will and/or moral responsibility viable in our natural (nonmiraculous) world?

The position being championed in this book is that our contemporary, nonmiraculous, naturalist (determinist) world system leaves no room for moral responsibility—though it leaves quite adequate space for individual freedom. This position denies the traditional connection between freedom and moral responsibility, and thus it does not fit into any of the three traditional categories (libertarian, soft determinist, hard determinist) on the issues of determinism (or naturalism), free will, and moral responsibility. Libertarians believe that determinism is incompatible with freedom and moral responsibility, but that determinism is false (we have a special, nondetermined, contracausal, nonnatural free will) and thus we are both free and morally responsible. Soft determinists (often called compatibilists) maintain that determinism (or at least naturalism) is true, but that it is compatible with human free will and moral responsibility. Hard determinists hold that determinism (naturalism) is certainly true, that it is fundamentally incompatible with free will and moral responsibility, and thus we are neither free nor morally responsible. The position taken here differs significantly from all the above. It is obviously not libertarian (since it is strictly naturalist-determinist and asserts the compatibility of individual freedom with naturalism-determinism). It is not soft determinist, since it vehemently denies that moral responsibility can be accommodated within a naturalist-determinist framework. And it is certainly not hard determinist: "hard determinism" usually designates a position asserting that *both* freedom and moral responsibility are incompatible with determinism (or naturalism); but the goal of this book is to drive a wedge between freedom and moral responsibility, affirming the former and denying the latter.

Since the position taken here departs from the traditional categories of "libertarian," "soft determinist," and "hard determinist," it would be convenient to give it a special label. "No-fault naturalism" seems a useful tag, for a couple of reasons. First, it places the focus on *naturalism* (rather than determinism). Second, the phrase "no-fault naturalism" will be a reminder that it is *moral responsibility*—not free will—that is incompatible with *naturalism* (and determinism). No-fault naturalism is the view that our natural world is quite compatible with individual free will but is fundamentally incompatible with moral responsibility. It insists that individuals can be and often are free, but denies that anyone is ever morally responsible: no one ever justly deserves blame, praise, punishment, or reward.

The arguments of this book are intended to sever the supposed links between freedom and moral responsibility: freedom (including free will and autonomy) will be retained and celebrated, while moral responsibility is banished. When compatibilist-naturalist individual freedom is clearly understood, then it will be obvious that moral responsibility is not implied by such freedom. (Thus if one still wishes to claim that we do have moral responsibility, that will require further arguments; merely establishing the compatibility of individual freedom with naturalism-determinism—which is what compatibilists have done thus far—fails to establish that moral responsibility can coexist with naturalism-determinism.) Furthermore, when moral responsibility is properly distinguished from individual freedom, most will find little to mourn in the loss of moral responsibility. Those claims are definitive of the no-fault naturalist view: first, that questions of individual freedom (and its compatibility with naturalism-determinism) are distinct from questions concerning moral responsibility; second, that individual freedom *is* compatible with naturalism, and that it is valuable; third, that moral responsibility is *not* compatible with naturalism; and, fourth, that we are better off without moral responsibility. In short, *no-fault naturalism* draws a sharp line between freedom and moral responsibility, supports and celebrates individual freedom, and denies and scorns moral responsibility.

Describing the individual freedom that is genuinely compatible with naturalism-determinism is the work of the next two chapters; demonstrating why moral responsibility is *not* compatible with naturalism-determinism requires several more chapters; showing why we are better off *without* moral responsibility will be the concluding task.

6

CHAPTER TWO

Two Views of Free Will

AT THE EXTREMES of philosophical perspective are radically opposed approaches to freedom and free will. The side of the angels proclaims an exalted freedom that seems too good for this world: a freedom (such as Kant's) that operates in the transcendent realm, not sullying itself in the empirical world; or a freedom confined to the miracle-working will of God, which it is blasphemous for mortals to pretend to understand; or a freedom of inexplicable mystery, as humans somehow choose themselves from an ethereal stance of existence without essence. In its contemporary manifestations this exalted view of freedom may be secularized, but never naturalized. It may be in the world but is not of the world. It is a free will that defies—and stands apart from and cannot be explained by—the operations of the natural world. For example, Peter Geach:

> When we hear of some new attempt to explain reasoning or language or choice naturalistically, we ought to react as if we were told that someone had squared the circle or proved the square root of 2 to be rational: only the mildest curiosity is in order—how well has the fallacy been concealed. (1977, p. 52)

For another example, Roderick Chisholm:

7

If we are responsible . . . then we have a prerogative which some would attribute only to God: each of us, when we really act, is a prime mover unmoved. In doing what we do, we cause certain events to happen, and nothing and no one, except we ourselves, causes us to cause those events to happen. (1975, p. 395)

And to underline the point that this is a freedom of choice that transcends natural phenomena and natural science, Chisholm goes on to state: "This means that, in one very strict sense of the terms, there can be no complete science of man" (p. 396). C. A. Campbell, in his brilliant account of this variety of free will, describes such free choice as a "*creative activity,* in which . . . nothing determines the act save the agent's doing of it"; the self, on this view, must "be taken as including *also* the authentic creative power of fashioning and re-fashioning 'character'" (1957, p. 177).

This view of free will may emphasize different points, depending on the concerns of the particular advocate: some philosophers (such as Richard Taylor [1974] and Peter van Inwagen [1983] and Alasdair MacIntyre [1957]) concentrate their claims of free creative choice on the powers of reason; others (like William Barrett [1961]) require creative free will for the creation of genuinely new and original works of art and literature; and still others (like Campbell and Chisholm) champion nonnatural creative free choice as a condition for responsibility. But a common thread runs through these diverse accounts: free will is a creative process, and creative in the *ab initio* manner that orthodox Christians and Jews reserve for God. However small and limited the sphere of genuine creative free will may be, and however seldom it is exercised, there is nonetheless an inexplicable spark of creative free will—which can be traced causally to nothing at all, for it operates apart from natural causal forces. This exalted sort of free will might be called "transcendent free will" to mark that insistence on transcendence of natural processes.

In stark contrast to the glories of creative free will, there is the

8

mundane "compatibilist autonomy." On this view, free will is not a special creative process carried out in a mysterious manner by some wondrous psychic power; instead, freedom is the natural exercise of one's wishes and desires in the natural world. It is perfectly compatible with a natural world in which all events (including all human behavior) are the determined product of a naturalist-mechanist causal system. One's will is just a matter of one's wants and desires, and freedom comes from being in circumstances that facilitate—or at least do not impede—the exercise of one's desires. If I want to go to the beach, then I act freely if nothing prevents me from fulfilling my desires (whether those desires stem from early childhood experiences or from the inheritance of the beach-loving-gene is nothing to the point). If, however, I am imprisoned, or someone holds a gun to my head and forbids me to move, or I am barred from the beach, then I cannot act freely. David Hume's is the classical statement of the position:

> What is meant by liberty, when applied to voluntary actions? We cannot surely mean that actions have so little connexion with motives, inclinations, and circumstances, that one does not follow with a certain degree of uniformity from the other, and that one affords no inference by which we can conclude the existence of the other. For these are plain and acknowledged matters of fact. By liberty, then, we can only mean *a power of acting or not acting, according to the determinations of the will;* that is, if we choose to remain at rest, we may; if we choose to move, we also may. Now this hypothetical liberty is universally allowed to belong to everyone who is not a prisoner and in chains. Here, then, is no subject of dispute. (Hume, 1902, p. 100)

Whatever one thinks of Hume's account of liberty, certainly his final statement is wrong: here indeed is a subject of vehement continuing dispute. But in this dispute, Hume has firmly established one pole—

9

what will here be called the compatibilist free will position. There is no mystery about the voluntary actions that we will: they are simply those that flow from our motives and inclinations, whatever those happen to be. The focus is on the conditions that facilitate or inhibit our acting according to the determinations of the will. We have liberty if we can act as we will to act. To the degree that circumstances frustrate our wills, we are to that degree deprived of liberty.

The compatibilist position has grown more sophisticated since Hume's eighteenth-century version. There is now enhanced understanding of the many ways in which the exercise of compatibilist free will can be frustrated. Not all hazards to freedom are in the form of chains and prison walls, real as such hazards are. Karl Marx, for example, pointed out the gross as well as subtle ways in which a repressive social-economic system could restrict individual exercise of free will. Another advance in the compatibilist account of autonomy has been the increased recognition of how internal psychological forces can inhibit personal freedom. Sigmund Freud made us aware that the free exercise of our wills might be thwarted not only by external chains and economic exploitation but also by conflicting desires and unconscious motives within ourselves.

Free will can be negated by chains, but contemporary compatibilists are also concerned with threats of unconscious desires, addictions, exploitative economic systems, and repressive social structures. It is no accident that those who *reject* transcendent autonomy —in favor of a more mundane freedom within the natural realm— are most alert to ways that freedom can be subtly circumscribed and free will deviously thwarted. Believers in transcendent free will need be less concerned about environmental influences that shape desires or restrict opportunities, for the pivotal act of autonomous choice occurs in splendid isolation from social and environmental influences. Even if desires and interests are shaped by cultural influences, through the exercise of transcendent free will one somehow rises above such influences and is liberated from them. A transcendent free will is detached from the controlling influences of the natural world, and thus makes it possible to oppose one's entire shaped character: transcendent autonomous choices are beyond control or explanation or prediction.

This may be seen most clearly by first looking through a glass darkly. C. A. Campbell has developed one of the most cogent and careful of the transcendent autonomy views, and in the course of defending his position he considers this objection: transcendent autonomy would destroy the possibility of accurate prediction of human behavior; but since we do make fairly accurate predictions, Campbell's theory of "contra-causal free will" must be false. Campbell first answers that in fact we do not make precise and reliable predictions of how humans will act in moral choice situations of conflict between desire and duty (the setting in which Campbell's transcendent autonomy is exercised); but then Campbell goes further:

It is obvious that where desire and duty are at odds, the felt "gap" (as it were) between the two may vary enormously in breadth in different cases. The moderate drinker and the chronic tippler may each want another glass, and each deem it his duty to abstain, but the felt gap between desire and duty in the case of the former is trivial beside the great gulf which is felt to separate them in the case of the latter. Hence it will take a far harder moral effort for the tippler than for the moderate drinker to achieve the same external result of abstention. So much is a matter of common agreement. And we are entitled, I think, to take it into account in prediction, on the simple principle that the harder the moral effort required to resist desire the less likely it is to occur. Thus in the example taken, most people would predict that the tippler will very probably succumb to his desires, whereas there is a reasonable likelihood that the moderate drinker will make the comparatively slight effort needed to resist them. So long as the prediction does not pretend to more than a measure of probability, there is nothing in our theory which would disallow it. (1957, p. 174)

This passage illustrates two things: first, the care with which Campbell has fashioned his theory of transcendent autonomy, to make room for external influences on behavior. Second, and most important, the fact that even though Campbell (and other champions of transcendent autonomy) may recognize the influence of conditioned history, still they do not regard it as the key factor. For—in Campbell's example—while it may be unlikely that the chronic tippler will suddenly exert moral effort and rise to duty and reverse his entire individual history, it is nonetheless a distinct and essential possibility. That is, for no other reason, for no other cause than autonomously deciding (in an ultimate and inexplicable fashion) to turn away from demon rum, the chronic tippler *may* vanquish the forces that shaped his life.

This examination of Campbell's sophisticated transcendent autonomy reveals two reasons why the believer in transcendent autonomy is not so likely to scrutinize freedom-limiting social-environmental forces. First, there is a sense of the futility of seeking diligently after natural causes for particular acts: there is always the possibility that no natural-environmental-social causes exist (it was a matter of transcendent autonomy). Second, it is (on the transcendent autonomy view) less important to seek the natural-environmental-social causes that might shape or circumscribe behavior: there is always the possibility of overcoming all such forces through an act of transcendent autonomous will. (At the crudest levels—far removed from the careful and cautious work of Campbell—are those believers in transcendent free will who justify their callous unconcern for social justice with the assertion that no matter what terrible social-economic circumstances shaped the individual, still it is finally just "up to her" what she does with her life, and it is her fault if she fails.)

Certainly not all believers in transcendent autonomy are blind to the forces that shape individuals and restrict freedom; obviously Campbell is not. But theorists who believe that *all* our behavior is the product of environmental forces are naturally more attentive to those forces and to the ways in which environment fosters or foils the exercise of free will.

CENTRAL TO THE DIFFERENCES between transcendent and compatibilist free will is the difference between what libertarians and compatibilists *want* from free will. Some of the desiderata are held in common by both the transcendent and the compatibilist camps; but there are also some substantial—and instructive—differences.

When we say that freedom and free will are goods, what are we commending? What is attractive about freedom and free will? For obvious reasons, we want to be free to follow our own wishes and desires. To be imprisoned is to have one's desires constantly and severely frustrated. The revulsion with which we view devices for locking bodies into rigid positions—chains and rings and pillories— stems from our horror of being unable even to move our arms and legs, the hideous constant frustration of desires we do not notice unless they are frustrated. So much is obvious, and is common ground both for those who favor an immanent compatibilist analysis of freedom and those who celebrate the transcendent.

In a broader sense, we want the "freedom to control our own lives." But while there continues to be some common ground between compatibilist and transcendent views on this goal, some basic differences also emerge. Some desires seem our own while others seem alien. My desire for chocolate chip cookies may be one that I abhor—my "better, truer self" favors tofu and brown rice—though it is certainly one of my desires. To the degree that I am compelled by desires of which I do not approve, I am not acting freely. Harry G. Frankfurt employs a hierarchical analysis of the will, noting that a drug addict may—at the level of effective willing—certainly desire drugs, but may also fervently desire (at a higher level) to be free of that addiction. In such a case, the addict will not be exercising free will in his use of drugs, even though there is no outside force compelling the addict to take drugs. And Frankfurt goes further: an addict who reflectively and deliberately and decisively favors a life of drug addiction may be acting freely—may be willing freely, may have the will he wants—even though drug addiction compels the addict's drug-taking behavior. So suppose that I have desires of which I approve, and that I reflectively and deliberately approve the sort of individual I am and the goals I have and the ways I act. Also, I have the opportunity to pursue those goals effectively. From the perspective of compatibilist autonomy, this is all the freedom one could wish.

This account of compatibilist free will requires further expla-nation and closer scrutiny, but that is for later chapters. For the moment, the important point is that such compatibilist freedom is not enough for proponents of transcendent freedom. For the ques-tion may still remain: how did I come to reflectively favor those desires, how is it that I now favor this sort of life and this type of character? The compatibilist will answer that that is a product of my cultural conditioning together with any genetic influences: I may have carefully reflected on my life and desires and goals, but that reflective process is in turn the result of the forces that shaped me. The transcendent theorist will find that unacceptable. On a tran-scendent view of free will, there must be some point at which I somehow step outside any environmental forces and autonomously choose the sort of person I wish to be: if the environment is the ultimate causal explanation, then the environment controls me—and that, for the transcendent theorist, is too much control. For the compatibilist, I now approve of my desires and character—causal origins be damned. The transcendent theorist wants a more radical free choice.

The conflict between compatibilist and transcendent views of freedom and free will can be elucidated by examining another key freedom issue: what is the significance of our behavior, what sort of effect do we have on the world? As Daniel Dennett puts it, we want to "make things happen" (1984). When shackled in an isolated cell there is little one can accomplish. But in less severe settings there can also be disturbing limits on our capacities to change things, to affect the world, to make things happen. If one is locked into a substandard socioeconomic status, with no opportunity to change it or advance out of it, then one has little opportunity to make things happen—and the result is likely to be lethargic depression. Seeing some effect from our acts is naturally reinforcing.[1] When such reinforcement is unavailable, lethargy sets in as the effort-making behavior is extinguished by lack of positive reinforcement. (Consider: a child's delight in learning that by pushing a button or pulling a string he can cause a light to turn on;[2] sitting mesmerized at a computer terminal, while modest key strokes yield dramatic effects.) But there are situations when we really can make things happen, when our behavior has an effect, when our efforts are rewarded by tangible results. As Skinner has noted (1978a), not merely is it important that we receive goods; what is essential is the way in which we receive those goods, that they result from—follow from—our own acts and efforts, and thus that they positively reinforce those acts. Otherwise, the receiving of goods can induce lethargy.[3] It is important not only that "good things happen to us," but also that we be instrumental in causing those good things to happen. (Dostoyevsky's Underground Man is so insistent on making things happen that he would be willing to sabotage events just to see some effect, even a bad one. The same phenomenon occurs on assembly lines, when workers feel that their efforts make no difference: they sabotage the line in order to have an effect.)

The believer in compatibilist autonomy—who favors naturalism-determinism—can consistently acknowledge that individuals do make things happen. Martin Luther King struggled valiantly to change the repressive system of racism he found in the United States. While he certainly did not succeed in eliminating racism, his efforts did have an effect: blacks gained greater opportunity to attend schools and universities, hold upper-level jobs, choose where they live. If one compares, for example, the Birmingham of 1954 with the Birmingham of 1984, one cannot doubt the dramatic effects of the work of King and others who participated in that struggle. For those who contributed to causing such remarkable and wonderful changes, the sense of accomplishment—of causing something to happen—must be very great. In this case, Martin Luther King (along with others) made a difference: their efforts bore fruit, their work has had a lasting and beneficial effect. In such complicated causal situations, it is impossible to say what would have happened had key circumstances been different: had there been no Martin Luther King, perhaps someone else would have stepped into the breach. Perhaps some other casual sequence might have produced like effects in a different situation; but in the causal situation as it actually developed, the work of Martin Luther King was a key factor in shaping subsequent events.

Consider this from the strictest naturalist—even determinist—perspective. Suppose it is agreed that King's work was entirely the product of the natural forces that shaped him. His indomitable will, his commitment to principle, his courage—all those qualities were shaped by his environmental contingencies. Given the full set of natural causes that shaped him (including genetic and short-term conditioning, and stretching back for millennia), as well as the environmental (including social) forces that constantly impinged upon him, Martin Luther King could not have done other than he did. But that does not diminish the fact that a key element of that causal sequence is named Martin Luther King, and that King's work made a difference in subsequent events. Martin Luther King's work is part of a natural process and is subject to naturalistic explanation—like everything else in the world; but Martin Luther King—as one ele-

16

ment of a natural system—did indeed make important things happen.

THERE IS ANOTHER important difference between what libertarians (who advocate transcendent free will) and compatibilists want from freedom. Even if it is granted that compatibilist freedom allows one to "make things happen," that will still not be enough for many libertarians. A remaining libertarian fear is that without a break in the naturalist-determinist system, the joyful openness and creativity and freshness of the world and of human behavior would be lost. William Barrett exemplifies this concern, claiming that when a philosophical proponent of determinism focuses too narrowly on moral responsibility, then:

> he omits, I think, one of the main motives in the rebellion against determinism, not only on the part of ordinary people but also of those modern philosophers who have been most vigorously opposed to the determinist position: namely, the desire for freshness, novelty, genuine creation—in short, an open rather than a closed universe. . . .
>
> It is worth while in this connection to recall the story by the Italian poet Leopardi about the Almanac Vendor. The vendor appears under a window hawking his wares, crying out that he has good predictions to sell for the year. A man leans out of the window and engages him in conversation: How long has the vendor been selling almanacs and making this same cry? "Twenty years, Excellency." And if he had the chance of living over any of those years? "No, Excellency, certainly not; not for all the money in the world." Here the man who sells predictions would not care, as a human being, to have those predictions true in detail. The point of the story is that even a good year—had we to live it over again with every detail fixed beforehand—would stifle us with bore-

dom: our food would taste dull to our palate, our most sponta-
neous talk sound as uninspired as the playback of a tape-recorded
conversation, and our words of love would sound hollow because
we should know beforehand the precise moment of fatigue when
they would expire. (1961, pp. 46–47)

There is an easy answer to Barrett's example: the fact that all
events in the world are determined does not imply that anyone can
actually predict those events in detail. Naturalists-determinists do
not suggest that each individual must know every detail of her future
life. The strict determinist position, like that of the poet in *The
Rubáiyát of Omar Khayyám*, verse 79, might indeed imply that it is
possible in principle for an omniscient being to predict all that will
follow:

> With Earth's first Clay They did the Last Man knead,
> And there of the Last Harvest sow'd the Seed:
> And the first Morning of Creation wrote
> What the Last Dawn of Reckoning shall read.

But the naturalist-determinist denies the existence of such an omniscient being; and in any case the determinist denies that humans
possess such knowledge.

Furthermore, there is no reason to suppose that determinism implies a universe devoid of freshness and novelty. Make the wheels of
determinism grind as inexorably as you wish—still, what they are
now grinding out is fresh and novel, new and surprising. In Eccle-
siastes the Preacher mourns that "there is nothing new under the
Sun"; but in a world that careens from one shattering scientific discovery to another, in which the arts thrive on novelty, in which social
events plunge from unanticipated crisis to cataclysmic change, that
is hardly our problem. The fact that it may be determined and inevitable does not diminish its freshness. Perhaps if we were merely

living out what we had already foreseen in detail, the bloom would indeed be off the rose; but such is not the case, and nothing about determinism implies that it is.

That is the easy answer, but the source of Barrett's concern is probably much deeper. Barrett champions "the desire for freshness, novelty, genuine creation—in short, an open rather than a closed universe." What will make it "an open rather than a closed universe" is not the novelty or freshness, but instead the "genuine creation." Barrett wants to be able to transcend all natural forces and causes and perform creative acts for which no natural explanation is possible. That is the deeper motivation for Barrett's opposition to determinism-naturalism, and two other concerns stem from that deeper concern. One is fear of control; the second is fear of fatalism. Both of these are closely connected to the desire to "make things happen."

The fear of control is the fear that in reality we are merely playing bit parts in a drama beyond our ken, that we are being used for someone else's purposes. T. S. Eliot writes in *Four Quartets*:

> Do not let me hear
> Of the wisdom of old men, but rather of their folly,
> Their fear of fear and frenzy, their fear of possession,
> Of belonging to another, or to others, or to God.

And for Barrett control by determined natural forces—control by long-term and short-term environmental shaping, control that is ultimately traced to forces outside the individual—seems uncomfortably close to being controlled by something alien. Robert Kane, in his excellent *Free Will and Values*, describes the concern, especially the fear of what he calls "covert non-constraining control":

In the extreme case of covert non-constraining control, the controlled agent is not even aware that there is a controller, or that his or her choices and actions are being controlled. The covert non-constraining controller in these cases is a behind the scenes manipulator who brings about certain wants, desires, beliefs, etc., in the agent, so that the agent will choose and act as he (the controller) plans. The controlled agent may not be aware that his behavior is being controlled or even that there is a person attempting to control his behavior. . . .

. . . Libertarians are . . . especially concerned about covert non-constraining control. . . . They want to know how the free agent can ensure against, or guarantee the absence of, CNC control of his or her will by another agent. (1985, p. 35)

Covert non-constraining control is not a pleasant prospect; but exactly why not? The reason is obvious enough, and does not require lamenting the absence of transcendent freedom. The controller may manipulate the controllee to benefit the controller at the controllee's expense. Perhaps the controller would be beneficent, and control me for my own good; but given the poor record of controllers— "absolute power corrupts absolutely" is not an empty slogan—I do not wish to take that chance. I know that I am genuinely concerned about my own best interests, however much I may fail to promote them; but I am not so sure that some covert controller will protect my interests rather than his own.

Fear of control was voiced over a century ago by Dostoyevsky in *Notes from Underground*:

What he [humanity] wants to preserve is precisely his noxious fancies and vulgar trivialities, if only to assure himself that men are still men . . . and not piano keys simply responding to the laws of nature. . . .

But even if man was nothing but a piano key, even if this could be demonstrated to him mathematically—even then, he wouldn't come to his senses but would pull some trick out of sheer ingratitude, just to make his point. . . .

Now, you may say that this too can be calculated in advance and entered on the timetable—chaos, swearing, and all—and that the very possibility of such a calculation would prevent it, so that sanity would prevail. Oh no! In that case man would go insane on purpose, just to be immune from reason. (1961, pp. 114–115)

The fear is similar to Kane's. The Underground Man does not want to be a piano key, played on by outside controlling forces. The metaphor is a useful one. Indeed we do not wish to be piano keys, for piano keys are manipulated for someone else's interests: the piano player—the controller—enjoys the music, but the piano key derives no benefits. Dostoyevsky is willing to undermine reason (Dostoyevsky opts for insanity, Barrett for inexplicable creativity, Kane for randomness) in order to thwart such control.

But it is time to exorcise such spirits. The "laws of nature" were not contrived by backroom politicians for selfish purposes; and the fearsome demon-neurologist who exerts selfish covert non-constraining control does not exist. In *Elbow Room* Daniel C. Dennett wisely counsels, "Please don't feed the bugbears"; and among the most gluttonous of philosophical bugbears or bogeymen is the "nefarious neurosurgeon" (also known as the "hideous hypnotist" and the "peremptory puppeteer"). Dennett's advice is sound:

I cannot prove that none of the bogeymen in this rogues' gallery really exist, any more than I can prove that the Devil, or Santa Claus, doesn't exist. But I am prepared to put on a sober face and assure anyone who needs assuring that there is absolutely no evidence to suggest that any of these horrible agents exists. . . . Whenever you spy a bogeyman in a philosophical example, check to see if this scary agent, who is surely fictitious, is really doing all the work. (1984, p. 10)

In the present case the bogeyman of covert non-constraining control *is* doing a lot of the work. If we shoo it away and look again, the prospect of determinism is not nearly so fearsome. Of course we are controlled by our environments (long-term evolutionary control and short-term conditioning control); but that environmental control is not some manipulator who may be tempted to exploit us. To the contrary, environmental control is likely to result in positive, not detrimental, effects. It shapes a species to be successful in its environment, and it shapes individual behavior that is likely to result in positive effects. (As Skinner has pointed out, the problem is often how to bring our behavior *more directly* under the control of long-term environmental contingencies.) That does not mean that we must adopt some Spencerian view of evolution and environmental contingencies as inevitably moving toward beneficent ends. It is possible that our species has evolved in ways that adapted it for living successfully in the world of ten thousand years ago but will prove fatal in an era of thermonuclear weaponry; and we know that short-term environmental contingencies can shape counterproductive superstitious behavior in pigeons as well as humans. But that is quite different from the spectre of an environment that slyly controls us for ulterior motives. We can recognize the environmental factors that shape us—and predict, control, and use them. That we do so is of course a result of our environment, but that does not make the environment a deviously manipulative agent.

The fear that determinism would destroy freshness also contains a fear of fatalism. That concern is closely related to the previous one. If we are destined to reach a certain fate—no matter how we seek to avoid it—then the most likely scenario is that we are being manipulated to that end by some devious controller. Like the spectre of a covert controller, fatalism is certainly disquieting. Its eerie sense of making us the helpless victims of an inevitable fate is brilliantly captured in a scene from Somerset Maugham's play *Sheppey*, in which Death is speaking:

There was a merchant in Bagdad who sent his servant to market to buy provisions and in a little while the servant came back, white and trembling, and said: "Master, just now when I was in the market-place I was jostled by a woman in the crowd and when I turned I saw it was Death that jostled me. She looked at me and made a threatening gesture; now, lend me your horse, and I will ride away from this city and avoid my fate. I will go to Samarra and there Death will not find me." The merchant lent him his horse, and the servant mounted it, and he dug his spurs in its flanks and as fast as the horse would gallop he went. Then the merchant went down to the market-place and he saw me standing in the crowd and he came to me and said: "Why did you make a threatening gesture to my servant when you saw him this morning?" "That was not a threatening gesture," I said, "it was only a start of surprise. I was astonished to see him in Bagdad, for I had an appointment with him tonight in Samarra."[4]

It is not surprising that fatalism and control should be fearful to us; in the Judaeo-Christian tradition both play prominent roles. For example, it is Pharaoh's fate to be the fall guy for Moses and Yahweh and the children of Israel. In playing out that fate, Pharaoh's "heart is hardened": he follows his own desires, but those desires are designed to make him a pawn of Yahweh's machinations. But the naturalist-determinist view does not hold such dangers; instead, the naturalist exorcises the powerful and malevolent deities who use us for their sport. If we are to be left to the caprice of Yahweh or other gods, and controlled for their "unfathomable" purposes, then indeed we have something to fear. But such is the stuff of miracles, not of naturalism. The natural environment that controls us accommodates us quite decently and seems well suited to our perceptual and theoretical capacities—which is hardly surprising, since those capacities evolved in response to precisely that environment, and those characteristics that were well suited for succeeding in that environment were more likely to be passed on.

So we are totally the product of a natural—perhaps determined—process; but we are not thus "predestined" to some ultimate frustrations contrived by fiendish forces or impetuous gods. Our efforts can and often do play a vital role in the course of events. The efforts we make (or fail to make) are the result of natural forces, of the environmental factors that shaped (determined) us. That does not imply that all our efforts are vain because they will be thwarted by cruel fate.

In fatalism, the fates conspire to bring about a specific result—no matter what we mortals do, no matter how we struggle, no matter how rapidly we ride, no matter how diligently we work. The work we do is a wheel that turns but has no effect on the operation of the machine. We are like children vigorously turning our back seat steering wheels while the real action is taking place up front. All our work makes no difference; it is unconnected with the real course of events: whether we steer carefully or carelessly, the car will reach its destination unaffected by our fantasy steering. No wonder that fatalism is disturbing. Even if the fates treat us kindly, what is lost is our significance in the world. But fatalism is a far cry from the naturalist-determinist position. On the latter view, we are assuredly and totally a part of the natural process. We do not stand above it as deities, nor are we impotent spectators of a drama played out by the fates. Instead, we play an active and effective part in the natural world. What happens in that world is partly—and sometimes quite substantially—the result of what we do.[5] What we do is also a result of natural processes, of course—including our social history and our earlier behavior and the earlier behavior of our ancestors and the various scenes of the natural drama that unfolded before our entrances and will continue after our exits. But we are players in that drama, and our acts not only influence but substantially constitute the course of that drama. And there is no outside author-director-manipulator pulling the strings of destiny, bringing the play to a fated climax no matter what we do. To the contrary, what we do is a key factor in determining subsequent scenes of the play—just as prior events (including prior human behavior) shaped our current acts.

Does that leave us, then, with "freshness and open possibilities"? Our acts are the determined-natural outcome of a determined-natural process; still, they can bring into existence events and paintings and poems and ideas that have never before existed and would not have existed but for our work and efforts and thought. Perhaps an omniscient being could have foreseen all that we have done; but in fact there is no omniscient being getting sneak previews, and hypothetical omniscience does not diminish freshness. Indeed, even if there were such a being, assuming that it kept its sneak previews to itself I should still find the drama of unfolding events new and entertaining. That is sufficiently fresh for me. In like manner, perhaps some omniscient "purblind trickster" could close off certain possibilities, could impose limits, could make the world a closed universe. But such a fanciful being imposes only fanciful limits. If our opportunities and vistas are limited only by our capacities and energies, then that is as much open opportunity as I desire.

But this may still not be enough for everyone. If ultimately the source of all our thinking and striving and imagining is rooted in past natural processes, some will find that intolerably confining. Here we reach an impasse that we shall bump into around several more corners. The differences that divide the transcendent libertarian from the naturalist run deep. For present purposes it is not necessary to convince intransigent libertarians of the adequacy of compatibilist-naturalist free will. But there are two points that are essential to note: first, that this compatibilist-naturalist free will is very different from the transcendent variety; and, second, that such compatibilist free will (which the no-fault naturalist favors) is genuinely valuable and offers what most people really want from free will—with one notable exception. One thing that some people want from free will is a foundation for moral responsibility, and, as will be argued in the next chapter, compatibilist free will cannot support moral responsibility (and perhaps transcendent free will can). However (as will also be argued) that is a virtue, rather than a defect, of compatibilist-naturalist free will; for when compatibilist free will is distinguished from moral responsibility and moral responsibility is judged on its own merits, few will regret that compatibilist free will is unencumbered by moral responsibility.

CHAPTER THREE

Individual Freedom Without Moral Responsibility

IN THE PREVIOUS CHAPTER compatibilist freedom was contrasted with transcendent freedom, and it was argued that freedom compatible with naturalism-determinism can satisfy all our reasonable demands for freedom: our choices and behavior can have real effects, fatalism is avoided, open possibilities are available. But compatibilists (soft determinists, such as Hume, Frankfurt, Dennett) believe that such freedom is also an adequate foundation for moral responsibility, and that belief is false. Convenient though the compatibilist account of individual freedom is, it is not an adequate foundation for moral responsibility: it is not even the right *type* of foundation for moral responsibility.

This chapter will extol the virtues of the naturalist-compatibilist account of individual free will; however, the main task of the chapter is to show that this quite workable account of individual freedom will not support claims of moral responsibility. Indeed, careful scrutiny of naturalist-compatibilist individual freedom reveals that it undercuts—rather than supports—moral responsibility.

There are solid practical reasons for our enduring belief in individual freedom. In this examination of the strengths of compatibilist individual freedom (prefatory to showing why such freedom does *not* support moral responsibility) the first question is: Why have we continued to believe in naturalist-compatibilist individual freedom? What is behind the enduring success of our common sense compatibilist notion of individual freedom? That question is not why the naturalist-compatibilist notion of individual freedom works better than the transcendent account. The advantages of the transcendent account are not of this workaday world: they are instead the dubious benefits of preserving embattled notions of special human status (transcendent, god-like free will) against the constant encroachments of biology and psychology and sociology. It is not difficult to see why the compatibilist account of individual freedom would prevail over such mysteries and obscurities. Instead, the query now posed is why the compatibilist account of individual free will has survived at all: why did not all notions of individual freedom wither in the blast of determinism and naturalism and mechanism? Why does the interest and focus on *individual* free behavior remain dominant, instead of being replaced by a more global interconnected view of causal relations? [1]

The most obvious answer is that every human individual carries a unique set of genes, and that has been the case far back into our evolutionary history. Concern for individual survival and individual success is an element of our process of evolutionary adaptation. Imagine a highly intelligent variety of bees in which all members of the hive have virtually identical genetic material (so that evolutionary pressure is exerted on the survival of various groups rather than on particular individuals). Such bees might find our notion of individual freedom strange and inconvenient and instead trace all causes to the activities of the swarm. (If one doubts that group identification could possibly replace individual free will, consider how easily scoundrels manipulate patriotic fervor to prompt willing human sacrifice for the supposed "good of the country"; and observe football fans who have never kicked a ball celebrating "our victory.")

A second—and more decisive—reason for our continued concern with individual freedom is the fact that environmental contingencies shape our behavior individually. I shall be delighted if you, my friend, drive your tee shot long and true down the middle of the fairway; but it is your behavior that is positively reinforced by the outcome, and your particular movements that are shaped. If (by accident) your severe shoulder hitch results in a splendid—and positively reinforcing—tee shot, then it is you (and not I, the friend who rejoices in your good fortune) who develops a flawed swing as you continue to make the movements that were positively reinforced. In short, conditioning-learning operates on an individual basis: environmental contingencies shape individuals one by one. The positive reinforcement that follows my specific behavior reinforces my *individual* pattern of behavior. If manna drops from the heavens purely by God's grace—with no respect to what any one of us was doing prior to the deity's manna drop—then *each* individual receiving the positively reinforcing manna will be positively reinforced for what each was doing immediately pre-manna. The same result—positively reinforcing manna—will shape each of us individually, and probably in quite different ways.

But manna rarely drops from the heavens. More often we are positively reinforced as a direct consequence of our own behavior. I hold the spoon upright, and am reinforced by eating the food rather than dropping it on my bib; thus upright spoon-holding is learned. I hold my finger firmly on the string, and am positively reinforced by a beautiful violin tone; and my fingering technique is shaped. I smile at my students, am positively reinforced by their increased attention, and become a more amiable lecturer. Our behavior is shaped by the relation between individual behavior and environmental effects; so we focus on the individual as a causal source.

Since operant conditioning shapes my behavior by positively reinforcing the individual behavior that immediately preceded the receiving of positive reinforcement (making it more likely that that behavior will recur), it is natural that I focus on my own individual behavior as a key causal source—natural, since (in *most* cases) it is my behavior that caused the subsequent positive reinforcement and (in all cases) it is my individual behavior that is in turn strengthened. In a similar manner, the success of operant conditioning in shaping the individual behavior of others also leads us to focus on the individual as the primary causal unit. If we wish to change behavior, we must focus on how the particular individual is being affected: what positive or aversive influences does the individual experience immediately after the relevant behavior. If I want Joe to talk more in class, I positively reinforce Joe's incipient acts of class participation: when he nods in agreement, I smile warmly on him; when he makes a small comment, I praise it and perhaps repeat it approvingly. Focusing on Joe's individual behavior is the most convenient and effective means of changing and controlling and explaining Joe's behavior. If we want to know why Joe is taciturn, we must examine the events that shaped him, what occurred immediately following his earlier speech behavior. If we wish to change his taciturn behavior, energy must be exerted at the same point—the events surrounding Joe's individual behavior.

To observe the workings of our useful notion of naturalist individual freedom, consider this variation on Harry G. Frankfurt's example of willing and unwilling drug addicts. Imagine three addicts: Felicity, Gretchen, and Harriet. Unknown to Felicity, someone slips addictive drugs into the glass of warm milk she drinks each evening; a few weeks later, Felicity discovers she is a drug addict and is unable to resist her desire for the addictive drug—though she hates the drug and her addiction. Gretchen is tempted by easy access to addictive drugs, tries them when her friends exert a bit of peer pressure, and discovers to her horror that her social dalliance has evolved into addiction: she likes the drugs, but now hates her addictive desire for drugs. Harriet resolved to become a drug addict, sought out the most addictive drugs she could acquire, and took them enthusiastically: she is now a drug addict, she likes being a drug addict, and she fervently approves her drug addiction.

Explanations of how each woman became an addict will be quite different. In Felicity's case, we need know nothing at all about her life history: the causes of Felicity's addiction have little if anything to do particularly with Felicity; she was merely the unlucky target. Gretchen's drug addiction has more to do with Gretchen, and to understand why Gretchen succumbed to peer pressure and why she chose to indulge in drugs we must know something of her conditioning history. Had Gretchen been made of sterner stuff (had she had a different conditioning history) she would have resisted the blandishments of dangerous drugs; on the other hand, had Gretchen not been in an environment that condoned and even encouraged drug experimentation and made drugs easily available, Gretchen would not have sought out drugs. An explanation of how Gretchen became a drug addict requires attention to her immediate environmental surroundings as well as her environmental-conditioning history. Harriet is at the other extreme from Felicity. Felicity's life history has little if anything to do with her addiction. In contrast, Harriet's life history—her cumulative record of environmental contingencies—is indispensable for explaining her addiction. Harriet does not become an addict because of current coercion or the immediate influence of a bad environment; instead, Harriet goes in search of drug addiction. Whether her immediate environment contains the opportunity and encouragement to use drugs (an essential factor in Gretchen's addiction) is irrelevant to Harriet's case. Harriet will do whatever is necessary to secure drugs and to become an addict. To explain her dedication to drug addiction will require probing deep into the forces that shaped her character and desires and commitments.

The differences among these women turn on the depth to which one must probe their individual histories to explain and understand their behavior. Felicity's individual history is irrelevant; Felicity has no individual freedom in her drug-taking. Gretchen to some degree acts freely from her own (conditioned) motives; her individual history is relevant to understanding her behavior. Harriet's history provides almost the entire story of her development of drug addiction, with immediate environmental contingencies eclipsed by the effects of long-term conditioning; Harriet is acting from profoundly personal and individual motivations, and her acts result from her individual free choice. In short, the difference in individual freedom among the three varies directly with the difference in degree to which explanation of their behavior depends on the *individual* (as shaped by the individual's conditioning history) rather than the immediate surroundings.

The same point can be seen in traditional compatibilist examples. Hume counts people as less responsible for the acts they do "casually and ignorantly," and attributes greater responsibility when the source of the act is the individual's formed character. When a ruffian presses a large-caliber pistol to my temple and orders me to drive her from the scene of the bank robbery, my compliance is a "casual and ignorant" sort of behavior: it does not stem from my own deliberate and reflective decision to participate in a holdup scheme, but is instead the product of the potent environmental forces currently controlling my behavior. When a bag of money is inadvertently left outside the bank, and I—in my penurious state, but with no thievish thoughts—happen to stroll by in the dark of the evening, then my act of absconding with the money does stem from my own desires and character. But that act of theft, prompted by very strong immediate environmental factors, is quite different from carefully plotting to rob a bank, seeking out the easiest target, laying plans over a course of weeks, and carrying out the dastardly deed at a time judiciously selected as the most opportune moment. In the latter case, my immediate surroundings are of little influence in controlling my bank-robbing behavior (they are the same in all relevant respects as those experienced by millions of other people who do not plot bank robberies). The explanation will have to be drawn from a study of my environmental history, not my immediate environment. Again, then, the key difference between the free thief and the coerced getaway driver is a difference in the degree to which individual conditioning history is relevant to understanding and explaining behavior. When the immediate environment (a powerful drug or a death threat) provides a full causal explanation of my behavior (with little or no reference to individual conditioning history required), then the act is not one of individual freedom.

The point of the above examples is this: there is a practically useful distinction between the willing addict and the unwilling addict, between deliberately planning a bank job and impulsively stealing a wad of bills, between compulsion by immediate circumstances and acting freely from deeply conditioned motives. That distinction is worth marking, as compatibilist accounts of freedom have made clear. It marks the important difference between behavior that is under the complete control of immediate (or very short-term) environmental contingencies and behavior that was shaped by longer-term conditioning-learning. The former behavior can be understood with little or no consideration of the individual's formed character and conditioning history; the latter ("free individual acts") requires knowledge of the individual's conditioning history and formed character for its explanation.

Our individualist conceptual system—with its notion of individual free will—is genuinely useful, and contemporary compatibilist elucidation of individual freedom enhances its usefulness. Indeed, if this were a Shakespearean drama rather than a dreary philosophical essay, the protagonist would now stop the action to extol the importance and the benefits of the naturalist-compatibilist account of individual free will and to praise the work of compatibilists like Frankfurt and Dennett who have contributed to that account. But, instead, the point to note here is that the system of compatibilist individual freedom is a matter of general—and genuine—*convenience*, not part of some fixed metaphysical order. We can imagine other systems, even if it is difficult to imagine that they might supplant our useful orientation toward individual freedom. The group focus of the intelligent bees is one imaginable system. Another is proposed by Spinoza (and perhaps others, such as the Taoists): the causal system is one unified whole, and it is intolerably shallow and myopic to regard individuals as causal units. The only adequate causal unit is the Whole (if Spinoza's God had a "point of view," it would have that one). Thus we might consider (with Spinoza) the cosmos as the only reasonable individual unit; or we might regard family or social units as basic. No doubt there are other alternatives.[2] In any case, I am not proposing that we substitute any of them for our current individualist view. That it is a convenient system is all the justification we need for our common compatibilist conceptualization of individual freedom.

NOTWITHSTANDING THE GENUINE CONVENIENCE of naturalist-compatibilist individual free will, it is now time to part company with the compatibilists. The problem is not with the compatibilist account of individual free will; rather, the problem is in what compatibilists try to *justify* with that account.

A basic error runs through the history of compatibilism: the belief that a workable compatibilist account of individual freedom automatically supports claims of moral responsibility. Compatibilists (and most incompatibilists) have assumed that free will and moral responsibility are so intertwined that they must flourish or wither together and that one only has to justify claims of individual freedom to thereby establish moral responsibility (or vice versa). For example, in Willard Gaylin's book *The Killing of Bonnie Garland* (an impassioned plea for moral responsibility and retributive punishment) the briefest paragraph is the following (quoted in full):

"Freedom demands responsibility; autonomy demands culpability" (1983, p. 338). The connection is regarded as so obvious that it need only be stated. But in fact individual freedom is in a radically different category from moral responsibility: justification of moral responsibility would require arguments distinct from and additional to those given in support of compatibilist individual freedom. I do not think such arguments *can* be given, at least not in the naturalist-determinist context in which compatibilist free will operates; but that will be argued in later chapters. The immediate claim is that the compatibilist justification of individual freedom does *not* justify claims of moral responsibility.[3]

ONE IS *morally* RESPONSIBLE for an act to the degree that it is morally right that one receive special benefit or detriment for it. Moral responsibility involves a moral judgment of what is *fair*: is it fair to treat a person in a special manner because of this act? Questions of compatibilist individual freedom are in a different category. Rather than questions of fairness, they are questions of the degree to which an individual's behavior is under the control of that individual (and the individual's strongest preferences) rather than the immediate control of the environment.

The confusion between compatibilist individual free will and claims of moral responsibility stems from the fact that both focus on the individual. But that similarity obscures a critical difference. The compatibilist account of individual free will focuses on the individual as a convenient (but by no means ultimate) unit of causal analysis. In contrast, the individualist beliefs at the foundation of moral responsibility are rooted in a metaphysical system that is rejected by naturalists-determinists: a metaphysical system in which individuals are the terminal causes of the acts for which they are morally responsible; in short, a system of transcendent rather than naturalist-compatibilist free will. The source of the confusion is that the individual has continued to be a convenient causal focus long after the transcendent metaphysical props (essential to moral responsibility) have been kicked away. Thus compatibilists—with individualist freedom still in hand—have failed to note that that convenient individual freedom lacks the metaphysical foundation that is necessary to bear the weight of moral responsibility.

From the perspective of moral responsibility, the individual is not merely a convenient focus: the individual is a special uncaused cause, a metaphysically fixed and primitive unit. If individuals exercise transcendent contracausal free will, then any causal account that relates to individuals *must* treat individuals as distinct and independent entities. A Spinozistic macroscopic view that grouped individuals together would exclude acts of contracausal free will. I am not mourning the demise of transcendent free will: losing such super freedom means losing a mysterious muddle that we can well do without. But scrapping that transcendent free will (in favor of compatibilist individual freedom) has consequences that have not been fully appreciated. The focus on individual freedom is ordinarily a convenient one, but it is only that—convenient, not fixed. And in many cases it is more convenient to focus on larger causal contexts in accounting for and changing behavior. (For example, the therapist who wonders why an individual repeatedly seeks out destructive relationships may find it essential to examine the rather remote causal history of that individual. And a society that wonders why so many individuals willfully favor a life of drug addiction must look at the social-economic-institutional forces that operate on the individuals.) Indeed, much of the convenience of the compatibilist notion of individual freedom stems from the fact that it can so easily move to larger and lengthier causal contexts. But if one is to hold an individual morally responsible, and assert that that individual justly deserves special treatment, then that move to larger causal contexts must not be so convenient; to the contrary, it must be blocked. Moral responsibility requires special grounds that justify differential treatment, that can support the claim that such differential treatment is fair. If the differences in two individuals are fundamentally and ultimately self-created, then that is the sort of difference that stops further inquiry and supports the justice of differential treatment. But if their differences can be traced to different causal-environmental histories that are not of their making and that are not differences that justify differential treatment, then such individual differences cannot support differences in just deserts, and thus cannot support moral responsibility.

Consider again the story of the three addicts: Felicity becomes an addict because someone in her immediate environment surreptitiously placed addictive drugs in her food (she is repulsed by her addictive state); Gretchen is tempted by her friends' encouragement to try drugs, and thus chooses to take drugs (and discovers to her horror that she has become addicted); and Harriet seeks out a life of drug addiction and fully approves of her state of addiction. As noted before, the degree of compatibilist individual freedom each exercises varies directly with the degree to which each individual's conditioning history must be probed in order to understand the individual's behavior. Felicity's drug addiction has little or no relation to her own choices, she does not act with individual freedom, and no study of her conditioning history is required in order to understand her behavior. In contrast, Harriet's drug addiction is almost totally the result of her quest for addiction, she does act with individual freedom, and an in-depth search of her conditioning background would be required in order to understand her behavior.

Generally, then, the greater the individual freedom the more deeply one's individual conditioning history must be probed in order to understand the free behavior.[4] And that is why any attempt to make compatibilist-naturalist individual freedom support moral responsibility is doomed to failure: it is precisely such probes of individual causal/conditioning history that undermine claims of moral responsibility and that claims of contracausal free will are designed to preclude. Far from providing a means of preventing such causal probes, careful scrutiny of individual freedom actually makes us more acutely aware of the need for such probes. The result is that causal factors are soon uncovered that are plainly inadequate for supporting claims that the individuals they have shaped deserve special treatment. Indeed, to hear of Harriet's appalling quest for enslavement to drugs certainly does not prompt us to drop any further questions about poor Harriet; to the contrary, such a case immediately demands further investigation into her background. And if Harriet affirms that her choice of drug addiction is not open to doubt or question and that it is a final and self-defining choice, that will only deepen our resolve to probe into her history for the causes of such purpose and resolve.

Thus it makes perfectly good sense that we regard the willing addict as acting freely (as acting from her own long-term conditioned desires and not from immediate environmental influences); but moral responsibility is something else entirely. For this example can also be used to point up the absurdity—and basic unfairness— of holding any of the women more or less (or to any degree) *morally* responsible for the addiction. I take it that no one (perhaps Sartre?) would blame poor Felicity for her addiction: it is obviously the result of forces over which she had no control. But precisely the same could be said for Harriet: her character and desires were ultimately shaped by forces (quite possibly in infancy, perhaps even genetic) that she certainly did not control. The difference is simply one of when the causal forces operated. Are they past causal forces, which shaped a particular individual whose conditioning history must be reckoned into any current explanation of behavior? Or are they current causal forces, in which only the immediate environmental forces (and not the individual's causal history) account for the behavior? Certainly there are important differences between willing and unwilling addicts, but the differences are not differences of moral responsibility.

The compatibilist error of linking individual freedom to moral responsibility is a natural mistake. *Transcendent* individual freedom *does* support moral responsibility, and since compatibilists also champion individual freedom (of a very different sort) it is an easy error to suppose that compatibilist individual freedom also supports moral responsibility. If Harriet's act of "willing addiction" is one of transcendent (contracausal) free will, then the act cannot be traced to environmental contingencies; instead, the act wholly originates in Harriet, and no further causal questions are allowed. But that marks the difference between the metaphysical basis for libertarian individual freedom and the convenience basis of compatibilist freedom. Compatibilist individual freedom—in contrast to transcendent freedom—does not establish a fixed and final source for behavior. To the contrary, on the compatibilist account of free individual behavior the causes for the behavior pass through the individual and back into the individual's conditioned history.

The compatibilist account of freedom—which does not limit inquiries into the causal history of free individual behavior—produces an insurmountable problem for contemporary compatibilist attempts to justify claims and ascriptions of moral responsibility. All willing and acting and reflecting (be they as completely and authentically the individual's own as the *compatibilist-naturalist* can make them) nonetheless result from circumstances for which it is unfair to blame or credit that individual. When such willing and acting result instead from contracausal transcendent free will, then the individual must be the stopping point for any causal analysis. But in contrast to the transcendent account, compatibilism (with its naturalist-determinist perspective) opens the way to seeking further explanation of compatibilist "free and authentic" behavior. Indeed, the compatibilist view—in which one's free behavior is that which is deeply learned-conditioned rather than generated by immediate circumstances— not only allows but promotes deeper causal explanations of free individual behavior, causal explanations that run far back into the individual's conditioning history and far beyond any plausible claim of moral responsibility. Thus a key problem for compatibilists (an insurmountable problem for any naturalist account) is how to justify the compatibilist decision to cut off causal accounts at what inevitably seems an arbitrary point.

Consider Frankfurt's brilliant account of the responsibility of the willing addict. Frankfurt uses the powerful example of an addict who is addicted to drugs (and thus will inevitably take drugs) but who has freedom and moral responsibility because he approves of his addiction. He has, in Frankfurt's felicitous phrase, "the will he wants to have" (1971, p. 15). This is the sort of example that shakes the dust from our concepts and makes us think more carefully: the standard example of the addict (in the grip of an uncontrollable desire) has been put to a decidedly nonstandard use. But when the dust clears, Frankfurt's account leaves a difficult question: *Why* does the willing addict favor drug addiction? When such a question is pushed it yields deep doubts about the moral responsibility of the willing addict. (The willing addict who has been shaped by an unkind environment to favor a life of drug addiction hardly seems the exemplar of moral responsibility.) Frankfurt employs desperate measures in his effort to answer that problem. He suggests that the willing addict "takes responsibility for" his addiction. But if Frankfurt is committed to avoiding the mysteries of transcendent autonomy, that "taking responsibility" must be the result of past causal forces and not some miraculous self-defining act. And if the "taking responsibility" is the product of environmental shaping, then we turn once again in this narrow radius: how can one be morally responsible for an act of "taking responsibility" that is the product of fortuitous environmental contingencies? Frankfurt also suggests that one might whole-heartedly identify with a particular sort of will in such a way that that identification "reverberates" through all the various levels of willing.[5] But the same problems emerge: perhaps one can "will" so strongly that no further questions occur to one concerning whether this is the sort of will one really wants ("I desire drugs, and I like the fact that I desire drugs, and I decisively approve of being the sort of individual who favors a life of drug addiction, and that's that"); but even in the face of such decisive willing—which effectively closes the matter for the willing individual—questions concerning moral responsibility remain. Jones decisively wills to be a drug addict, and that willing reverberates through all levels of Jones' willing in such a way that Jones will not question his own will; but is Jones morally responsible for this decisive willing? Since the source of Jones' decisive willing can be readily traced to environmental contingencies not of Jones' making, is it fair to blame Jones for his profound and unswerving devotion to drug addiction?

Frankfurt's example of the willing addict is a dramatic one, but the very drama of the example undermines Frankfurt's efforts to put a stop to inquiries into the willing addict's past. If an addict makes a decisive, reverberating affirmation of drug addiction, and on the basis of that affirmation refuses to deliberate further about whether he prefers drug addiction, that will indeed call a halt to the addict's deliberations; but it will certainly not call a halt to our efforts to understand the addict's choice of addiction. It will instead prompt deeper scrutiny of the addict's past. ("An unwilling addict is one thing; but this guy genuinely seems to prefer addiction. It is not just the effect of the drugs he likes; he actually likes being enslaved to drugs. I must discover the experiences, conditioning, genes, or whatever it was that caused such deep and decisive commitment to willful drug addiction.") Far from such decisive commitments' cutting off the causal inquiries that undermine moral responsibility, those "reverberating" commitments will stimulate such inquiries. That is, they will stimulate such inquiries unless the decisive commitments are instances of transcendent free willing; in that case, all further causal inquiry *is* effectively blocked. But that is *not* the sort of decisive willing that naturalist-compatibilists are proposing. And that is precisely the point: attempting to ground moral responsibility on decisive willing requires the transcendent willing that compatibilists—

for good reason—reject. To suppose that compatibilist decisive willing can halt the inquiry into the causal contingencies that undermine moral responsibility is to treat compatibilist willing as if it were transcendent free will.

We need not turn to such fanciful cases as willing addicts to find instances of "decisive willing" that cut off further deliberation. Fundamentalist Christian sects are on the upsurge. When a believer from this movement is questioned or challenged concerning her bizarre system of religious beliefs, the believer typically rejects the questions decisively, often voicing this slogan with heart-felt sincerity: "The Bible says it, I believe it, and that settles it!" Like the commitment of Frankfurt's willing addict, this commitment to a system of belief is profound, and the decisive commitment does block—indeed, bar—further consideration and reflection; and obviously the sect-member identifies with and approves of this commitment. But while such decisive willing blocks further inquiries on the part of the decisive willer, it does not prevent *our* search into the causal background of the willing believer. When such a search is conducted, then causal forces inconsistent with moral responsibility are quickly found. When encountering such decisive willful rejection of further deliberation, the reflective individual is certainly not moved to conclude that such decisive willing is the end of the story. Rather than regarding the decisive willing of the religious enthusiast as unfathomable grounds for moral responsibility, such decisive willing prompts questions and curiosity about the stifling educational history or authoritarian childhood or desperate fears that caused such adamant and stultifying willing of belief.

It is not coincidence that Daniel Dennett also seeks some sort of "decisive willing" that can cut off further questions. For Dennett senses—as does Frankfurt—the constant threat to compatibilist moral responsibility: the danger of further questions concerning *why* one wills decisively. Such questions soon lead to causes for such decisive "acts of willing," and those causes are environmental contingencies for which the willing agent is not morally responsible.

Dennett's quest for a means of establishing compatibilist moral responsibility (a moral responsibility compatible with mechanism and naturalism, and not requiring any transcendent miraculous acts), leads him to focus on the act of *stopping* a deliberative process and *acting* on the choice that the deliberative process has generated at that point. Dennett describes the benefits of his approach thus:

> Finally, the model I propose points to the multiplicity of decisions that encircle our moral decisions and suggests that in many cases our ultimate decision as to which way to act is less important phenomenologically as a contributor to our sense of free will than the prior decision affecting our deliberation process itself: the decision, for instance, not to consider any further, to terminate deliberation; or the decision to ignore certain lines of inquiry. (1978, p. 297)

Dennett maintains that "these prior and subsidiary decisions contribute to our sense of ourselves as responsible free agents" through the fact that we decide to stop deliberating and act "in the full knowledge that the eventualities may prove that I decided in error, but with the acceptance of responsibility in any case" (p. 297). But what can such decisions actually contribute to "our sense of ourselves as responsible free agents," to our "acceptance of responsibility"? Such decisions may contribute substantially to our sense of ourselves as *free,* and indeed may even instill in us a "*sense* of ourselves as *responsible* free agents." But they will do nothing to establish that we actually have moral responsibility. The first confusion is between acting freely and being morally responsible. As already discussed, one may indeed act freely in deciding to cease deliberations (the decision comes from deeply entrenched motives, and is neither coerced nor

43

accidental); but being morally responsible is something else again. Leaving that aside, it is quite possible that one's decision to stop deliberating may promote a "*sense* of ourselves as *responsible*." That *sense* of responsibility stems from the same confusion that bedevils Frankfurt's efforts to establish that the willing addict is morally responsible. When one freely and willfully decides to stop deliberating and choose, that does indeed contribute to a *sense* of moral responsibility—precisely because it seems to *block* further inquiry and deliberation (just as an act of transcendent free will justifies moral responsibility by closing inquiry into any causal sources other than the miraculously self-caused actor). Thus it is not surprising that a decision to stop deliberating and choose—which consequently stops further inquiry into causes, at least for the choosing individual— should give one a *sense* of moral responsibility. But it is a false sense, because the *compatibilist* free act of choosing to stop deliberation is not a transcendent act of willing; instead, we can quite intelligently ask why an individual chose not to deliberate further, and the answers we shall find when pursuing those questions are answers that undercut claims of moral responsibility.

Consider more closely Dennett's claim of moral responsibility. Where exactly does moral responsibility come from in this compatibilist account of choices made after choosing to stop deliberations? Either the responsibility must rest on the rational deliberation process that weighs the relative importance of various considerations, or the responsibility stems from the decision to stop or continue the generation of considerations. But the former cannot be the source— at least for Dennett—because Dennett obviously does not think that a process of rational deliberation in itself establishes moral responsibility. If it could, then the business about choosing to stop deliberating would be superfluous, as moral responsibility would emerge from the rational operations themselves. But the latter interpretation—that the responsibility emerges from the decision to stop deliberation—fares no better. The capacity and/or inclination for prolonged deliberation (or the tendency to deliberative lethargy) is learned, conditioned by one's environmental contingencies, controlled by the degree of reward accompanying past deliberations, determined by whether such further deliberations were reinforced (and on what schedule of reinforcement) or instead were extinguished. And it hardly seems fair to credit or blame an individual— hold an individual morally responsible—for such contingencies.

The decision "to terminate deliberation," that "I've considered this matter enough and now I'm going to act," does contribute to one's sense that the action taken is one's own and is the result of one's own decision. That is, Dennett is correct that such processes are an important element of one's "sense of authorship" of one's decisions and behaviors. But (like Frankfurt's) Dennett's contribution to the phenomenological analysis of the "sense of authorship" does not establish moral responsibility. It may be agreed that lethargic Harry's decision to stop deliberating and act is *his;* but it is something else again to hold Harry morally responsible, blameworthy, for his decision, especially when we consider Harry's unfortunate history and how it contributes to Harry's hasty and ill-considered decisions. Unlike transcendent authenticity and freedom, the compatibilist authenticity and freedom elucidated by Frankfurt and Dennett do not block such responsibility-undermining inquiries. To the contrary, compatibilist freedom invites exactly such inquiries.

One last example of the common compatibilist failure to distinguish individual freedom from moral responsibility: Jonathan Glover (1970) offers the following response to any no-fault naturalist effort to trace bad behavior back to conditions/causes that the individual could not control. Glover states the problem thus:

> It is only where a bad act or omission results from a bad desire (or lack of good desire) that one should be blamed. But a bad desire may be one that the agent desires to change, yet is unable to do so. It is only when he does not desire to change his first desire that

he should be blamed. But how about his second-order desire? Has he the ability to alter this? One can see the possibility of regress. (1970, p. 80)

But Glover rejects the regress—the search back into the individual's causal history to a point at which the individual's subsequent behavior is shaped by causes he does not control—with the following argument:

> Looked at in this way, it may appear that one would only be entitled to blame someone after an infinitely protracted investigation of his psychology. But, since it is up to us to decide when to disapprove of people, we can make a cut-off where we choose. We might say that a person is blameworthy where his bad action was one he desired to perform . . . and where this desire was not one he desired to change (rather than one he was unable to change [had he wanted to change it]). We might decide to reject as irrelevant to our attitudes any investigation of his ability or desire to change this second-order desire. (1970, pp. 80–81)

The key error centers in the assertion that, "since it is up to us to decide when to disapprove of people, we can make a cut-off where we choose" on the question of what *caused* such bad characteristics. Glover is quite willing to acknowledge that such "cut-off" decisions are "perhaps arbitrary" (p. 81); and he is right in thinking that such an admission does not undermine our decision of "when to disapprove of people." What counts as exercise of *individual* freedom (and as an act or characteristic of a specific individual) is indeed a question of what sort of individuation is most convenient; and an individual who freely acts in a vicious manner can justifiably be judged a morally bad individual. But it does not follow that the morally bad individual, who freely chooses to act viciously, *deserves blame*.

The fatal error is in supposing that we can immediately move from individual freedom to moral responsibility—that establishing the legitimacy of arbitrary cut-off points for questions of individuation and individual freedom thereby establishes that such arbitrary cut-offs of causal inquiry are also justified when dealing with questions of just deserts and moral responsibility. We cannot be so cavalier about judgments of moral responsibility. In judgments of just deserts, the degree of arbitrariness is precisely the degree of injustice. One must be able to explain why it is fair that an individual should receive special (detrimental) treatment, and arbitrary cut-off points are not the explanation. Certainly we can decide to disapprove of someone, no matter what the individual's history. It is quite legitimate to disapprove of a vicious and merciless killer, who acts from his own selfish and cruel desires; and the only question that need be asked in that context is whether the killer is actually like that, whether the killer has such desires (and is not being coerced by someone who holds his family hostage). But when the question is instead whether it is fair and just to *blame* the killer, then questions of causal history cannot be so easily ruled out.[6] Knowing only his own motives and acts, we can legitimately judge the merciless murderer to be a bad person who freely chooses to kill. But the convenience of that individual focus does not justify blocking inquiries into his causal history when considering whether he deserves blame (is morally responsible). And when we find that he experienced the most hideous sorts of systematic abuse from birth to adulthood, that undermines the belief that he deserves blame (though it does not alter our judgment that he is a bad and vicious person).

Glover wrestles with the same problem that bedevils Frankfurt and Dennett and other perceptive compatibilists who try to reconcile moral responsibility with naturalism: how can we cut off further causal inquiry before it leads to shaping forces for which the individual is obviously not morally responsible? But there is no compatibilist analog of the libertarian contracausal barrier to further causal questions. Like Frankfurt (reverberating commitments) and Dennett

47

(decisions to cut off deliberation), Glover struggles gamely with the right question; but the struggle is in vain.

WHEN WE MOVE from compatibilist attributions of individual freedom to claims of moral responsibility, we have moved across a deep chasm: rather than being an easy and immediate consequence of individual freedom, claims of moral responsibility fall into an entirely different category. Claims of moral responsibility are moral claims, are claims concerning the fairness and justice of treating an individual in a special manner. The justification of such special treatment requires a special foundation: the general convenience of the compatibilist focus on individual free will is not such a foundation.

This difference has been overlooked because the shift from the traditional transcendent notion of freedom to the compatibilist notion of individual freedom has masked an important difference between the two notions of free individual acts. The notion of contracausal free will is the perfect match for moral responsibility. In order to justify claims of moral responsibility, it must be shown that the morally responsible individual has some special individual quality that justifies special treatment of that individual, that makes such treatment fair. Contracausal free will fills that need admirably: it makes the individual an irreducibly distinct actor; it blocks any effort to push the causal explanation of the individual's behavior to a larger causal/environmental context. With contracausal free will, the individual makes choices *ab initio,* and thus has the special status required to justify claims of moral responsibility. But the compatibilist notion of individual freedom is of a very different sort: it is a convenient focus, but not a necessary stopping place. In particular, the *individual* is no longer a metaphysical-moral given. We are not individual uncaused causes, we are not individual images of God, we are not ultimate stopping points for causal explanations. Compatibilist individual freedom is convenient and functional and valuable for many purposes; but it cannot support moral responsibility.[7]

To prevent any misunderstanding, I want to emphasize that this denial of moral responsibility is neither an attack on nor a disparagement of naturalist-compatibilist individual freedom-autonomy. This is *not* a suggestion that since naturalist-compatibilist individual free will cannot support moral responsibility, therefore the compatibilist account of free will is fatally flawed; still less is it a suggestion that the compatibilist account of free will must be abandoned and transcendent free will embraced in order to save moral responsibility. To the contrary, I consider its *in*compatibility with moral responsibility to be one of many excellent features of the naturalist-compatibilist account of individual free will. (When moral responsibility is examined on its own, without the reflected light of individual free will, few will find it worth saving.) In contrast to moral responsibility, individual free will or autonomy (as elucidated by the brilliant work of Hume, Frankfurt, Dennett, Dworkin, and others) is a very useful notion, and I think it is possible to give strong moral arguments in favor of preserving, protecting, and enhancing such individual freedom. Such naturalist-compatibilist individual free will is psychologically healthy, morally worthy, and philosophically sound. (The attack on moral responsibility is not an attack on individual free will; instead—it will be argued in later chapters—the demise of moral responsibility is likely to strengthen individual free will.) But the major claim being made in this chapter should also be clear: naturalist-compatibilist individual free will does not provide an easy, obvious, immediate foundation for moral responsibility; to the contrary, the nature of naturalist individual free will (in contrast to transcendent free will) is such that there are at least *prima facie* reasons for thinking that moral responsibility cannot be reconciled with that account of free will. The remainder of this book is largely an attempt to show that there are even deeper reasons for keeping naturalist-compatibilist freedom while denying moral responsibility.

CHAPTER FOUR

The Value of Freedom Without Moral Responsibility

C. A. CAMPBELL ASSERTS that concern with free will is largely a function of concern with moral responsibility:

> It is not seriously disputable that the kind of freedom in question is the freedom which is commonly recognised to be in some sense a precondition of moral responsibility. Clearly, it is on account of this integral connection with moral responsibility that such exceptional importance has always been felt to attach to the Free Will problem. (1957, p. 159)

If one's major reason for valuing freedom is to provide a foundation for moral responsibility—for reward, punishment, credit, blame, and just deserts—then naturalist-compatibilist freedom will not be satisfactory. But the desire to preserve moral responsibility often stems from the erroneous belief that moral responsibility is inseparable from freedom, and that loss of moral responsibility means loss of freedom. When freedom is carefully distinguished from moral responsibility, then moral responsibility—viewed on its own—has few charms. Freedom (compatibilist freedom) is genuinely valuable; but it can be retained while moral responsibility is junked.

This chapter examines some outstanding representatives of contemporary compatibilism, in order to make clearer both the value of naturalist-compatibilist individual freedom and the futility of trying to establish moral responsibility on the basis of such freedom. The goal is to winnow the wheat of compatibilist individual freedom from the moral responsibility chaff.

Daniel Dennett's compatibilism focuses on reason, reflection, deliberation. A reasoning human can ask herself questions, be moved by reasons, reflect on evidence, consider the consistency and coherence of her beliefs. Dennett argues that the control and adaptability and options afforded by such intelligence are the stuff of free choice. And indeed, such intelligence *is* at the core of individual freedom and "authentic" (or autonomous) individual behavior: there is no better (naturalist-determinist) way of making an act distinctively my own than by reflectively and deliberately and rationally favoring it. But even the strong individual freedom that stems from intelligent deliberation will not support *moral* responsibility.[1]

Dennett insists that the skills of reflective deliberation and self-control *can* support moral responsibility. He starts by imagining the following dialogue:

> When the talented succeed, it is not because they are lucky, but because they are talented. Ah, but they are lucky to be talented in the first place! Not always. Some talented performers are made, not born; some have diligently trained for hours every day for years on end to achieve their prowess. . . . Ah, but they were lucky to be born with the gumption and drive required to develop their skill in training themselves. Not always. Some aren't born with that temperament, but learn it from a wise teacher or coach. Ah, but then they are lucky to have the intelligence required to comprehend the lesson of that good coach. (1984, p. 96)

And so on. And then Dennett draws the moral of the tale:

As this petulant little dialogue exhibits, there is a tendency to treat "lucky" and "unlucky" as complementary and exhaustive, leaving no room for skill at all. On this view nothing in principle could count as skill or the result of skill. This is a mistake. Once one recognizes that there is elbow room for skill in between lucky success and unlucky failure, the troubling argument that seems to show that no one could ever be responsible evaporates. Luck averages out and skill will tell in the end. (1984, p. 97)

Since the effects of good or bad luck are usually cumulative, it is certainly doubtful that "luck averages out"; but that is a topic for a later chapter (Chapter Nine). There is a more immediate problem with Dennett's interpretation of the no-fault naturalist (responsibility-denying) view in the "petulant little dialogue." The no-fault naturalist denies neither the existence nor the importance of skill; rather, what is denied is that anyone is *morally responsible* for having skill: skill is the result of good luck (ultimately one *is* just lucky to have the drive, the good coach, the intelligence). *Given* the skill, subsequent events are more likely the result of skill than of luck. The skillful player does make the winning shot: it is that player's own deliberate and practiced act; it is performed freely and skillfully and is not mere luck. The free skillful player makes things happen and plays a significant and deliberate role in the outcome. But it is quite a different thing to claim that the player deserves credit (is morally responsible) for either the skill or its effects.

There is no moral responsibility for skill, but that does not lessen its worth. One's efforts—particularly skillful efforts—can indeed make things happen. It is important to recognize that, and it is important that individuals believe that their own skillful efforts can and do have significant effects: important because those having such beliefs are likely to make stronger and more successful efforts, and important also because a vital element in psychological well-being is belief that one's efforts and skills can achieve worthwhile results.[2]

But while it is certainly valuable to have skill and to be able to make things happen and to *recognize* that one can make things happen, it does not follow that anyone is ever morally responsible for having (or lacking) skill.

There is also (as Dennett notes) such a thing as skill in deliberation and self-control, and those with high skill levels will be more likely to behave well: it is not just a "matter of luck" that one acts virtuously or viciously. But whether one has the background, the influences, the environment, the training, the good fortune to develop such skills of deliberation and self-control *is* a matter of luck and is not something for which one is morally responsible. On a naturalist view, what produces the difference between the "gifted" individual of careful deliberation and strong self-control and the profligate whose intemperate and ill-considered behavior is a constant danger? Ultimately the difference will be found in causes—genetic make-up, early family life, perhaps intervention on the part of teachers or spiritual leaders—that cannot support claims of just deserts–moral responsibility. Or perhaps one develops deliberative skills through strenuous practice, while the other neglects such efforts; but, again, we soon encounter earlier controlling factors fitting one to make such efforts and the other to neglect them. We may admire the individual's skills in deliberation and self-control (we may think them genuine qualities of the individual, a result not merely of immediate pressures but instead a deeply conditioned character trait); but it does not follow that we must regard the individual as morally responsible—as justly deserving special treatment or benefit—for those skills.

Only when individual freedom and moral responsibility are run together does it seem plausible to suppose that deliberation establishes moral responsibility. Having the desirable skills of careful deliberation and self-control is indeed to be a free person—one who has reflected on and approved his choices, who has a strong sense of being in control, and whose acts are not mere luck but instead the result of deliberate exercise of skills. There are no better grounds for individual freedom, and Dennett's elucidation of such freedom is an important contribution. But there is another question: is one morally responsible for being so reflectively and profoundly free? Whether one has or lacks the desirable skills (and thus what one does or does not achieve through one's skills) is a matter of good or bad luck in heredity, childhood, environment, not something for which one is morally responsible, unless it is supposed that one is morally responsible—deserves special treatment—for good or bad luck.

Dennett's compatibilism shows the other half of the problems generated by confusing naturalist individual freedom with moral responsibility. Because of that confusion, Dennett fears that the denial of moral responsibility entails the denial of skill (and the denial that skillful behavior can "make things happen"). Thus Dennett winds up insisting on moral responsibility when what he really wants is just naturalist-compatibilist freedom.

AS A SECOND EXAMPLE of the virtues of contemporary compatibilist accounts of freedom and the vices of confusing compatibilist freedom with moral responsibility, consider Frankfurt's superb discussion of higher-order identification with desires and acts. Frankfurt's famous "willing addict" approves of and identifies with his addictive desire for drugs and has thus "made this will his own" (1971, p. 19). It does not matter—for individual free choice—that the willing addict does not have open "alternate possibilities": his addiction compels him to take drugs whether he wishes to or not. He cannot act otherwise, but his higher-order approval of the drug-taking (and of the desire that prompts it) makes it his own. According to Frankfurt:

> To the extent that a person identifies himself with the springs of his actions, he takes responsibility for those actions and acquires moral responsibility for them; moreover, the question of how the

actions and his identifications with their springs are caused is irrelevant to the questions of whether he performs the actions freely
or is morally responsible for performing them. (1975, p. 122)

Frankfurt has noted a key element of free individual behavior:
identification with one's motives, the sense that one's effective desires
are one's own, the power of acting in a manner that reflects what
one wishes to be.[3] And Frankfurt cogently argues that one may act
freely—in the sense that one identifies with one's desires—no matter how the desire and identification were caused. But note the last
passage quoted above: "the question of how the actions and his identifications with their springs are caused is irrelevant to the questions
of whether he performs the actions freely or is morally responsible
for performing them." Here Frankfurt makes the key mistake—confusing compatibilist freedom with moral responsibility. Frankfurt
does show that causal considerations are not the key factors in establishing compatibilist individual freedom. It does not follow that they
are unimportant for questions of moral responsibility.

The willing addict acts freely. That is, if we wish to understand
the willing addict's behavior, we must focus on the addict's own (reflectively approved) motivational system and not on coercive alien
forces acting against the addict's own deepest desires: the willing addict's desires are *authentically* his own. However, there is
a further question: does the willing addict *deserve blame* for his
choices? (Is it fair to treat the willing addict in a special, detrimental manner?) Causal considerations are relevant to that question. Under what circumstances does one become a *willing* addict?
Such an individual has had rougher handling by his environment-
conditioning-circumstances than has the reform-minded addict. The
addict who wills nonaddiction has experienced joys and successes
apart from drugs and prefers those successful and interesting and
positively reinforcing alternative activities to drug addiction; but
the willing addict—because of a particularly painful or deprived

background, or because all early efforts resulted in discouraging and desire-extinguishing failure and frustration—has been deprived of other interests and pleasures. The unwilling addict wants to pursue other options and interests; the willing addict prefers the enslavement of drug addiction to the hideous void of life without drug addiction. The "choosing" of drug addiction may appear a heroic affirmation of individuality; but when a more sober inquiry removes the romantic lenses, such willing can be seen to result from shrinking options and deadened desires. Such causal history may not affect our ascription of compatibilist individual freedom and authenticity to the addict who chooses and affirms drug addiction. The motivation for taking drugs comes from deep within the willing addict, and whatever the causal history that shaped those desires, they are now the willing addict's own desires (the motives are not to be found in the immediate environmental circumstances). But to suggest that the addict's history of shriveled hopes has no bearing on questions of *blame* seems both hard-hearted and ethically implausible. And note that challenging the suggested causal history will accomplish nothing. I believe such a causal history (of interests extinguished by failure and frustration) is the most likely one for a willing addict. But nothing is gained by attacking that causal account as inaccurate or fanciful; for one who claims that Frankfurt's second-order willing establishes moral responsibility must show that the suggested causal history is irrelevant, rather than false.

Frankfurt's analysis does square with our immediate reaction to willing addicts. If the willing addict were an alcoholic, A.A. would refuse assistance. Unless he "really wants to stop," they will make no effort to help. And we might also be inclined to wash our hands of such a wretch: "He likes the way he is, he doesn't want to change; I would be willing to help if he would make some effort, but if he doesn't care why should I?" We feel more sympathy for and more willingness to help the addict who is struggling to overcome addiction. (This is not surprising, given the fact that the addict who does not want to change is a much less promising candidate for reform: helping efforts can also undergo extinction.) But while we may be justified in devoting limited treatment facilities and energies to the most promising subjects, who want to change (and in any case there are good reasons to be very wary of imposing treatment[4]), we are not justified in blaming the least promising subjects.

DENYING THAT FRANKFURT has established grounds for compatibilist moral responsibility does not mean denying the importance of what Frankfurt *has* elucidated—"compatibilist authenticity." Certainly it is important when people identify with and approve of their own desires and characters; and it is important to establish that such authenticity[5] is possible within (is compatible with) a determinist-naturalist context. But the importance of such compatibilist authenticity notwithstanding, it is not moral responsibility.[6]

The struggle of American blacks for freedom and dignity offers a significant illustration of the importance of compatibilist authenticity, and of why such authenticity does not support moral responsibility. Living in a culture which—in song and story, advertisement and beauty pageant—glorified white characteristics and disparaged black features, many blacks came to regard their own racial characteristics as alien and distasteful. Through emphasis on the attractiveness of distinctively black features, blacks came to identify with and favor their own racial characteristics. Such identification with one's appearance is an important element in personal satisfaction and dignity, and it is obviously a good thing for blacks to identify with and approve of black characteristics; but that can hardly justify taking credit (moral responsibility) for one's physical characteristics.

The same distinction applies when desires and volitions—rather than physical characteristics—are the focus of authenticity and responsibility. If a black man should desire "white" features, then one might pity that individual for being so much the dupe of a racist culture. But if that person's desires go much deeper—he wills to have such desires, is so thoroughly the tool of racist values that he regards those unfulfilled longings as his best element, they are desires with which he strongly identifies and he has no wish to eliminate them— then we would correctly regard such desires as deeply characteristic of him and authentically his own. But we should be even further from holding him morally responsible for such volitions: an individual so thoroughly debased by the culture that exploits him is surely more to be pitied than censured. The willing slave whose resistance has been destroyed does not thereby acquire moral responsibility.[7]

Frankfurt makes a cogent case for the value of individual freedom and authenticity in our determinist-naturalist world. But the common mistake of linking freedom to moral responsibility leads him to suppose that moral responsibility must be saved in order to preserve such freedom. When Frankfurt's account is purged of dubious claims for moral responsibility, then the strength and value of compatibilist-naturalist individual freedom (which such compatibilists as Frankfurt and Dennett do much to elucidate) is even plainer.

THIS CHAPTER ENDS with an example that dramatically marks the distance between compatibilist freedom and moral responsibility. Imagine two individuals, Saul and Paul, who are reflectively living honorable lives. They are both kidnapped by a cult of Wotan worshippers, a thoroughly despicable group who are dedicated to everything low and dastardly. Saul is kidnapped first, and he successfully resists the efforts of the cult to convert him to their cause (they use propaganda and crude brainwashing techniques but are not successful). Six months after he is kidnapped, Saul escapes and returns to his morally exemplary life. A year after Saul is kidnapped the Wotan worshippers abduct Paul. By this time their conversion techniques have become much more potent (they are now using drugs, or subliminal techniques, or whatever). Paul succumbs to those techniques, renounces his previously held principles, and becomes an enthusiastic convert to the ways of Wotan. Saul and Paul, *prior* to their abductions, were all but indistinguishable: they held similar principles for similar reasons, and they held them with similar degrees of reflectiveness, steadfastness, and self-control. Had Paul been subjected to the conversion techniques experienced by Saul, Paul would have successfully resisted; and had Saul been kidnapped when Paul was kidnapped, he would have succumbed.

In neither case are we dealing with conversion techniques that turn the subject into a zombie. In the case of Paul the techniques are certainly powerful: they radically alter Paul's preferences, desires, feelings, sympathies. But they leave the individual's reasoning and reflective and deliberative powers intact. (It would be a mistake to suppose that such radical changes must destroy rationality. A person's basic values may change—from a radical youth to a reactionary old age, from deep faith to agnosticism—without diminishing her rational capacities. Certainly some who undergo such profound belief changes are reflective and deliberative and self-controlled during both stages. From a naturalist-determinist perspective there is no reason to suppose that accelerating or controlling such a process would be impossible in principle.)

So Paul is a reflective and conscientious and enthusiastic member of the Wotan cult. He regards his past attitudes as silly and sentimental and is delighted that he now finds in himself a stoney temperament. He approves of his current acts, is delighted at his good fortune in being kidnapped by the Wotan worshippers (otherwise he would have remained in the views he now despises), and considers the cult's Draconian conversion measures justified by the marvelous result.

Paul acts freely: he identifies with his desires, and his higher-order volitions approve of his first-order desires; he reflectively approves of his acts; he exhibits impressive self-control; and he is resolutely committed to the Wotanian program and strives to deepen that commitment. But while Paul now acts freely (by quite reasonable and convenient compatibilist standards of freedom), his moral responsibility is at least doubtful. Any one of us, under the same circumstances, would have also become enthusiastic worshippers of Wotan. And it is sheer accident that Saul had the good fortune to be kidnapped earlier, before the conversion techniques were perfected. Can Saul claim that he deserves praise for his upstanding behavior and that Paul deserves blame for his despicable acts?

Naturalist-compatibilist moral responsibility is undermined by this example, and it cannot be shored up with further requirements. Michael Levin maintains that cases of implanted desires fail, because as soon as the victim goes on "internal power" and recognizes the source of the desire the victim will reject the desire; and if the victim is not allowed to recognize the source, then that impairs rationality and the example fails (1979, pp. 250f.). But the kidnapping case is well protected against the first horn of Levin's dilemma. Paul can be placed—as Levin legitimately demands—on full "internal power" in such a manner that Paul reasons and examines causal histories and acts from his own internalized desires. In such circumstances it does not follow that Paul will, as Levin assumes, "presumably want to be rid of wire-induced desires." For Paul—so thorough is his conversion—may be grateful to his captors for the desires they implanted in him. He may recognize that (under his old "benighted" outlook) no *rational* persuasion techniques could have so radically altered his views and thus be glad (given his profound disgust with his earlier views) that his captors adopted such extreme methods of changing his outlook. Thus Paul's wires may be arranged so skillfully that the compatibilist advocate of moral responsibility will be required—counterintuitively and unfairly—to find Paul morally responsible and deserving of opprobrium.[8]

CHAPTER FIVE

Responsibility:
The Nonmoral Varieties

THE PREVIOUS CHAPTERS ARGUE that there is no moral responsibility for anyone anytime, and the following chapters will press that claim forward. But it is also important to note some other uses of "responsibility" that are not being challenged. It is important, first, because the other senses of "responsibility" may continue to be useful when moral responsibility is abandoned. Second, the arguments that will be offered against *moral* responsibility must not be misinterpreted as opposing those other types of responsibility. Third—and most important—arguments for the *other* senses of responsibility are often mistakenly thought to support *moral* responsibility.

IN *Elbow Room* DANIEL DENNETT develops several fresh and interesting arguments for moral responsibility. Among them is the following. Dennett notes that we are all "the 'gifted' ones":

> That is, I take it that all my readers are members, like me, in the community of reason-givers and considerers. We are all gifted with the powers of deliberation, or we wouldn't be here (in the adult world of books and readers). . . .

We gifted ones are good at deliberation and self-control, and so we expect a good deal of each other in these regards. On the basis of those expectations we place gifted ones in positions of trust and responsibility, and then we *count on them* to do the right thing. . . .
We are not totally responsible for being responsible, of course. . . . After all, a mugger might leap out of an alley and brain me tomorrow. I would then be unlucky enough to lose my status as a responsible citizen through no fault or error of my own. (1984, p. 98)

Dennett's disarming disclaimer is the clue to the problem: "We are not totally responsible for being responsible." (In fact we are not at all responsible for being responsible, but let that pass for the moment.) Dennett is here using two different senses of "responsible"; and, as a result, Dennett's case for the "responsibility" of "we gifted ones" is not a case for our *moral* responsibility.

We do indeed place gifted ones in "positions of trust and responsibility"; but that sort of responsibility has little or nothing to do with desert and blame and credit: it is not moral responsibility. Instead, such positions of trust confer special *role*-responsibility.[1] H. L. A. Hart describes role-responsibility thus:

A sea captain is responsible for the safety of his ship, and this is his responsibility, or one of his responsibilities. . . . A sentry [is responsible] for alerting the guard at the enemy's approach; a clerk for keeping the accounts of his firm. These examples of a person's responsibilities suggest the generalization that, whenever a person occupies a distinctive place or office in a social organization, to which specific duties are attached to provide for the welfare of others or to advance in some specific way the aims or purposes of the organization, he is properly said to be responsible for the performance of these duties, or for doing what is necessary to fulfil them. . . . If two friends, out on a mountaineering expedition, agree that the one shall look after the food and the other the maps, then the one is correctly said to be responsible for the food, and the other for the maps, and I would classify this as a case of role-responsibility. (1968, p. 212)

When the nature of role-responsibility is recognized, there is nothing strange in saying that an individual is not morally responsible for failing her role-responsibility. Role-responsibility and moral responsibility are distinct issues. To determine whether one has role-responsibility requires examining the role one is playing and the duties of that role. But determining whether one is morally responsible poses the quite different question of whether one deserves special treatment for one's behavior. Jones may "have responsibility" (role-responsibility) for picking up the key to the lecture hall; but we may—consistent with ascriptions of responsibility in that sense— also hold that Jones is not morally responsible (not to be blamed) for forgetting to pick it up (the poor man's memory is failing). It *is* his role-responsibility, but he is not responsible (not morally responsible) for failing to discharge it. In short, there are "responsible" persons who have substantial "responsibilities" and who have been placed in such positions of "responsibility" because they are self-controlled, deliberate, trustworthy. But all of that is a matter of role-responsibility and must not be confused with moral responsibility. Establishing that Joan is a wonderfully (role)-responsible person does not establish that she is morally responsible for those good qualities, any more than establishing that Jeff is terribly irresponsible establishes that Jeff deserves blame (is morally responsible) for that serious flaw. Thus proving the existence and usefulness of role-responsibility will not prove the viability and benefits of moral responsibility.

This confusion of role with moral responsibility has bedeviled some of the most innovative and influential recent work on responsibility, in which defenders of responsibility have focused on *taking* responsibility. Rather than asking whether a given individual *has* moral responsibility, the question becomes how one might claim or acquire or develop or *take* responsibility. In this type of argument for responsibility, the claim is that people can and do sometimes simply take responsibility. When I knowingly and willingly take responsibility for my acts or character or desires or choices, then they become my responsibility (no matter what part my past history may have played in shaping such character and causing such acts). For example, in his insightful account of taking responsibility, Frankfurt asserts:

> To the extent that a person identifies himself with the springs of his actions, he takes responsibility for those actions and acquires responsibility for them; moreover, the question of how the actions and his identifications with their springs is caused is irrelevant to the questions of whether he performs the actions freely or is morally responsible for performing them. (Frankfurt, 1975, p. 122)

In short, one takes responsibility by claiming, identifying with, asserting as one's own.

Along similar lines Dennett also emphasizes the taking of responsibility:

> What we want when we want free will is the power to decide our courses of action, and to decide them wisely, in the light of our expectations and desires. We want to be in control of ourselves, and not under the control of others. We want to be agents, capable of initiating, and taking responsibility for, projects and deeds. (1984, p. 169)

And consider one other compatibilist attempt to save responsibility from naturalism-determinism by "taking" responsibility.

Edward Madden insists that moral responsibility can be saved from determinist challenges by means of "the existentialist insight":

> namely, that in normal or non-neurotic behavior the point is not that man *is* responsible but that he *becomes* responsible as the price of maturity, of no longer being a child, and thus that he does *accept* responsibility for the consequences of his personality and character even though he had no control over their formation. (1973, pp. 110–111)

So responsibility, from this "taking" perspective, is not a static property but is instead an active acquisition process. And this perspective is certainly a helpful one, especially in elucidating what it is we actually want in the way of individual free will and free choice and self-control.

Such claims make sense when the responsibility taken is role-responsibility; but when role-responsibility is then confused with moral responsibility, the resulting claims of "taking (moral) responsibility" become nonsense.

Consider a situation in which it is legitimate to speak of "taking responsibility." To use Hart's example, I can "take responsibility" for looking after the maps during a mountaineering expedition. In such a case, I am the one who is responsible for obtaining accurate maps and keeping them safe during the trek. That is my responsibility because I took it. But that is quite different from saying that I have moral responsibility for taking care of the maps, that I deserve credit for scrupulously caring for the maps or blame for losing them. It is certainly meaningful to say that I am responsible for the maps (role-responsible), yet I am not responsible (not morally responsible, deserve no blame) for abysmally failing to carry out the duties of map-keeper: "He took responsibility for the maps; but with his advancing senility, he is not (morally) responsible for failing at that responsibility."

One can assert and take role-responsibility, in at least some settings; but one cannot simply assert and take moral responsibility. To see the absurdity of the latter, consider a player who "takes responsibility" for covering center field. The player is naturally so swift and sure-handed and clear-eyed that she effortlessly catches every ball hit to center field. She has splendidly fulfilled the duties for which she took responsibility; but it is something else again to claim that she deserves credit or praise for what she has done. One might argue that she is so wonderfully swift and skillful that she should have covered the entire outfield, and not merely center field, and that thus she deserves no praise for lethargically performing so far below her natural capacities. Or one might object that her wondrous skills are purely genetic (she smokes and never exercises), and thus she deserves no credit for her splendid play. Such claims may be completely false and misdirected; but the point is that she could not *answer* such denials of her moral responsibility for her acts merely by asserting that she is *taking responsibility* for them. An eight-foot-tall basketball player with enormously long arms might well take responsibility for blocking any shots near the basket; but it is something else for him to claim moral responsibility (to claim that he deserves credit and praise) for carrying out a role for which his genes admirably suited him.

In one setting the temptation to confuse taking role-responsibility with acquiring moral responsibility becomes particularly seductive. There are cases in which we do not merely "take responsibility" for a social task or duty, but indeed even "take responsibility" for our own individual development and destiny. In such cases we "hold ourselves responsible" for what we are and what we become. At first glance this appears the magic key to deserving full credit and blame for whatever one does and whatever one becomes. It is not. Such super role-responsibility comes no closer to establishing moral responsibility than do any of the other uses of role-responsibility. In fact, such cases of taking role-responsibility for self-development accentuate rather than ameliorate the problems with moral responsibility. If one "takes responsibility" for one's own future and development, then one does indeed take the role of setting one's future course and shaping one's future character: one is responsible—role-responsible—for one's self. But I may take such responsibility (that is, I assert that *I* will make the decisions about my own life, I will *not* be under a therapist's or guru's or parent's or teacher's or lover's direction) while still not being morally responsible for the fact that my own guidance of my life is effective or faulty.[2] Taking role-responsibility for the direction of my own life is no more to establish that I am morally responsible for the direction my life takes than taking role-responsibility for the maps makes me morally responsible for doing that task well or ill. This is obvious enough when it is considered soberly, with the distinction between role-responsibility and moral responsibility clearly in view. But when glorious phrases like "I take responsibility for myself and for what I shall become" are bandied about, then such obvious points become obscured. One can take *role*-responsibility for covering center field or preparing a lecture or planning one's own life and character; but one can not take *moral* responsibility for any of those tasks.

To summarize the above points: one may take (role)-responsibility for building a boat or building a character (including one's own future character); but whether one has *moral* responsibility for such building (for the way in which the task is carried out or for taking on the role-responsibility) is another matter. If the boat sinks, or sets speed records, we shall look to the builder (who had role-responsibility) for the causes and reasons; if the life goes wrong, we shall in similar fashion look to the planner who took role-responsibility for it. But while such inquiries will certainly be at least a step in the explanation of boat and life development, we can also go further and look at the shaping of the builder's or planner's talents. If the boat sank, we look to the boat designer's faulty work for the proximate cause; but we may also look further and discover that the designer received severely flawed training in her boat-building studies. If the individual's life goes down the "lost highway" (of country music lore) then we may look to the individual who took role-responsibility for that life in order to understand why it went wrong; but we may again go further and examine what shaped the role-responsible individual into such a poor life-planner. In both cases, finding who is role-responsible will leave those further questions entirely open and will not establish *moral* responsibility.[3]

It is important to note that there is nothing wrong with taking role-responsibility for one's self; to the contrary, it has many advantages. For example, one is more likely to be vigilantly concerned with one's future development than is anyone else. Also, the very process of taking responsibility for one's own development and future may enhance one's powers of self-control and deliberation.[4] If I rely on myself to plan my future (rather than passively following the direction of others) I am likely to develop my capacities for careful planning and reflective deliberation in the process. But the genuine advantages of such role-responsibility for one's self are not points in favor of moral responsibility.

There is obviously more to say about developing one's self, and about claims that such self-development might support claims of moral responsibility for one's own acts and developed character. (Chapter Six will be devoted to that issue.) The claim here is not that self-development cannot support moral responsibility. (It cannot, but that will be argued later and is not now being claimed.) Rather, the claim is only that the legitimate assertion of role-responsibility for the development of one's self is *not* the same as (and does not establish, and should not be confused with) asserting *moral* responsibility for the development of self. I may be role-responsible for my self-development, yet not be morally responsible for carrying out that project well or ill. If one still maintains that role-responsibility does somehow lead to moral responsibility, then that will require further argument—argument that those who confuse role-responsibility with moral responsibility have failed to give, because the ambiguous use of "responsibility" has concealed the need for such argument.

When role-responsibility is distinguished from moral responsibility, another problem can be eliminated. People worry about loss of moral responsibility for many reasons—all bad—and it will require the remainder of the book to deal with the most substantial of them. Having distinguished role-responsibility from moral responsibility, we can eliminate one reason for worrying about the denial of moral responsibility. As noted above, role-responsibility is important; and, as Dennett points out, "we gifted ones" are big-time players in the role-responsibility game: "We gifted ones are good at deliberation and self-control, and so we expect a good deal of each other in these regards. On the basis of those expectations we place gifted ones in positions of trust and responsibility." Our positions of trust and responsibility—our role-responsibilities—are vital to fulfilling our goals, being in control, "making things happen." So if it is denied that one can ever have role-responsibility, then one has good reason to be disturbed: to be denied role-responsibility would mean being denied "positions of trust and responsibility" in which we can influence events. (That is most obviously and horribly the case if my role-responsibility for my own self-development is denied.) Furthermore, when we consider the grounds on which role-responsibility is denied—defective capacities for deliberation and self-control—it is again reasonable to resent claims that one cannot qualify for role-responsibility. Obviously, then, denial of the capacity for role-responsibility is something to resent: it means one cannot effectively deliberate, cannot exercise restraint, cannot carry out one's plans and promises. To be so regarded is not only to be categorized as defective but also to be denied the opportunity to make things happen. But denial of moral responsibility entails no such difficulty. Role-responsibility is denied on the basis of defect. In contrast, the (universal) no-fault naturalist denial of moral responsibility carries no implication of defect or inadequacy: no one is ever morally responsible, no matter how psychologically and rationally sound that person may be. The most splendidly role-responsible individual is not morally responsible for her strong role-responsibility.

FAILURE TO DISTINGUISH CAREFULLY between role and moral responsibility has also been the source of accountability muddles. One sense of "being responsible" is "being accountable": one is "responsible for" an act if "accountable" for it, if one can be "held to account" for the act and reasonably expected to give an account or explanation or justification for the act. But this accountability sense of responsibility is role-responsibility (rather than moral responsibility). Being expected to "give an account" of an act implies the act is part of one's rational plans and purposes. One is not moved by demons or obsessions or madness, one has not been coerced or deceived or tricked into the act; instead, this is an act that is an element of one's own reasoned plan of life. And to make and have plans for one's life is precisely to be *role-responsible* for one's life. I am the proximate cause of the behavior, and the role-responsibility for my plans and acts is my own (no one else has role-responsibility for my life). But the profound differences between role-responsibility and moral responsibility remain. One may have role-responsibility for one's own acts, and thus be the individual best suited to give (at least a proximate) account of one's behavior, yet not be morally responsible for the skill (or lack of skill) with which one discharges one's role-responsibility.

IN ADDITION TO THE PROBLEMS caused by confusion of role-responsibility with moral responsibility, there is another ambiguity that sometimes sets discussions of moral responsibility at cross purposes.

In this book, "moral responsibility" is used in its central and most common meaning: "moral responsibility" justifies or even requires special treatment or special deserts. It is fair for the morally responsible individual who acts virtuously to receive greater benefits and fewer detriments than are accorded the morally responsible person who behaves viciously. This might be called "moral-judgment responsibility." However, there is another sense of "moral responsibility" that must be distinguished from moral-judgment responsibility.

The sense of "moral responsibility" that is to be distinguished from moral-judgment responsibility might be called "moral-act responsibility." Moral-act responsibility designates a particular sphere of responsibility—responsibility for distinctively moral (or immoral) behavior. H. L. A. Hart uses this second sense of "moral-act responsibility" (though he does not call it that, and he doesn't distinguish it from moral-judgment responsibility) in the following passage:

> Thus a man may be morally as well as legally responsible for the maintenance of his wife and children, but a host's responsibility for the comfort of his guests, and a referee's responsibility for the control of the players is neither legal nor moral. (1968*b*, pp. 213–214)

In this use, one might be responsible for discovering a new element—but since discovering or failing to discover a new element is not ordinarily regarded as a moral issue, one would not be morally responsible (moral-act responsible) for that nonmoral act. There is no *moral* responsibility because the act is not within the special domain of moral/immoral behavior. The discovery of new elements is not like returning a lost diamond or bearing false witness or stealing from the poor box. If I search diligently for a new element without success, I shall not be morally responsible (moral-act responsible) for my failure, simply because morality does not enter into it one way or the other. In this use of moral responsibility, "moral" marks the domain of interest: it is moral, as opposed to, say, aesthetic or legal.

The other sense of "moral responsibility" (here called moral-judgment responsibility) is quite different from moral-act responsibility, in both intension and extension. The moral-judgment sense of moral responsibility (which is the focus of this book) is not concerned with the types of acts for which one is responsible (moral as opposed to nonmoral); instead, moral-judgment responsibility focuses on the process by which responsibility is assigned. In this sense one is *morally* responsible (moral-judgment responsible) for an act if it is judged morally right to assign one blame, praise, credit, punishment. In moral-judgment responsibility the question is not whether the *act* falls within the domain of moral concern; rather, the question is whether it is judged fair and just that special treatment (blame, punishment, praise, or reward) should be given for that act. Thus it might be claimed that one is moral-judgment responsible for an act that is nonmoral: Edward is moral-judgment responsible for writing the poem (a nonmoral act) because he deserves the praise for writing such fine verse, he deserves the poetry prize, he deserves the glory. On the other hand, Alice is moral-act responsible for the theft of the ring (of her own volition she committed a morally bad act) but not moral-judgment responsible (when we consider her unfortunate background we decide she is more to be pitied than censured).

The confusion of moral-act responsibility with moral-judgment responsibility has been a source of confusion on two fronts. First, it has obscured the real conflict between compatibilists and incompatibilists. In the classic compatibilist arguments of David Hume, the compatibility of determinism with moral responsibility is easily established: we find an act that is morally bad, and then we seek the immediate cause of that act; the responsible source is just the point at which punishment is efficacious. Contemporary compatibilists have greatly refined Hume's argument, but the crux of the position remains the same: this is a morally bad act; this individual is the source of that act (perhaps not the ultimate or final source, but the causal forces nonetheless operate from that individual's desires/will); thus this individual is responsible; the individual is responsible for a moral (or immoral) act, and thus this individual is morally responsible. It follows that determinism is obviously compatible with moral responsibility—that is, with moral-act responsibility. But when incompatibilists (no-fault naturalists) deny moral responsibility, they are not denying moral-act responsibility. They acknowledge that there are morally bad (and good) acts and that it is quite reasonable and practical to trace the responsibility (the proximate cause) for those acts to the individuals who will them (although no-fault naturalists will insist that the significant causal path by no means ends at that individual). No-fault naturalists instead are concerned with moral-judgment responsibility. For them the question is not whether an individual can be the (proximate) source of a morally bad act. Rather, the question is whether it is morally right—is it fair, is it just—to blame or punish an individual for being moral-act responsible. And when the no-fault naturalist considers that the individual who committed the morally bad act did so as a result of causal forces that were ultimately a matter of bad luck (the individual willed the morally bad act, but the individual's will is the product of causal forces, etc.) then the no-fault naturalist considers it unfair to blame that individual. For the no-fault naturalist moral responsibility is a moral question—and a moral question of a particular type. It is not a question of whether the acts committed by the individual have moral standing; rather, it is a question of the moral rightness or wrongness, the justice, of treating an individual in a special manner because of acts that are ultimately the product of chance. Of course, that does not settle the debate concerning compatibilism. One might still decide that it *is* just to blame or punish. The point here is only that such decisions will have to be based on more than merely finding that an individual is the source of a morally bad act (is moral-act responsible). That is, those who doubt moral-*judgment* responsibility will not be convinced by demonstrations of moral-*act* responsibility.

The other side of that coin is also important: moral responsibility is nonexistent, but the moral responsibility being denied is moral-*judgment* responsibility. The no-fault naturalist does not deny moral-act responsibility, and thus does not deny the category of moral acts. It is sometimes claimed that the denial of moral responsibility entails the denial of all moral judgments and moral considerations. That claim is false—but that will be argued in Chapter Twelve. However, one source of that mistaken claim is confusion of moral-judgment responsibility with moral-act responsibility, resulting in the mistaken belief that no-fault naturalists deny moral-*act* responsibility. *If* the no-fault naturalist denied moral-act responsibility, then a likely grounds for such denial would be the denial of the entire category of moral acts. Thus recognizing the distinction between moral-act responsibility and moral-judgment responsibility should eliminate at least one source of the mistaken belief that anyone who challenges moral responsibility must reject not only moral responsibility but all moral claims whatsoever.

WITH THIS CLARIFICATION of exactly what is being rejected—moral-judgment responsibility, not moral-act responsibility; moral responsibility, not role-responsibility; moral responsibility, not individual freedom—and what is being preserved, the groundwork is now laid for arguments against moral responsibility. The next few chapters will argue that moral responsibility is an empty category and that the best compatibilist efforts to preserve moral responsibility fail; following that demolition project, the last chapters will show why the view is better after moral responsibility has been razed and will sketch plans for an attractive alternative to be placed on that site.

CHAPTER SIX

Self-Making and Its Limits

PAUL (OF CHAPTER FOUR) is not morally responsible, since his vicious character is not of his own making. But defenders of compatibilist moral responsibility might still insist that, while moral responsibility is perhaps too widely claimed and ascribed, it should not be denied altogether: there are cases in which individuals *make themselves,* and thus are morally responsible for who they are and what they do. No mysterious transcendent autonomy is required. We daily engage in making ourselves and developing our own characters. When our characters are substantially of our own making we bear substantial moral responsibility for the result.

That is an attractive position: it attempts to save moral responsibility without appealing to mysterious transempirical powers. Aristotle proposes that sort of account in *The Nicomachean Ethics.* He asserts that the careless and negligent are to blame (are morally responsible) for such carelessness, and then considers a possible objection:

You may say that very likely he could not help it, he is just that sort of man. But there is an answer to that. Such people have only themselves to blame for having acquired a character like that by loose living, just as they have only themselves to blame for being unjust, if they make a practice of unjust behavior, or intemperate, if they spend their time in drinking or other forms of dissipation. It is their persistent activities in certain directions that make them what they are. . . . The man, then, must be a perfect fool who is unaware that people's characters take their bias from the steady direction of their activities. If a man, well aware of what he is doing, behaves in such a way that he is bound to become unjust, we can only say that he is voluntarily unjust.

. . . When once you have thrown a stone, it is gone for good and all. Still it lay with yourself to let it lie instead of picking it up and throwing it; the origin of the act was in you. Similarly it was open to the dishonest and dissolute fellow to avoid becoming such a character; so that his original action was voluntary. (Aristotle, 1955, Bk. III: chap. 5)

But for all its immediate charms, closer scrutiny reveals the deeper flaws of this attempt to base moral responsibility on "self-making." It accomplishes nothing except to push back the inevitable question: why does one choose the path of dissipation, while the other takes the path of righteousness? Since the flaws in this position are not far below the surface, the interesting question becomes: why should such a stopgap measure hold such enduring appeal? The answer lies, again, in the confusion of moral responsibility with individual freedom.

It is quite clear why Aristotle's effort to find the dissolute's moral responsibility in earlier choices will not work. Everyone agrees (in Aristotle's example) that the dissolute fellow could not now resist strong drink. But Aristotle insists that he may still be blamed—held morally responsible for his bad acts and his ruined character—because when he took the early steps toward such a dissolute life he certainly could have resisted temptation and chosen otherwise. But why, then, did the dissolute individual take that fatal first step? In what sense might he have avoided it? How could he be morally responsible for it? Those become the crucial questions—and they are questions that Aristotle does not answer. They demand answers; and since "making one's self" is invoked to justify moral responsibility *without* the mysteries of transcendent autonomy, they demand *nonmysterious* answers.

May and June both encounter the opportunity to experiment with dangerous drugs. May resists, and June succumbs; to borrow an image from Robert Frost, their paths diverged at that point, "and that has made all the difference." Aristotle now holds June morally responsible for her drug-addicted behavior, on the grounds of that earlier choice: so what is it about that earlier choice that provides grounds for moral responsibility? Why did May choose one path, June the other; and what feature of their choices justifies blaming one and praising the other?

The most popular answer is that May "made the effort" to resist, while June did not. At this early (pre-debauchery) stage, a modest degree of effort would suffice to resist temptation (later, even a very strong effort of will would not be sufficient to resist the entrenched charms of debauchery); but since at an earlier stage a quite modest and nonextraordinary degree of effort would have been sufficient to put aside the temptation, June is morally responsible for not having made that small degree of effort—and thus is morally responsible for the terrible long-terms results. Still, *why* did May exert the *small* effort, while June did not? What sort of account can we give for that common phenomenon: keeping in mind that the account must be *non*mysterious and must justify claims of moral responsibility (and differences in just deserts) for May and June.

A variety of plausible accounts can be given; but none that will support moral responsibility. Perhaps June did not recognize the drugs as a danger. She had less understanding of the process of addiction, or she overestimated her ability to control the process. Or possibly she was more susceptible to peer pressure, being less self-confident or more desperate for the approval of her friends. Or maybe she was a wishy-washy kid, easily led. Or a devil-may-care sort, willing to try anything. These are rough and ready suggestions, at best. But rough as they are, it should be clear that there is nothing in any of them that provides grounds for moral responsibility. If the difference was May's greater knowledge or perceptiveness, then that was May's good fortune and June's bad, but it is no basis for saying that one deserves reproach and the other praise. (The former may be bright, the latter dull; and those may be convenient and legitimate characterizations of the two individuals. But it does not follow that they are morally responsible for their different degrees of intelligence.) If one is more carefree, the other more sober and deliberative, that does not support claims of credit and blame.

It may be tempting to answer that such differences can support moral responsibility—that it all depends on *how* the one became more reflective and deliberative and knowledgable, the other less. But that leads to a vicious regress. If one perceived more clearly the joys of a life of caution and reflection, then why? Must we trace the causes of that to further choices? When we finally find—as we must, if we abjure mystery—that the causes of those choices stem from an environment not of the girls' making, then we are back to the original problem that drove compatibilists back into earlier choices in search of moral responsibility. If instead one asserts that tracing the choices back is not the right path to take (that just *here* is the key choice, and one is morally responsible for that choice, and the past causal history is largely irrelevant) then the question now becomes: What is it about this particular choice that justifies moral responsibility? What sort of nonmysterious account can be given of such a special act of choice or will?

The best attempts at such an account focus on our sense that we (some of us) do (sometimes) take stock of our situations, evaluate our lives, consider the way we are proceeding, and deliberately decide to continue or make some changes.[1] Whether we then continue in the same pattern or make substantial changes in our lives is thus up to us, and turns on the fundamental choices we make at such decisive junctures. If I don't like my personal relations, my career plans, my "life style," even my desires and personality—I can change them. If I decide to repudiate my tendency to indolence and procrastination, I can set up programs that will stimulate me to work more energetically and systematically. If I find that I am driving my friends away with my suspicious or malicious or parsimonious manner, then I can work on changing such character traits. Not everyone is so fortunate, of course. I might have fallen so far into dissolution that I lack the capacity to change; or I might be in a deadening and stultifying situation that I am powerless to change (imagine being marooned on Gilligan's Island); or I might have commitments (such as to parents or children) that force me to work long hours in a deadening job in order to provide for them. People who read philosophy are among the fortunate: they generally do have opportunities and capacities and resources that open up different options. (They can, for example, usually change jobs/careers; they can afford psychotherapy if they want to change some aspect of their personalities and are not sure how to do it; they can hire a coach to improve their tennis games, if they decide that will give new direction to their lives.) Not everyone enjoys such good fortune; but people who do have such open possibilities and the means of exploring them have drawn off generous measures of freedom and individual authenticity: this is my life, and if I don't approve of it I can change it to something that I do favor. That seems about as much freedom as one could reasonably ask.

However, while it is possible to develop a quite plausible and intelligible and nonmysterious account of self-constructive freedom, that account will not support moral responsibility. To see why requires looking more closely at self-constructive free will and its inadequacy as a foundation for moral responsibility.

Stuart Hampshire offers a persuasive and perceptive account of self-constructive free will, but combines it with the mistaken assumption that establishment of such free will can support claims and ascriptions of moral responsibility:

> There is a sense in which a man is responsible for any condition that he would be able to change if he tried, even if the condition was originally the effect of causes outside his control. If this principle were abandoned, one aspect of the distinction between human beings as intentional agents and animals, which are not intentional agents, would have been lost. Human beings can identify their own limitations, as one feature of the world among others to be self-consciously accepted, or, if possible, deliberately changed, rather than simply responded to. They can understand the causes of the limitations of their own thought and interests, and they may either acquiesce in these limitations or they may try to change them. . . . Every man has a responsibility to look at all times for the best action of which he is capable at that time, and not to acquiesce in his natural and his socially conditioned limitations of thought and interest without having tried to overcome them. (1967, pp. 185–186)

Thus Hampshire endeavors to acknowledge the social-environmental factors that shape us, while preserving grounds for moral responsibility:

> My character is still something for which I am responsible, chosen from a number of alternatives open to me. If I had thought that my history, and the external causes influencing me, were in any respect bad in their effects, I could at least have tried to find the means to prevent or to minimise their effect. As soon as I have identified these influences as determining influences, I am thereby faced with the choice of acquiescing or of trying to find means of diverting or nullifying their effects. (1967, p. 187)

Hampshire's analysis contributes much to our notion of freedom and self-control, and I shall now celebrate that analysis—prior to arguing that it does nothing for moral responsibility.

Hampshire makes clear that what is wanted of freedom is not freedom from our past (unless that past was so pathologically horrific or painful that we wish to renounce our entire history). Instead, we want to know that we are not the pawns or puppets of our pasts. (Indeed, many people have a particular interest in the ways in which they have either lived out the traditions and expectations and influences of their earlier history—"I followed in my father's and grandfather's footsteps in studying the law," for example—or have rejected the traditions and patterns of life of their background—"I am the first in my family to have married outside my faith"). I may regret various things about my past (I may wish, for example, that my undergraduate college had required more science courses, or that my high school tennis coach had improved my backhand, or that my parents had more strongly encouraged my music lessons); but that is quite different from wishing to obliterate all past memories and influences. Wishing for such a wiping of the slate is to wish to be a cipher, to be nothing at all. (Longing to be "reincarnated" as someone completely different is longing for one's individual mortality.) Whether I prefer to continue the path I have started or rebel against it at significant points, there still must be something there recognizable as me, the product of my past and my present. I have no wish to start from pure nothingness: that would mean the elimination of me, and the creature that springs into being from nothingness might be an interesting one, but I am not willing to be replaced by it.

In nonpathological, ordinary cases it is not the existence of past influences and shaping that worries us; rather, it is the fear that we are merely puppets jerked about by the strings of our past. Hampshire cogently argues that such fears are largely groundless: we can, normally, consider and evaluate our past influences; and we can, if we judge them deleterious, endeavor—often successfully—to eliminate or at least ameliorate their influence. If I judge the influence of my childhood friends to be narrowing and stifling, I can attempt to make new friends; if I find that my childhood has instilled prejudice against a race or gender or ethnic group, then I can diligently pursue measures—such as spending more time with members of such groups, reading books or papers by them, watching films or dramas that present them sympathetically—that will lessen or eliminate that unwanted prejudice; if I find that I have developed a troublesome tendency to procrastinate or eat junk food or watch too much television, then I can try a variety of measures to correct those problems, from simply cultivating other interests to setting up a token economy by which a friend rewards me as my behavior gradually approximates the desired end. Thus if I wish I can change. I am not a prisoner of my early environment and upbringing, for I can take effective measures to change my behavior and desires and interests.

All of that is worth noting, for two reasons: First, people often worry—needlessly, as the above points indicate—that they are trapped in a web of past influences that prevents them from making desired changes. Second, noting the possibilities for self-change is important because it sets the stage for showing that even the strongest compatibilist account of individual freedom (and self-control and self-making and self-evaluation) leads not one step closer to moral responsibility.

The sort of freedom and self-control described by Hampshire will not—for all its merits—support moral responsibility. In the first place, this sort of individual self-evaluation and self-improvement and self-scrutiny is something of a luxury item. The hurly-burly of everyday life—of getting and spending, commuting and computing, helping the P.T.A. and worrying about the C.I.A.—leaves most people little time or energy for reflective self-evaluation. (An individual who does carefully evaluate the direction her life is taking and decide to make changes will probably be sent to a therapist for help with her "mid-life crisis.") And even with time and inclination, self-scrutiny is likely to be stifled by the stultifying and pervasive effects of television and religion and consumerism. Popular "self-improvement" books focus on how to achieve one's desires (how to have more friends, more money, more influence, fewer worries) rather than on critical evaluation of desires and goals. In the academy, where there is more time and opportunity for reflective self-evaluation, the serious scrutiny of one's own life and goals and values is rare (compared, say, to the serious scrutiny of epistemology or subatomic particles or microeconomics—or moral responsibility, for that matter). In short, most people do not reflectively examine their own lives and goals and directions and influences. Of course some people diverge radically from their childhood training and move in unusual directions, but seldom because of careful evaluation of themselves and their histories and their goals. So even if reflective self-evaluation—and the opportunities it affords for change—*could* support moral responsibility, that would still leave moral responsibility confined to the rather narrow range of those who engage in such reflective activities. Of course one might claim that those who do not engage in such self-reflection and self-evaluation have made a reflective choice not to do so; but that sort of claim is enormously implausible (would it be an *unconscious* reflective choice?). And, as the next section will show, if the claim were true it would still not establish moral responsibility.

Reflective self-evaluation will not establish broad moral responsibility, since it is not broadly practiced. But in fact it will not even establish moral responsibility for those who practice self-scrutiny zealously and effectively. The first issue, as noted above, is whether one engages in such self-evaluation at all, and if so to what degree. Whatever the causes leading to self-evaluation, it hardly seems likely that one will find grounds for holding an individual morally responsible for engaging or failing to engage in such evaluative practices. Why is it that one carefully scrutinizes his life and background and goals and another does not? The answer cannot turn on a reflective decision to self-evaluate; or at least it cannot turn on such a decision without turning in a tight circle. Perhaps it is because one is more reflective "by nature," or one was brought up in an environment that positively reinforced such self-evaluation, or because one's dynamic philosophy professor brought vividly to life the notion that "the unexamined life is not worth living." Whatever, none of that seems the stuff of moral responsibility. One's good fortune in genetics or early childhood or educational background does not give one a special desert status; in fact, those *are* special benefits, not grounds for *deserving* special benefits. Besides, if we were morally responsible for the causes that stimulated self-evaluation—which cannot without regress include self-evaluation—then we could be morally responsible *without* self-evaluation; in that case, all of the complicated claims about how self-evaluation supports moral responsibility would be merely a scenic but superfluous detour.

But it might still be claimed that those who do engage in such self-evaluation (for whatever causes) are both free and morally responsible. (One might not be morally responsible for being—or not being—morally responsible; nonetheless, those who carry out careful self-evaluation and exercise—or fail to exercise—self-control are morally responsible.) But even that narrow band of moral responsibility cannot be sustained. For the question now becomes one of the quality of one's self-evaluation and self-control—and, for that, one is not morally responsible.

Suppose that one does indeed reflect upon, and reflectively approve, one's values and goals and direction of life—but that one does it poorly. There are lots of ways that might happen. Perhaps one lacks the imaginative capacity or the variety of experiences necessary to consider alternatives adequately; or possibly one is stifled by religious or political or cultural dogmas to such an extent that the dangerous glint of heterodoxy prevents serious consideration of alternatives; or possibly one does consider other alternatives, but with inadequate care and depth due to limitations in intellectual capacity and energy, so that the evaluations of competing alternatives are seriously flawed, with key features of each one omitted. But is one morally responsible for being such a poor judge, for lacking depth of perception? Of course one might say that the analysis should be pushed back: how did this individual become such a dud at considered judgment? Shouldn't that individual have chosen a different sort of life earlier, and thus become better at this important skill? But that line will not work here: for here we are going back, by hypothesis, to the earliest formative choices that shape later choices. Some individuals then choose badly and nonreflectively, and those choices have consequences that then reverberate through all their later choices (by damaging their development of reflective judgment); but how can they be held morally responsible for being so lousy, at this first choice stage, at making careful reflective choices?

Differences in capacity for making intelligent reflective choices seem, then, a weak foundation for grounding moral responsibility. But this chapter is somewhat preliminary. The usual focus of those who insist on moral responsibility through self-making is not on intelligence or emotions or values, but instead on effort. That is obviously the case with Hampshire, as noted above:

> My character is still something for which I am responsible, chosen from a number of alternatives open to me. If I had thought that my history, and the external causes influencing me, were in any respect bad in their effects, I could at least have tried to find the means to prevent or to minimise their effect. As soon as I have identified these influences as determining influences, I am thereby faced with the choice of acquiescing or of trying to find means of diverting or nullifying their effects. (1967, p. 187)

It is on that point that the plausibility or implausibility of self-making ultimately turns. I am not morally responsible for my initial intelligence or emotions or values, but I am responsible for making an effort to evaluate and—if necessary—change my character and desires and even abilities. With the issue so conveniently focused, it is now time to examine the plausibility of the effort approach to self-making. The next chapter will examine effort—efforts at self-making as well as less exotic varieties—as a basis for moral responsibility. As will be argued, effort accomplishes much: but even the best efforts cannot sustain claims of moral responsibility and just deserts.

CHAPTER SEVEN

Why the Best Efforts Cannot Support Moral Responsibility

EFFORT SEEMS THE MOST immediately and enduringly plausible foundation for moral responsibility and just deserts.[1] It is obvious that people differ in strengths and talents, intelligence and dexterity. It is also obvious that such differences result from causal factors (genetic makeup, early childhood, family environment) for which the individuals are not responsible. But effort seems a different matter. I cannot sing like Luciano Pavarotti, not if I struggle with voice lessons and breathing exercises until the crack of doom. Nonetheless, I can—it seems—exert just as much effort as Pavarotti does. The results may still be decidedly mediocre, and my best performance will be woefully bad when compared to Pavarotti's worst. But it is up to me to exert the effort, in a manner in which it is not up to me how tall or fleet or musically talented I am. I am responsible for *trying*.

This position appeals to many careful and fair-minded people who have struggled with the problem of just deserts; and no one has made the case for effort as the basis of just deserts more eloquently or cogently than James Rachels. His arguments can serve as a strong representative of the position:

According to the view I am defending, we may deserve things by working for them, but not simply by being naturally intelligent or talented or lucky in some other way. Now it may be thought that this view is inconsistent, because whether someone is willing to work is just another matter of luck, in much the same way that intelligence and talent are matters of luck. . . . So if a person does not deserve anything on account of his intelligence or natural abilities, how can he deserve anything on account of his industriousness? Isn't willingness to work just another matter of luck?

The first thing to notice here is that people do not deserve things on account of their *willingness* to work, but only on account of their actually having worked. . . . Therefore it is no objection to the view I am defending to say that willingness to work is a character trait that one does not merit. For, on this view, the basis of desert is not a character trait of any kind, not even industriousness. The basis of desert is a person's past actions.

Now it may be that some people have been so psychologically devastated by a combination of poor native endowment and unfortunate family and social circumstances that they no longer have the capacity for making anything of their lives. If one of these people has a job, for example, and doesn't work very hard at it, it's no use blaming him because, as we would say, he just hasn't got it in him to do any better. On the other hand, there are those in whom the capacity for effort has not been extinguished. Among those, some choose to work hard, and others, who *could* so choose, do not. It is true of everyone in this latter class that he is *able,* as Rawls puts it, "to strive conscientiously." The explanation of why some strive, while others don't, has to do with their own choices. When I say that those who work hard are more deserving of success, promotions, etc., than those who don't, I have in mind comparisons made among people in the latter class, in whom the capacity for effort has not been extinguished. (1978, pp. 157–158)

Rachels sets out the effort-makes-desert position perspicuously; but the problems of the position are also clear. The most severe of those problems is this: even if the focus is to be on *making an effort* (rather than on *capacity* to make an effort), how can it be maintained that such effort-making is not merely "another matter of luck" (and thus not a just basis for claims of just deserts and moral responsibility) like making a brilliant play or singing a splendid solo? Of course none of those is a matter of luck in the simple way that winning the lottery is a matter of luck; whether one plays brilliantly or sings beautifully or works industriously is the result of one's own capacities. But if brilliant athletic or musical performances are not an adequate basis for just deserts because they stem from one's good genetic-environmental luck in having the talents and capacities for such brilliant performances, then how can dilatory or diligent work be an adequate basis for just deserts, when the capacities that give rise to such work are equally the product of good genetic-environmental luck?

Rachels attempts to finesse that issue. He asserts that he is considering only those with the capacity for effort, who then choose to either work hard or not work hard. But that finesse will not go through, for two reasons. First, the notion of "choosing" to work hard is more a philosophic embellishment than an actual phenomenon; and, second, even if there are occasions of "choosing" to work hard, that will raise more questions than it answers.

In our workaday world the experience of "choosing to make an effort" is a rare one at best. The only thing in my experience that comes close is when during tennis I blow an easy forehand, and then exhort myself to try harder. Even then it seems more like reminding myself to concentrate and watch the ball, rather than choosing to exert more effort. Certainly on most occasions when we exert effort (or fail to exert effort) no process of "choosing" to exert effort occurs prior to the effort-exerting. We just do—or do not—exert the effort. Neither when I work diligently nor when I dawdle do I first *choose* which to do; rather, I just do it. Occasionally, in disgust at my own lethargy, I may berate myself and resolve to work harder; but even that is less like choosing to exert effort than simply taking useful steps to make more sustained efforts.

Only under the (conscious or unconscious) influence of superautonomous contracausal free will does it seem natural and plausible to speak of "choosing to exert effort." The transcendently autonomous self is totally in control: it never just "does" anything, for that would lead to questions about the conditioning history that caused the self to do that; instead, it "chooses" every act, and those choices come from its very own self, and no further questions are allowed. As Rachels puts it: "The explanation of why some strive, while others don't, has to do with their own choices." End of story, halt to further causal inquiry: the responsible source has been reached and no further questions are appropriate. But here we are considering compatibilist positions, which abjure the mysteries of transcendent free will and endeavor to establish both freedom and moral responsibility within a naturalist-determinist framework. And so (for compatibilists, including Rachels) "their own choices" cannot be final and inexplicable, and the question of *why* such choices were made must be a legitimate one.

The model of the "choosing self"—who constantly makes choices about what degree of effort to exert—distorts our perspective in another way. That model encourages us to view the choosing self as making choices about the degree of effort to exert on each individual project: this much effort here, a little less on that project, maximum effort on something else. But that again is part of the model of the individual chooser making self-originating choices for each aspect of her life. Such a model may fit the requirements of the morally responsible self, but it is alien to our common experience. People do not make an effort here and withhold an effort there; rather, some people are industrious and others lethargic, and there are many degrees between. Some people are simply more industrious than others—not on one project or another (that is the influence of the model of each individual making individual and independent choices) but instead quite generally. When we are concerned about questions of just deserts and moral responsibility, we are primarily concerned with that general characteristic of diligence and energy. The question is not so much why I exert (or fail to exert) effort on this particular project; rather, the question is why I am industrious (or lethargic) in pursuing my own projects and goals, *whatever* they may be. Some people take their projects and goals very seriously, and others do not; but that is precisely the stuff of industry or lethargy. A key element of lethargy is finding nothing very significant or worthwhile or worth doing (or, if one does consider something worth doing, one doubts one's capacity to do it). The effort-making person finds projects worthwhile and confidently endeavors to bring them to fruition.

When the transcendently autonomous choosing model loosens its grip, then pertinent questions can be considered. And that raises the second reason for doubting attempts to make effort the foundation for moral responsibility and just deserts: Why does one person exert effort, and another dawdle? If the answer is that one chooses to exert (or withhold) effort, and that that is an inexplicable act of transcendent free will, then the discussion grinds to a halt—or at least it moves to a different plane, and becomes an issue of whether the empiricist-naturalist-determinist model is ultimately preferable to the transcendent-miraculous-first cause model. But if one rejects such appeals to transcendent autonomy, then questions concerning why one does or does not exert effort (or why one "chooses to exert effort") cannot be suppressed.

When that question is asked—"*Why* does one person make efforts while another does not?"—the advocates of effort-based moral responsibility get a bit touchy. There is a tendency to reject such queries as absurd or even a bit improper. But *if* inquiries about the causes for good (and bad) efforts are to be ruled out of order, then on what grounds? For the believer in transcendent free will, the grounds are that such efforts (or choices to make or withhold effort) are the sorts of creative acts that are miraculously self-caused, and for which no causal antecedents exist. But such grounds are not available to the compatibilist-naturalist who wants to block inquiries into the background causes of effort-making. The *sense* that such inquiries are illegitimate is probably the result of confusing the convenient individualist basis for compatibilist freedom with the requisite metaphysical basis for individual moral responsibility (as discussed in Chapter Three). If so, then it is not surprising that compatibilists should become touchy when someone insists on looking further into the causal history: such inquiries severely challenge claims of moral responsibility for effort, and place more weight on a shaky individualist metaphysics that is already in danger of collapsing under the weight of naturalism-determinism.

When we rudely ignore all objections and pursue the *causes* of effort-making, we discover that they are not difficult to find—and we also discover why compatibilist advocates of moral responsibility would prefer not to find them. The causes of effort-making (and of greater and lesser degrees of effort-making) may be less obvious than the causes of height or swiftness or a splendid operatic performance, but they are not difficult to trace. Effort (or lack of effort) is the product of fortunate (or unfortunate) contingencies of reinforcement. When an act is positively reinforced (rewarded), the act is more likely to be repeated. When a behavior is sometimes positively reinforced and sometimes not, that schedule of reinforcement shapes "dedication" to performing the behavior. (If the reinforcement schedule is gradually "stretched," in such a manner that an increasing number of behavioral repetitions are required for reinforcement, then the subject is likely to become obsessively "dedicated" to that task.) When a behavior is repeated a number of times with no positive reinforcement, the behavior is likely to be extinguished. The fortunate child who is given challenging but not impossible intellectual tasks will have her intellectual efforts occasionally (but not invariably) positively reinforced, and will ultimately become pertinacious in pursuit of solutions (will be intellectually dedicated); the child whose tasks are too easy will show some effort, but will probably not sustain that effort over a long period; and the child who is given tasks that are much too difficult (and who thus experiences no positive reinforcement) makes no effort at all. Thus when dedicated effort is scrutinized, it becomes obvious that—like height or speed or intelligence—it is the product of good or bad fortune, and not something for which the individual deserves praise or blame.

The individual who "won't even try" is certainly frustrating. The student who struggles diligently with a difficult mathematics assignment is one with whom we easily sympathize, and we eagerly offer help and encouragement. But the student who takes one look at the problem and closes his book gets little help and little patience: "I can't help you if you won't even *try* to work it!" Our frustration with the student who will not try is understandable. Just as the student has learned a helplessness response to mathematics, in the same manner a tutor may learn a helplessness response—"there's no use trying to help him"—with helpless students. But even a cursory examination of how individuals lose the ability to make an effort (of how "learned helplessness" develops) should undermine any claims that effort (or failure to exert effort) is a good foundation for moral responsibility.

Learned helplessness is easily taught in the animal learning laboratory, and its effects are dramatic. A dog develops learned helplessness when subjected to inescapable shock (it is placed in a restraining harness and subjected to a series of painful shocks that it can do nothing to avoid). If the dog is then placed in a shuttle box (a two-sided chamber with a barrier between the sides, in which the dog can escape shock by leaping over the barrier) the dog runs about for a few seconds, and then gives up: it lies down and whines helplessly. When the dog is next placed in the shuttle box, it will make even less effort to escape before giving up. In contrast, a dog that has not been subjected to such inescapable shock races about until it leaps the barrier; on subsequent tests, it leaps the barrier more quickly; soon it leaps the barrier immediately, or even before the onset of the shock. If a week passes between the imposition of a single inescapable shock and being placed in a shuttle box, then the dog tends to escape normally. If, however, the dog receives several sessions of inescapable shock prior to being placed in the shuttle box, then the dog's inability to escape the shock will persist for weeks. After repeated sessions of inescapable shock, followed by sessions in a shuttle box in which the dog "could escape if it tried" but instead accepts the shock passively, the dog will be profoundly helpless in avoiding shock. When the barrier is removed, the dog will not go to the other side to avoid shock. When the dog is called to the other side during shock—or even offered food—it will not respond (Seligman, 1975, pp. 21–27, 46).

It is not difficult to see the parallels with human learned helplessness. The woman who passively accepts her husband's brutal beatings may seem almost to "deserve" them: "She knows what is going to happen if she stays with him; and yet she won't make any effort to leave. We have offered her a place to live, and encouraged her to leave, but she won't make any effort to help herself." But while we might naively think that after repeated beatings the woman would finally learn to escape, in fact the opposite is the case: repeated inescapable trauma teaches helplessness rather than resolve. When we discover that the woman was an abused child, we may be even more amazed: how could she stay with a brutal husband after the terrible experiences of her brutalized childhood? But when we look more closely at the effects of that early childhood conditioning, there is nothing surprising about the learned helplessness that persists in adulthood. (Of course we hope she seeks therapy, and if she is lucky her friends will encourage it; but no one should blame her if she does not make such efforts.)

With some knowledge of the dynamics of learned helplessness, we may be less tempted to indulge in the banal remarks that often accompany claims that making effort establishes moral responsibility. When we observe a student "give up trying" after one failed effort at writing a dissertation or solving a deductive logic problem or reading a difficult assignment, we are likely to conclude that she should not give up and certainly could try harder and more persistently: after all, "I had a problem just yesterday that I couldn't solve on the first try; but *I* kept trying until I got it; and so should she; it's her own fault for giving up too easily. When I was faced with the same difficulty, I persevered, and so should she." But when we look closely at the details of learned helplessness, then we may begin to see that some of the supposedly similar circumstances were in fact profoundly different. A dog subjected to one episode of inescapable shock escapes energetically and effectively when placed in a shuttle box; but a dog that has been subjected to repeated inescapable shocks gives up and cowers. An observer who sees only the shuttle box behavior (and not the earlier history) might conclude that the situations of the two dogs are similar and that since one escaped "the other should also." When we observe the difference between our own perseverance and another's quitting, we may observe only that we are responding quite differently to a single failure, and forget that our failure was preceded by many successes and the other person's failure was the last in a string of frustrating failures.

When one makes repeated futile efforts to obtain a reward or avoid pain, one learns that efforts are futile; when one receives rewards independently of efforts, one learns the same lesson (Seligman, 1975, pp. 23–37). That is, whether one learns effort-making or helplessness (and whether one learns a deeply entrenched or shallow perseverance, or a profound or mild degree of helplessness) is a function of the *effects* of one's efforts. Thus whether one learns industry or lethargy is a function of what *follows* from one's efforts—and what follows from our efforts depends on the situation in which those

97

efforts are exerted (whether in an environment that rewards efforts or one in which efforts have no effect, whether in the presence of a delighted and responsive parent or in a situation of neglect, whether in fertile or barren soil). But whether an individual's early situation (particularly the vital formative stages) is one in which effort is or is not rewarded is *not* something for which the individual is morally responsible. In short, whether one now makes an effort depends on the effects of earlier efforts—effects that were positive in some cases, aversive in others, but that in any case were the good or bad fortune of the effort-maker and are not grounds for moral responsibility.

WITHIN THE NATURALIST-DETERMINIST FRAMEWORK, it is not difficult to give an account of why one person exerts the crucial effort and another does not; however, it is impossible to give a naturalist account of such a difference that does not involve causal factors for which the individuals obviously are not morally responsible. Sensing that difficulty, the naturalist (compatibilist) advocates of moral responsibility are sometimes pushed to an interesting stratagem: they make the critical level of effort exertion so tiny that it all but escapes notice—and there have been ingenious efforts at reducing the degree of effort required to very low voltage indeed. Paul Secord, for example, provides a marvelous account of how a small nudge can have profound consequences. Secord maintains that people can autonomously *enable* themselves to perform difficult tasks (and overcome difficulties) by a process of "self-intervention":

> Enablements of performance include both capacity and desire; the act cannot be performed unless P has both the capacity to perform and is also able to generate sufficient motivation to carry it out. And those acts that P cannot perform are in that category because P either lacks the capacity or because P cannot generate the motivation to do them. (1984, p. 30)

Secord then discusses in detail acts that P cannot perform because of lack of motivation:

> All actions are contingent upon internal states, circumstantial conditions, and situational contexts. Suppose that some of the acts that P *can* perform will change the situation so as to facilitate the performance of acts that previously could not be performed. This would occur either because of a change in P's internal state or in the prevailing external circumstances, P may now have sufficient motivation to execute the act. In that case, self-intervention would have occurred because P performed some acts that were in P's power to perform, and these acts created new facilitative conditions that brought the hitherto blocked act within P's power to execute. We can say that what P does is to create enabling conditions for executing the desired act. Self-intervention, then, would take the form of doing what one *can* do in order to create conditions that enable what one cannot ordinarily do. (1984, p. 30)

Secord's proposal is a promising one, up to a crucial unexplained point. To illustrate what Secord's model can—and cannot—provide, consider the following case.

If I lack the motivation to complete my dissertation, I may give to a reliable friend some checks made out to the Heritage Foundation (the charity I most abhor) with instructions to mail a check on the last day of each month unless I have finished an additional dissertation chapter. If I have the capacity to write, then this (relatively easy) enabling process may fire my motivation to the necessary level. This is an instructive model of self-intervention, but how does it account for why one person does and another does not take the initial small step, make the relatively small effort, to set the process in motion?

If we seek Secord's answer to that question, the most promising place to look is in the process of self-intervention, where Secord's multi-level analysis does its work. In Secord's system the crucial autonomous act enters in a second-level guiding operation. In the primary, immediate level of action I have the capacity to write my dissertation, but due to insufficient motivation I fail to exercise that capacity. I can, however, get some leverage on that motivation by operating at a higher level of self-intervention. I *can* make the necessary effort to set in motion an enabling process: I have the capacity and also the necessary motivation (writing a few checks requires less motivation than writing a dissertation). Through this autonomous self-control process, I gain control over activities that were otherwise beyond my motivational limits. It is rather like a system of pulleys, in which a small and quite possible effort eventually generates sufficient force to move weighty obstacles. As Secord describes it:

> The principle that, in order to enable the performance of previously inhibited acts, . . . P does what P *can* do so as to facilitate . . . these acts *is* very useful. Certain familiar processes may work because they fit this principle. They may often take a stepwise form, with each successive act making the next act easier to perform. (1984, p. 31)

This is inventive and appealing. It offers a plausible account of how a relatively small autonomous act can have far-reaching repercussions, and shows how—through the multi-step enabling process that the small autonomous act sets in motion—actions of considerable magnitude and difficulty can be generated. Unfortunately, the proposal has a fatal flaw: it leaves the crucial origin of the small initiating effort a mystery. The key problem is not how a tiny effortful act can cause further effects; rather, the problem is how the original effort-making act is initiated. Secord's enabling process and multiple levels will keep the account rolling, but he offers no means of starting it.

The shape of the hole remaining in Secord's account may be outlined by the following example. Bob and Alice are both working on dissertations, and both are struggling. They make excuses, duck their advisors, indulge wide ranges of avoidance behavior. But Alice overcomes her problem by creating an extra impetus. She gives postdated checks to a friend, with instructions to return them on the first day of each month only if a dissertation chapter has been submitted. The additional motivation has its effect: she is positively reinforced for completing a chapter, successive chapters are thus easier to do, and Alice lives happily ever after in the groves of academe. Bob, however, initiates no such program, continues to stew in dissertation procrastination, and comes to a bad end. The different outcomes are not surprising, given the differences in their situations once Alice does (and Bob does not) initiate a special motivation program. *Given* that difference, it is neither surprising nor difficult to explain (in behavioral terms) why their paths should then sharply diverge. But what is the explanation for Alice's initiation of the program and Bob's continuing slide into indolence? Secord offers no answer to the crucial question: why is Alice's power activated and why does Bob's remain dormant? Secord's position leaves this a mystery.[2] It need not remain one; as noted earlier, we do know something about the natural causes that would shape such different behaviors—but such causes do not support moral responsibility.

ONE ADDITIONAL—and especially noteworthy—version of effort-establishes-desert must be examined. George Sher suggests the following as "the correct explanation of why the diligent ought to succeed. They ought to succeed because their sustained efforts are substantial investments of themselves—the ultimate sources of value —in the outcomes they seek" (1987, p. 62). This is an attractive position that takes seriously the task of explaining why effort establishes desert. And essentially Sher's answer is: one justly deserves a return on one's *investment* (of one's energies and capacities, indeed of one's self). Sher's argument derives its plausibility from its analogy with capital investment: I deserve a return on my capital investment proportionate to that investment, and if I invest more than someone else I deserve proportionately more than that smaller investor. In an analogous manner, if I invest more of my own sustained effort—more of myself—in an enterprise, then I am proportionately more deserving of the fruits of success than the less diligent and consequently smaller investor of self. However, those claims can be sustained only if the differences in available investment capital (both the self-capital of effort and the monetary capital) are themselves fair and just. (That is a necessary condition; it may not be sufficient, but that is more than need be argued here.) And that is certainly not always, if indeed it is ever, the case. To take an obvious example, if because of racism or sexism an individual has been consistently deprived of success and accomplishment, and the individuals's efforts have thus consistently been in vain, then that individual is quite likely to become lethargic (effort-making behavior will undergo extinction). Such an individual will have less available self-investment capital of diligence and effort (and obviously the individual does not justly deserve that smaller share of capital). To then assert that the individual deserves less (for having made less self-investment) is as unfair and unjust as claiming that the robber baron (or the heirs of such ill-gotten wealth) now justly deserve larger shares of goods as "just returns on their investments." In both cases, the just returns claims are legitimate only within the system of presuppositions: that the starting capital distribution is itself just. If one questions the fairness of how both sorts of investment capital were accumulated, and probes into the reasons behind the different distributions of capital, the justice of both systems is seen to be doubtful. And of course the example of the individual whose reduced diligence-capital resulted from racism and sexism was merely an illustration; for the point is that, as argued earlier, all the capacities (including the capacity for hard work) of all individuals result from causal histories and environmental contingencies for which the individual cannot reasonably be held morally responsible.

THE CONCLUSION IS THAT those who make heroic efforts do not justly deserve greater reward than do layabouts. But it does not follow that it must be wrong to reward game effort; much less does it follow that indolence is equal in worth to industry. The latter point will be taken up in Chapter Twelve; for the interim, I shall state baldly that dedicated effort *is* a good thing, and in particular dedicated effort for a morally good end is a morally good thing, and the fact that no one is morally responsible for such good efforts—and that no one justly deserves reward for such good efforts—in no way diminishes the moral good of the effort. But for the moment, consider the first point: that even though no one is morally responsible and no one justly deserves credit for making dedicated, sustained efforts, it does not follow that such efforts should not be rewarded. In order to explain that claim, consider the following story. Imagine a more realistic account of the story of the tortoise and the hare, in which the lazy and arrogant hare breaks training, smokes heavily, and runs lethargically—but still beats the hard-working tortoise by twenty lengths. In such a case, we might well say: "The (defeated) tortoise really deserves praise; he has dedication and courage and perseverance, even though he doesn't have much speed." But we never say: "The (defeated) hare really deserves praise; he is very speedy, even though he doesn't have much drive and dedication." At first glance this difference seems curious: dedication and speed equally result from factors beyond one's control. But it is not difficult to account for the difference. We praise the defeated but hard-working tortoise because hard work and dedication are desirable qualities that can be sustained and strengthened through the positive reinforcement of praise; but we regard speediness as a trait that cannot be strengthened by praise. Furthermore, we temper our praise for the speedy but lazy hare because we are afraid of reinforcing bad habits. We praise the dedicated but slow athlete because dedicated effort can be extinguished without positive reinforcement, and thus it is important to sustain that dedication through at least some praise. But the indolent hare's swiftness will not be extinguished by lack of praise, while the hare's indolence may become more entrenched if he is praised even when he loses. It is useful to praise a dedicated but unsuccessful athlete, and it is counterproductive to praise a talented but indolent player; but none of that has any bearing on just deserts. At the level of just deserts, no one deserves any more (nor any less) praise, censure, benefits, or detriments than anyone else.

It is vitally important that people *learn* to exert effort, and (what amounts to the same thing) it is vitally important that people learn that their own efforts can have positive effects (and that their own lack of effort can cause failure).[3] But whether one has learned that (and thus exerts effort and perseveres) or has not learned that his own effort can make things happen (because of earlier failed efforts) is not something for which one is morally responsible. A central element of a happy and healthy life is learning that one can—by one's own efforts—make things happen; and learning that lesson is important and is inherently rewarding. But whether or not one learns the lesson is not something for which one *deserves* reward or punishment.

Some may now insist that that gives away the game for just deserts and moral responsibility—that if it is granted that praise and reward can sometimes be useful, that is all the compatibilist requires. After all, the compatibilist was not in search of some ultimate metaphysical grounding for claims of desert and moral responsibility. If they are useful, then they are justified. However, such a conclusion does not follow from what has been granted concerning the occasional usefulness of praise. For what has been granted about the usefulness of praise is *not* that it is useful to employ praise and blame and reward and punishment in accordance with traditional desert claims; rather, it is only granted that use of praise may sometimes be beneficial. That does not justify claims of just deserts and moral responsibility—just as the usefulness of conditioning a pigeon's behavior by giving a food pellet to the hungry pigeon (rewarding the pigeon) does not establish that the pigeon deserves the reward and attains moral responsibility for its behavior. But that is a point that requires more argument; and that argument must await a later chapter (Chapter Ten).

ADAMANT ADVOCATES of effort-establishes-desert may still insist that hard workers justly deserve more than do the lazy: simply making the effort (whatever the source of the effort and of the effort-making ability) is the basis for moral responsibility and just deserts; if you make an effort, then by so doing you *make* your own just deserts. The causes for one's energy and the other's lethargy, the backgrounds that make one diligent and the other desultory, are irrelevant: the simple fact is that if one works hard and the other does not, then the former deserves rewards that the other does not deserve. If someone continues to insist on that, and to insist that the backgrounds that shaped and radically differentiated the talents and capacities of the two are simply irrelevant, then perhaps we have reached an ethical impasse. But I trust that few who consider the situation carefully will think such background causes irrelevant. The capacity to exert strenuous and sustained effort is certainly a desirable capacity, and it commonly yields positive results. To suppose that it is fair and morally just that one who has and exercises that capacity (through the good fortune of well-structured early environmental contingencies) receive and deserve greater reward than the less fortunate lethargic individual seems a very peculiar supposition. It would be similar to giving one typist a computer with laser printer, and another a beat-up manual portable with keys that stick, and then claiming that the one who accomplished more was justly deserving of greater reward: after all, he just did more, and we're not interested in why. It sounds plausible to claim that people justly deserve special reward not because of their capacity for hard work, but rather because they have worked hard; but when that reasonable-sounding assertion is scrutinized it is seen to be unfair and implausible. For in a similar manner we could say that it is not because of his computer that the first clerical worker deserves greater reward (than the second with the shoddy typewriter); rather, it is because he actually does more work, accomplishes more. It's his work, his accomplishment, that we are rewarding; not his potential or capacity for accomplishment. But in fact the former does not justly deserve greater reward than the latter—neither for his greater work nor for his greater capacity for work. And if I start (and am not morally responsible for so starting) with less capacity for effort than you and due to that lesser capacity actually exert less effort, then it is wrong to claim that I justly deserve less than you.

PEOPLE OFTEN HAVE a deep feeling—perhaps beyond the depths that philosophical argument can plumb—that *effort* must be a fair basis for differences in just deserts. This last section is not a final argument against effort-establishes-just-deserts; rather, it is an attempt to discover—and dislodge—the source of that feeling. There is one vital element that funds the visceral feeling that the indolent are less deserving (should justly receive less) than the industrious. That is the sense that layabouts are receiving the goods and joys of sloth, and that if they also deserve the same as the industrious then the indolent receive special and *unequal* benefits. There is the feeling that the indolent individual would then enjoy the goods of indolence and still have an equal claim on the fruits of her more industrious neighbors. If the indolent deserve goods equal to those of the industrious, while at the same time the indolent enjoy the pleasures of indolence as the industrious take up the burdens of labor; then that seems to provide a double reward for the dilatory while the diligent suffer the penalty of hard work.

But that account of the situation—the industrious are deprived of the joys of indolence and so must be compensated by special deserts—is psychologically false. It seems plausible only if one supposes that people step outside their conditioning histories and somehow "make choices" either to exert effort or to idle about. "I think I would enjoy the pleasures of sloth; I choose that over enthusiastic effort." The image of individuals weighing up the benefits of sloth over industry, and then making a choice of lethargy (which must be respected, and given its "just reward" or, as the case may be, its just deprivation) is hideously false and has wrought much wrong. People do not choose lethargy, any more than they choose the deep depression that is its common accompaniment. When efforts are extinguished due to absence of positive reinforcement, then no productive behaviors are shaped into effective secondary reinforcers, and the resulting decreased effort spirals down into further reduction of positive reinforcement. In such cases people sink into patterns of lethargy that are not easily escaped. The "benefits" of lethargy are an illusion. A pattern of lethargic behavior is not like the energetic worker's restful and restoring week at the beach. A refreshing vacation from satisfying (positively reinforced and reinforcing) work is one thing; it is quite another to be drawn into the morass of indolence, in which one feels no desire or inclination to accomplish anything. The latter is not an attractive alternative to energetic industrious work, with benefits that might be chosen over those of diligence; rather, it is a depressing and deadening sink.

We turn to behavioral psychology for a better account of why one is industrious and the other lethargic, but few will need any evidence beyond their own experiences to recognize that lethargy is not an attractive option with its own special benefits package. We all know people who are quite "lazy" and others who have gone from energetic and enthusiastic hard work to lethargy. None of us would be

willing to trade positions—not even if our lethargic friend is a finan-
cially secure lottery winner. Indolence is not its own reward, and our
experiences of "episodic indolence" attest to that. We are happiest
when working most enthusiastically and diligently.[4] Those occasions
when nothing seems very interesting or worthwhile, when one feels
like lying in bed all day—such periods are not recalled as the most
satisfying days of one's life.

The claim here is not that there is something inherently satisfying
and fulfilling about hard work. Rather, the point is that *if* one is
industrious, then one has experienced (and continues to experience)
the right pattern of reward-reinforcement to *make* one's work inherently satisfying. (There is nothing about hard work in itself that
guarantees satisfaction, as the common occurrence of burn-out abun-
dantly demonstrates.) To work enthusiastically at tasks that have
been reinforced in the right manner (so that the effort itself has become a conditioned positive reinforcer) is to experience a substantial
part of a very satisfactory life.

The moral of all this is that the abolition of just deserts would not
mean that the indolent would be entitled to equal benefits in *addition* to the joys of indolence: indolence is a burden, not a benefit. To
the contrary, if one bases just deserts on efforts, and then rewards
the industrious and deprives the lethargic, then those who "make
no effort" suffer a double misfortune. First, they are unfortunate
for not having the interests and capacities and patterns of positive
reinforcement that would give them the pleasure of satisfying, effortful work. Second, they are deprived of benefits for having suffered
the first misfortune. To base claims and ascriptions of just deserts
on effort-making is to follow a policy that (as will be argued later)
is inefficient; the point of this chapter is that such a policy is also
fundamentally unjust.

CHAPTER EIGHT

Nonjust Deserts

HAVING JUST EXAMINED why *effort* does not establish just deserts and moral responsibility, I want at this point to note some desert claims that are *not* being denied—some legitimate uses of "desert" that are quite different from the empty category of *just* deserts. (Chapter Five noted some legitimate senses of "responsibility" other than moral responsibility; this chapter describes legitimate senses of *non*just deserts.)

Desert questions usually focus on *what* is deserved (a prize, grade, reward, punishment) or *who* is deserving (who crossed the finish line first, had the original idea, threw the first punch). While both considerations are important, there is a more fundamental question that is often neglected: which *sense* of "deserves" is at issue?

Alice, Barbara, Carol, and Dianne engage in a foot race. Alice races brilliantly and finishes first; Barbara runs in a muddy lane and is soundly beaten; Carol struggles courageously but is outclassed; and Dianne is both slow and lethargic. Yet all four may be *deserving*, in four different senses of "deserves."

The first meaning of "deserves" is emphasized by soft determinists. The winner deserves the spoils. It matters not that Alice's speediness is her good genetic luck (she smokes three packs a day and avoids exercise): she won the race fair and square and thus deserves the prize. This first sense of deserving—in which the only questions are what was accomplished, who did what—might be called "act-deserving."[1] The winner of the race is act-deserving if she followed the rules and finished first. Whether her training was dedicated or desultory, whether her speed comes from her genes or her environment, whether she had the advantages of superb coaching or overcame the trials of impoverishment: all such questions of personal history are irrelevant. She is the speediest on this day, she won the race, she act-deserves the reward.

But in some cases there is no question that the winner act-deserves the victory, yet we are loath to say—in another sense of "deserves"— that she *deserves* it. "Yes, Alice won the race, and everything was according to the rules, and Alice act-deserves the prize. However, Alice didn't deserve to win: she drew a favorable starting position and her faster rivals were unable to overcome her initial advantage." Lanes are assigned by luck of the draw, that's one of the recognized rules of the game. Alice act-deserves the prize (she played fair and won the race), but in another sense one of her rivals is more deserving. When the most talented loses a fair contest to a luckier rival, then the former "*talent*-deserves" to win. (In harness racing a horse that draws the extremely disadvantageous outside post position may lose though it paces farther and faster than a less talented rival on the rail. The lucky inside horse still act-deserves the prize, but the outside horse is more talent-deserving.)[2]

A third sense of "deserves" was discussed in the previous chapter. In the revised story of the tortoise and hare, the lazy but speedy hare easily bests the slow but gamely dedicated tortoise. In such a case the hare act-deserves the win (the race was not rigged). Furthermore, the hare talent-deserves the victory (the tortoise was not a speedy victim of bad racing luck). Nonetheless, we may legitimately say: "The tortoise deserved to win."

In what sense of "deserves" does the tortoise deserve victory? The tortoise is more deserving because he tried harder, trained more diligently, raced with more grit and determination. He deserves victory because while less talented he "made the most" of his talent: factors beyond his control (in this case, species-specific genetic factors) deprived him of victory. The tortoise is neither act- nor talent-deserving, but he "*effort*-deserves"[3] to win.

However, questions of desert do not end at effort-deserving. The limits of effort-deserving are made evident by the question: under what conditions would one deserve praise for dedication or spirit? The causes of dedication and perseverance may be less obvious than are the causes of speediness or beauty, but (as noted in the previous chapter) when the sources of dedication are scrutinized, it becomes obvious that—like height or speediness—such characteristics are the product of good or bad fortune and not characteristics for which the individual deserves praise or blame. That is the point the no-fault naturalist is making by saying that no one (fast or slow, dedicated or desultory) *deserves* praise or blame, reward or punishment. It is a distinct and additional sense of "deserves" and should be called by a different name: "justice-deserves.[4]

WHEN *non*JUSTICE SENSES of deserving (act-deserving, talent-deserving, and effort-deserving) are distinguished from justice-deserving, it becomes clear what compatibilist arguments accomplish—and what they fail to accomplish. They do show that the nonjustice senses of deserving are compatible with determinism; they do not prove that determinism is compatible with justice-deserving. Consider three examples.

First, Walter Stace's argument that there is no conflict between determinism and desert: "You do not excuse a man for doing wrong because, knowing his character, you felt certain beforehand that he would do it. Nor do you deprive a man of a reward or prize because, knowing his goodness or his capabilities, you felt certain beforehand that he would win it" (1952). Of course we do not deprive an individual of a prize because his talents made him an odds-on favorite. We give the speedy hare the prize and acknowledge that he deserves (act-deserves) the victory. But there is an important further question: not whether the hare act-deserves the prize, but is he more *justice*-deserving?

Moving from act-deserving to talent-deserving, Les Holborow argues that it is false that "the basis on which a man claims that he deserves something must itself be something he deserves." Holborow offers this counterexample: "The musical child deserves an appropriate musical education not because he deserves his talent, but merely because he *has* it" (1975, p. 161). That is indeed all the justification required for talent-deserving claims, but it does not justify differences in justice-deserving. (It is one thing to claim that a good musical ear talent-deserves special training; quite another to argue that one is justice-deserving of special benefits or praise for such natural endowments.) Again, the error is in treating one sense of "deserves" (in this case, talent-deserves) as if it exhausted desert questions.

As a third example, consider James Rachels' claims (discussed in the previous chapter) for effort-deserving in his rejection of the view that "willingness to work is just another matter of luck":

> The first thing to notice here is that people do not deserve things on account of their *willingness* to work, but only on account of their actually having worked. The candidate for promotion does not deserve it because he has been willing to work hard in his old job, or because he is willing to work hard in the new job. Rather he deserves the promotion because he actually *has* worked hard. Therefore it is no objection to the view I am defending to say that willingness to work is a character trait that one does not merit. For, on this view, the basis of desert is not a character trait of any kind, not even industriousness. The basis of desert is a person's past actions. (1978, p. 158)

Rachels is exactly right, so long as we are considering exclusively effort-deserving. If the contest is one in which the victory goes to the hardest worker, then the one who did the hardest work effort-deserves the promotion. If someone more talented at hard work fails to work as hard (because of an illness), that is unfortunate but irrelevant. The basis of effort-deserving is a person's past actions, and the one who strives hardest effort-deserves the prize. But it is a mistake to suppose that conclusions drawn from effort-deserving also apply to justice-deserving. As argued in the previous chapter, whether the contest rewards speed, good looks, or dedication, no one *justice*-deserves the advantages or disadvantages that determine the order of finish. In effort-deserving contexts we are interested only in what the individual actually did, no matter what her initial advantages or disadvantages; but in justice-deserving contexts the fact that a harder worker is luckily endowed with greater willingness to work or other special talents will have a strong bearing on what desert conclusions are drawn. Whether one produces a hard day's work or a winning effort, there are no differences in justice-deserts.

No-fault naturalists (and hard determinists) insist that all are exactly equal in *justice*-deserts. Individuals may vary in what is act-deserved and talent-deserved and effort-deserved, but all justice-deserve precisely the same. Or another way of putting it: no one justice-deserves anything at all.[5] However, that claim has been challenged by Daniel Dennett, who offers the following example:

> Imagine trying to change the rules of basketball in the following way: if the referees decide that a particular basket was just a lucky shot, they disallow the points, and if they notice that bad luck is dogging one of the teams, they give that team compensatory privileges. A perfectly pointless effort at reform, of course, which would not appeal to anybody's sense of fairness. In sports

we accept luck, and are content to plan and strive while making due allowance for luck—which is, after all, the same for everyone; no one actually *has more luck* than anyone else, even though some *have been* lucky enough to start off with more talent. But that is fair too, we think. We don't suppose that the only fair contest is between perfectly matched opponents; the strength of one may defeat the finesse of the other, or vice versa. Roughly comparable overall prowess is all we demand. And if on some particular occasion the particular strengths of one count for more than the particular strengths of the other, that is "too bad" for the latter, but not at all unfair. (1984, p. 96)

Before we are swept away by the charm of Dennett's example, two problems should be noted. The first is simply: luck does not equal out. It is not true that "the strength of one" is balanced by "the finesse of the other": there are many cases in which strength and finesse are combined against weak, clumsy competitors. However, that issue will be the topic of the next chapter. The current concern is with the second reason why Dennett's example fails: it confuses act-deserving with justice-deserving. Certainly Dennett is correct that "trying to change the rules of basketball" so that the referees give compensatory privileges to an unlucky team would be "a perfectly pointless effort at reform." Sport is more interesting if the talent-deserving team does not invariably win. And if "the particular strengths" of one team enable it to triumph over another team the result is not considered "unfair." But the reason is that in sports our focus is commonly on act-deserving. Confining our attention to act-deserving yields a more satisfactory game with greater pleasure for its participants and fans, and that is probably sufficient reason to play the game in that manner. (To insist that the winner be justice-deserving would require a never-ending sequence of overtime periods, each ending with the score precisely even. Justice-deserving is very important, but it would yield tedious sport.) Dennett's points are well taken so long as they are confined to cases in which act-deserving is the appropriate concern; but it is a mistake to extend claims that are true at the act-deserving level to more expansive conclusions about deserving.

REJECTION OF DIFFERENCES in justice-deserving does not entail the abandonment of other senses of "deserves." To the contrary, when all the senses of deserving are properly distinguished we shall not be tempted to abandon useful senses of "deserves" (the hard-determinist tendency) nor tempted to find too much deserving in one sense of "deserves" (the soft-determinist temptation). Indeed, no-fault naturalists (and hard determinists) should emphasize, rather than disparage, the other (nonjustice) senses of "deserves." Those other senses provide the means of answering the most common objection to no-fault naturalism. It seems at least *prima facie* obvious that people sometimes deserve something, so that one who denies deserving must bear the burden of proof.[6] When the other legitimate senses of "deserves" are distinguished from justice-deserving the burden of proof is shifted. The no-fault naturalist notes several senses of "deserves" in which desert-differences are meaningful and useful; it will be up to libertarians and intransigent soft determinists to find grounds for this extraordinary notion of differences in justice-deserving.

Aside from their utility in lifting the burden of proof from weary no-fault naturalist shoulders, what use is there for the nonjustice senses of "deserves"? Act-deserving will continue to be useful in many contexts: obviously in competitive sporting events, but there are other situations in which we are interested exclusively in results and act-deserving is the appropriate focus. If I submit a paper to a friend I want an evaluation of the end product. Whether my talents are large or small, my work habits zealous or languorous, my background privileged or deprived: all that is irrelevant.

Talent-deserving will also retain its usefulness. If a superior horse loses to an inferior rival (due to bad racing luck), we say that the inferior act-deserves the trophy. But it will be useful to remember that the superior horse has more talent. It will affect our future wagers and our selections for breeding stock. If an individual has special musical talent it is important that it be recognized and nurtured: such an individual talent-deserves special musical education. But it is also important to remember exactly what sort of deserving that is, and what it will and will not justify. The musically talented may talent-deserve special training, but that is not grounds for special justice-deserts, and certainly it does not justify special luxuries for the superior musician.

The effort-deserving category will remain particularly important. It is useful (as noted in the previous chapter) to praise a dedicated but unsuccessful athlete as effort-deserving, and it is counterproductive to praise a talented but indolent player; but none of that has any bearing on justice-deserving. At the level of justice-deserving, no one deserves any more (nor any less) praise, censure, benefits, or detriments than anyone else.

These deserving distinctions can dissolve a vexing question posed by Michael Slote: should "an ideally just distribution of goods in society" be based on "*success* in contributing to society" or on "conscientious *efforts* to contribute to society"? With the deserving-distinctions in hand, it is easy to see "why that issue is so difficult to resolve in any definitive and universal way" (1973, pp. 323ff.). The dilemma it poses is false. Neither success nor effort provides ideally just distribution. Slote mistakenly supposes that one of those standards for deserving must be the standard for just distribution—the problem is deciding which one. Thus he proceeds to develop a series of cases in an effort to decide which type of deserving is truly justice-deserving, and he effectively demonstrates that our intuitions pull us in opposite directions. If two persons make equally dedicated efforts at helping me find my lost watch, they seem to deserve equal thanks no matter which one luckily happens to stumble on the watch; but, on the other hand, the person who actually finds and returns my watch does seem deserving of some special gratitude. Such contrary cases seem to make desert questions impossible to resolve. But when we recognize that act-deserving and effort-deserving—important as they are—are not justice-deserving, the supposed quandary disappears. If the game is one in which success is largely a matter of luck (as in finding a lost object or buying a lottery ticket) yet we wish to play the game and reward the winner, then the successful player deserves (act-deserves) the prize/praise. In another context we may find it worthwhile to praise/reinforce/reward effort, and that will be sufficient to establish that a person effort-deserves reward. It is only when we try to make act-deserving or effort-deserving carry the burden of justice-deserving that questions about desert seem impossibly difficult.

It might be thought that the above claims for the utility of nonjustice-deserts show that those types of deserving are not really *desert* categories at all. After all, one does not deserve something because it is socially useful that one have it. As Feinberg notes, it may be that a teacher ought to give a student a high grade because the mother of the student is a neurotic who will be broken-hearted if the student receives a low grade; but the social utility of the high grade certainly does not show that the student deserves a high grade (Feinberg, 1970*b*, pp. 58–60). Thus if the justification for effort-deserts is its social utility, that seems to show that effort-deserving is not genuine desert. But such a criticism would be mistaken. The above arguments for the utility of effort-deserving and act-deserving and talent-deserving do not suggest that we praise the effort-deserving individual because it is useful to do so. Under the practice of effort-desert, the individual who makes an effort effort-deserves praise *for that effort,* not because of the social usefulness of praising effort. The *practice* of recognizing effort-deserving is justified by its social utility; but the individual desert claims—made within each deserving practice—must be justified by the acts or abilities of the person deserving praise, not by social utility. If—within the practice—we dispensed praise on the basis of social utility rather than outstanding acts or efforts, we would be participating in a very different practice (not a deserving practice at all).

WHEN THE DESERVING DISTINCTIONS are noted our apparently muddled and contradictory practices of rewarding can be seen to serve varying and useful functions. We handicap the better horse with substantially more weight than its less successful rivals are assigned; and when a less talented rival edges the high-weighted favorite, we think the less talented winner deserves the prize. On the other hand, we assign the superior team the home ice advantage in the Stanley Cup Playoffs and think the more talented winners deserving of their advantage and their victory. Are these contradictory? Only if one mistakenly supposes that both are supposed to match *justice*-deserving. The more talented horse is assigned more weight because such a handicap makes the race exciting. The more successful team is given home ice advantage because that provides an incentive for the teams to play hard during the regular season. Those are the rules we find it useful to play by in these games, and the winner act-deserves the prize in both cases. Justice-deserving has nothing to do with it.

Questions about justice-deserving can be raised in such contexts, but they are questions of the extent to which we should *deviate* from justice-deserving. That is, since no one justice-deserves more than anyone else, to what extent should our society include games and practices and training programs in which the more act-deserving/talent-deserving/effort-deserving receive special rewards? If we are to deal with that question effectively it is essential that it not be confused with the question of what sort of system is just. People are, or may be, willing to approve of some deviations from perfect justice-deserving under some circumstances. For example, we might wish to have competitive sports and awards for victors, or provide special training for those with special talents, or reward/reinforce certain desirable behaviors (including the behavior of making a strong effort). When and to what degree and on what basis we might approve such uneven distribution of benefits is certainly a difficult question, but it becomes impossible if we fail to recognize the question for what it is: a question not of what system fits justice-deserts, but instead of the degree to which our practices should deviate from justice-deserving.

WE MAY CONTINUE to conclude that an individual act-deserves the victory, and if we find games with those rules worth playing we shall reward the winner. We may praise dedication as effort-deserving, as a means of reinforcing a characteristic that we find desirable and that we believe can be strengthened through positive reinforcement. And we may provide special training for the development of talents we deem it desirable to develop. But we should not be tempted to suppose that the more act-deserving or talent-deserving or effort-deserving also have a just claim to more goods. Recognizing that no one justice-deserves more or less than another, we shall be careful to limit the reinforcers necessary to make act-deserving and talent-deserving and effort-deserving functional: strong justification will be required for any deviation from the egalitarian distribution norm. And if the reinforcers are properly scheduled and the dangers of unequal distribution recognized[7] then such deviations from the egalitarian standard will be very small indeed.

CHAPTER NINE

Racing Luck and Just Deserts

AN IMPORTANT PART of the argument against moral responsibility is the claim that people wind up in different positions because they start at different points (and are subsequently shaped by different environments). In life's race, the different results people achieve are due to "uneven starts." Since people start unequally—at starting points not of their own choosing or making—they are not morally responsible (do not justly deserve blame or credit) for the finish. This "uneven starts" position is stated elegantly by John Rawls:

> It seems to be one of the fixed points of our considered judgments that no one deserves his place in the distribution of native endowments, any more than one deserves one's initial starting place in society. The assertion that a man deserves the superior character that enables him to make the effort to cultivate his abilities is equally problematic; for his character depends in large part upon fortunate family and social circumstances for which he can claim no credit. (1971, p. 104)

The "uneven starts" claim involves more than starting points. Not only do people start unevenly; they also (to continue the metaphor) race in "unequal lanes." The child of loving, intelligent, economically successful parents not only starts with important advantages (including better prenatal care), but is likely to continue to enjoy special benefits: better early education, the best in health and dental and dietary care, private music lessons, access to the latest technology, abundant encouragement and attention, extensive travel, an intellectually stimulating home environment, funds for college and graduate study, introduction to "well-connected" people, and perhaps entry into a particularly desirable firm. The lucky racer in the "uneven start" not only gains an initial advantage but then races in the better lane throughout the contest.

The claim that uneven starts undermine just deserts has not escaped challenge. Libertarians have disputed it on the grounds that we can rise above and soar beyond any environmental influences through acts of transcendent contracausal free will—acts of free will that lift us out of the mundane world of natural contingencies and natural causes and into the rarefied sphere of self-caused causes and moral responsibility. However, focusing on recent challenges from the naturalist-compatibilist camp, this chapter will defend the claim that uneven starts really do undermine moral responsibility.

Daniel Dennett (1984) and George Sher (1979 and 1987) offer distinct but similar defenses of just deserts, and each develops a spirited and innovative challenge to the "uneven starts" claims. For both Dennett and Sher, the crucial point is that even if starting points are not precisely even, still in at least some cases what we do—what we accomplish—really does depend on our own efforts. While not every accomplishment is open to everyone (I could never be a power forward in the National Basketball Association) there are still avenues of success open to most (if not quite all) of us, and it is up to us what we do with those open possibilities. Thus—according to Dennett and Sher—we can justly claim to deserve the fruits of our success (and perhaps also the bitter fruits of our failures). There are differences in starting points, but those differences do not eliminate moral responsibility.

Dennett challenges the uneven start basis for denying moral responsibility thus:

One may be tempted to say, there are two sorts of differences in an agent's circumstances that are merely matters of luck: how much initial strength or talent or character one is lucky enough to be born with, and how many lucky breaks one encounters during one's period of self-creation. One way or the other, it seems, these factors must conspire to defeat any self-styled agent's claim of personal responsibility for his own character. . . .

Suppose—what certainly seems to be true—that people are born with noticeably different cognitive endowments and propensities to develop character traits. . . . Is this "hideously unfair" . . . or is this bound to lead to something hideously unfair? Not necessarily. (1984, p. 95)

Dennett then offers an insidiously charming example to show why such differences in starting points and subsequent "lucky breaks" do not vitiate just deserts and moral responsibility:

Imagine a footrace in which the starting line was staggered: those with birthdays in January start a yard ahead of those born in February, and eleven yards ahead of those born in December. Surely no one can help being born in one month rather than another. Isn't this markedly unfair? Yes, if the race is a hundred yard dash. No, if it's a marathon. In a marathon such a relatively small initial advantage would count for nothing, since one can reliably expect other fortuitous breaks to have even greater effects. . . . Is it fair enough not to be worth worrying about? Of course. After all, luck averages out in the long run. (1984, p. 95)

It seems churlish to poke at Dennett's delightful example; but in truth the effects of small initial differences on long-range character development are not at all analogous to staggered starting positions in a marathon. Initial differences in life's race are more often amplified than canceled out. The initially more alert individual engages in exploratory activities that are reinforced, and thus becomes increasingly inquisitive; the eager student is positively reinforcing for her teacher and receives extra attention; the lad who steals a few coins is a suspect when other coins are lost; the better soccer player sharpens skills and develops stamina in competition, while her less talented teammate's skills and stamina and confidence gradually erode on the bench. The small gap widens. Not always, of course; I am not claiming a "slippery slope" down which the initially disadvantaged inexorably slide: subsequent influences—later "racing luck"—sometimes overbalance initial disadvantages. But small initial differences should not be lightly dismissed as making little or no difference in the essentially "fair and equal" marathon race of life. Rather than Dennett's equal-luck marathon, a better analogy might be a horse race on a muddy track, in which the slow starters are additionally handicapped by the mud kicked onto them by the early speed.

Sher develops an argument similar to Dennett's. He, like Dennett, grants that such differences exist; and he also attempts to neutralize such differences in order to preserve claims of just deserts and moral responsibility. But Sher does not apeal merely to "racing luck"; rather, he offers specific suggestions for how such initial differences can be overcome. Sher suggests that an individual with less effort-making ability can negate that disadvantage by greater vigilance or by taking special steps to increase motivation and avoid distractions. And he later extends that claim to "other differences in initial ability as well":

Even if M is initially stronger or more intelligent than N, this difference will only entail that M does not deserve what he has achieved relative to N if the difference between them has made it impossible for N to achieve as much as M. However, differences

in strength, intelligence, and other native gifts are rarely so pro-
nounced as to have this effect. The far more common effect of such
differences is merely to make it more *difficult* for the less talented
person to reach a given level of attainment. He must work harder,
husband his resources more carefully, plan more shrewdly, and so
on. (1987, pp. 31–32)

That is an appealing scenario: the slow tortoise uses his greater
perseverance to nose out the speedier hare, the weak rabbit outwits
the powerful bear, the player of modest talents excels through endurance and effort and perhaps guile. Such stories are heart-warming
and even inspiring: usually they are also fables. The less talented are
not likely to develop greater diligence and perseverance, for those
qualities are the conditioned product of successful past efforts, and
those who are initially less talented are likely to experience fewer successes and consequently less positive reinforcement for their efforts.
Thus less talent is more likely linked to lethargy than to perseverance. In similar fashion, less talent is not likely to be offset by greater
shrewdness; to the contrary, the more talented are also more likely
to have opportunities to develop "court savvy." Shrewd play is a
function of playing time, which is likely to be a function of initial
talent.

The basic flaw in the arguments of both Dennett and Sher is the
tendency to treat individual characteristics as if they were handed
out one at a time by lottery. In fact, talents and abilities (as well
as faults and liabilities) have a cumulative effect. Rather than the
hare's speed being offset by the tortoise's endurance, the speedy hare
is likely to be a more successful racer and thus a more positively
reinforced and frequent racer—and thus also better conditioned.

A sober look at the actual operation of early "luck" and initial talents raises serious doubts concerning claims that "luck balances out." But there is a more fundamental reason why such claims
cannot sustain naturalist-compatibilist moral responsibility. On the

naturalist-compatibilist-determinist view—which rejects all appeals to contracausal free will and unconditioned self-creation—all differences in finishes *must* be the product of starting positions and/or racing luck, and those are not adequate foundations for moral responsibility and just deserts. Back to Dennett's marathon metaphor: when Rachel finished ahead of Sarah, why did that occur? Certainly it may be—as Dennett would emphasize—that Rachel trained harder, in which case Rachel is now a better marathoner, and it is *not* just a "matter of luck" that she finished faster. However, it *is* ultimately a matter of luck that Rachel had more diligence, better discipline, greater capacity for hard work. For if the causes are not to be traced to some self-caused cause then they must result from fortunate circumstances or early childhood influences (or even genetic factors) for which it is absurd to claim moral responsibility and on the basis of which one cannot claim just deserts. If the naturalist-compatibilist decides that advantages and disadvantages are roughly comparable, and that racing luck has roughly balanced out, then the naturalist-compatibilist must also expect that the results will be roughly even. Any difference in those results must stem from some difference in starting points or racing luck, neither of which support moral responsibility. (The "fair starts" myth is a natural companion to the libertarian's transcendent free will: if the start is roughly equal then significant differences in results can be attributed to individual contracausal free will. In contrast, the naturalist rejection of transcendent free acts prompts a search for the important differences in starting points or "racing lanes" that caused the variance in results.)

IT IS A MISTAKE to suppose that "luck balances out," that weaknesses in one capacity are balanced by other strengths, and that claims of moral responsibility and just deserts can thus be justified. However, it is *not* a mistake to tell our children the story of the gritty tortoise nosing out the indolent hare, and it is not a mistake to emphasize that disadvantageous starting points can be and some-times are overcome. That is important for two reasons. First, it helps overcome any lingering fears of fatalism. As noted in Chapter Two, some fear that determinism-naturalism makes us helpless pawns of our early environmental-genetic influences. But that is certainly not the inevitable result that many people fear. *If* one strongly desires to break away from the influences and habits of one's early con-ditioning, then quite often—through effort and planning—one can actually do so. The individual who feels stifled by lack of education can take steps to correct that situation—and (usually) by effort and work the individual can indeed remedy educational deficiencies and achieve the education he desires. So one need not feel trapped by one's conditioning-environmental history.[1] However, the capacity to work hard to overcome such deficiencies, the intelligence to plan an educational program, the perseverance to carry it out, and—espe-cially—the original desire to gain an education: all of that is itself the complex product of environmental contingencies for which one is not morally responsible. Quite commonly one can achieve one's goals; but one is not morally responsible for such achievements (or failures) and cannot claim special reward as one's "just deserts." Strenuous efforts really can make things happen. It does not follow that one is morally responsible for the effort or its effects.

The second reason that it is important to emphasize what can be accomplished by those who "really try"—even against bad luck and initial disadvantages—is that emphasis on the possibility of achievements may foster those achievements. Such verbal encour-agement should not be overemphasized. Inspiring bedtime stories are no substitute for the early experience of well-ordered, interest-ing, and progressively more difficult tasks at which individuals can succeed through exerting modest effort. Early effort-enhancing ex-periences are the key to developing perseverance (and repeated early failure is the key to later lethargy). Still, inspiring stories and en-couraging words have their uses. One of my childhood favorites was the story of Dick Whittington, who rose from poverty to become "thrice Lord Mayor of London town," using only his wits, his hard work, and his lucky mouse-chasing cat. It's a good children's story, with a useful message: if you keep trying, luck will come your way; and through pluck and wit and a bit of luck, one may overcome enormous obstacles and make a great success. The story is a good one, despite the fact that in actuality childhood poverty is likely to produce lethargy, as early deprivation results in early failures and thus the extinguishing of effort-making behavior and the deadening of desires and dreams. Still, we should continue telling the story of Dick Whittington. Children who have the good fortune to hear it may be somewhat more likely to develop perseverance. But we should not draw the wrong moral from the story. People can succeed through pluck and effort and wit; and if one has the good fortune to develop such characteristics (through hearing the right bedtime stories and experiencing the right early successes) then one really can accomplish things and achieve important goals. Such worthwhile accomplishments do not, however, justly deserve special credit or reward, since the means of achieving them (perseverance and intelligence) are the result of one's good luck.

In sum, there is every reason to promote (compatibilist) free will and the importance of individual effort. We *can* make things happen—and those who have the good fortune to learn that lesson are more likely to make successful efforts. But such compatibilist freedom does not establish moral responsibility. Whether the result is diligent accomplishment or lethargic failure, the influence of uneven starts and unequal racing lanes undercuts credit and blame.

CHAPTER TEN

Denying Moral Responsibility and Enhancing Moral Behavior

ATTEMPTS TO ESTABLISH moral responsibility and just deserts (within a naturalistic framework) run aground on the fact that our characters and behavior are the products of complex causes for which we are not morally responsible. It is unfair to reward Saul and punish Paul (Chapter Four) or praise Rachel and blame Sarah (Chapter Nine) when their character and behavioral differences are products of earlier environments for which neither is morally responsible. Their behavior is the result of their good or bad fortune in early environments and subsequent environmental contingencies. Since it would be unfair to blame or credit them for the past influences that shaped their current behavior, it is unfair to blame or credit them for the results.

However, some "forward-looking" advocates of moral responsibility have challenged the above argument. These champions of moral responsibility emphasize the future benefits of desert-responsibility practices: rewarding and punishing shapes better future behavior, and that is all the justification those practices require. Moritz Schlick states the classical justification of the position:

Hence the question regarding responsibility is the question: Who, in a given case, is to be punished? Who is to be considered the true wrongdoer? This problem is not identical with that regarding the original instigator of the act; for the great-grandparents of the man, from whom he inherited his character, might in the end be the cause, or the statesmen who are responsible for his social milieu, and so forth. But the "doer" is the one *upon whom the motive must have acted* in order, with certainty, to have prevented the act. . . . Consideration of remote causes is of no help here, for in the first place their actual contribution cannot be determined, and in the second place they are generally out of reach. Rather, we must find the person in whom the decisive junction of causes lies. The question of who is responsible is the question concerning *the correct point of application of the motive.* And the important thing is that in this its meaning is completely exhausted. (1939)

More recently Dennett has stated the position even more persuasively, making it appear that it is the skeptic about moral responsibility who is obsessed with antiquated theological notions of moral responsibility and guilt. Forget such stuff, Dennett argues, and hold people morally responsible simply because it *works:*

Instead of investigating, endlessly, in an attempt to *discover* whether or not a particular trait is of someone's making—instead of trying to assay exactly to what degree a particular self is self-made—we simply *hold* people responsible for their conduct. . . . And we are rewarded for adopting this strategy by the higher proportion of "responsible" behavior we thereby inculcate. (1984, p. 164)

This certainly sounds progressive: it is not your past, your place of origin, nor your family tree that we care about; what counts is what you do now, and that immediate behavior establishes your just deserts. If you now act virtuously, that behavior will be sustained through reward. Vicious behavior will be discouraged through punishment. Forget the past: it's your behavior today (and tomorrow) that matters.

Dennett and Schlick champion what will be called pragmatic moral responsibility. They exhort us to drop our obsession with discovering remote causes for behavior, drop any concern with whether people are ultimately and metaphysically morally responsible: focus instead on the benefits when we "simply hold people morally responsible" and treat individuals as justly deserving of credit or blame for their own acts. The higher proportion of good, beneficial, socially responsible behavior engendered by individual moral responsibility is all the justification such practices require.

This pragmatic approach to moral responsibility has a tough-minded, forward-looking appeal; however, closer examination reveals two basic flaws. First, it is not fair; and, second, it is not genuinely useful, for the strategy of denying moral responsibility is more efficient in increasing the "proportion of 'responsible' behavior." Advocates of the pragmatic approach to moral responsibility may shrug off the fairness objection; but the second—moral responsibility is impractical—challenges champions of pragmatic moral responsibility on their chosen ground. Before plunging into that fray, consider the first objection: ascriptions of moral responsibility and just deserts are *unfair*.

Dennett claims that moral responsibility *is* fair, because it yields good results: everyone benefits from the institution of moral responsibility–just deserts; what could be fairer? Or as Dennett succinctly phrases it: "My claim here is in effect that *holding people responsible* is the best game in town" (1984, p. 162). And if we try to distinguish between the game's being "the best available" and "really justified," Dennett will have none of that; he considers that objection and then replies:

Skepticism about the very possibility of culpability arises from a misplaced reverence for an absolutist ideal: the concept of total, before-the-eyes-of-God Guilt. The fact that *that* condition is never to be met in this world should not mislead us into skepticism about the integrity of our institution of moral responsibility. (1984, p. 165)

Contra Dennett, one need not look through a god's omniscient eyes to see the unfairness of moral responsibility, the injustice of "just deserts." Considerably shorter perspectives will suffice. Consider, for example, those who have been the victims of racism or sexism. Suppose that we now adopt pragmatic moral responsibility and ignore the severe disadvantages imposed on the victims of such discrimination. (That is not to suggest that those who favor pragmatic moral responsibility support such discrimination. The point is that pragmatic moral responsibility bids us ignore such history—indeed almost all social and individual environmental history—when holding people morally responsible for what they do *now*.) From the perspective of pragmatic moral responsibility, the victim of racism or sexism will be accorded full moral responsibility for what she now does, just as the beneficiary of racist and sexist practices (the child whose superior educational opportunities were paid for at the expense of those excluded) will also be morally responsible for her present and future behavior. Forget the past; it's what you do now that counts. But even a glance at the past will show the unfairness of such practices. To suggest that *now* everyone is equal in moral responsibility—and rewards and punishments, benefits and deprivations, credit and blame will now be dispensed strictly on the basis of what each individual does—is transparently unfair. If pragmatic moral responsibility claims imply anything at all, they imply that the individual who *now* works harder and more skillfully *justly deserves more* than the individual who now works with less skill and diligence: the just deserts of both depend entirely on what they now do and accomplish, without regard for their histories and whether those histories are "before-the-eyes-of-God" fair and equal. But even if it were true that such practices produced better behavior (and it is *not* true, as will be argued next), it would still be unfair to deprive the victim of discrimination of equal benefits, since her comparative lack of skills and diligence are the products of a discriminatory system that deprived her of the opportunity to develop skills and to experience effort-enhancing success.

If individuals are abstracted from their histories and environments and placed in bloodless settings as "responsible agents," then it seems easy to ridicule qualms about moral responsibility. But a close look at real individuals shows they are shaped by environments that are not of their own making and for which they are not responsible—environments often containing discrimination and privilege, arbitrary handicaps and advantages, the benefits of careful nurturing and the detriments of harsh treatment. That casts a different light on the suggestion that we ignore individual conditioning histories and simply treat people as morally responsible. Even if the practices of moral responsibility were beneficial, those benefits would be purchased at too high a price in injustice. (I am not claiming that those who have suffered discrimination now "deserve" special benefits. No one justly deserves anything, or, alternatively, everyone's just deserts are precisely equal. However, it is also true that the victims of discrimination did not deserve to be treated unfairly, and they certainly do not deserve to suffer continuing bad effects from such mistreatment. I favor remedying—as much as possible—the bad effects of such mistreatment, simply on the grounds that such mistreatment and its effects are wrong. It is wrong for one to be subjected to reduced opportunities and inequitable benefits, whether as a result of racism or sexism or for some other reason; and one can campaign for the elimination of such wrongs without appealing to dubious notions of moral responsibility and just deserts.)

THE ABOVE ARGUMENT is to show that a social policy of "holding morally responsible" is unfair; before turning to arguments to show that "holding responsible" is also *impractical*, it is important to note one more possible source of confusion in Dennett's suggestion that "we simply *hold* people responsible" in order to inculcate a "higher proportion of 'responsible' behavior." In one sense it is obviously true that "holding people responsible" is a good means of nurturing "responsible" behavior. But Dennett is right to place scare quotes around that sort of "responsible" behavior, for it involves role-responsibility—not the moral responsibility Dennett hopes to establish.

As noted in Chapter Five, role-responsibility is quite important: having role-responsibilities is central to having influence and position and opportunity in society. Furthermore, when we "hold people responsible" (role-responsible) we do indeed shape more "responsible" behavior: by learning to play important social roles (including particularly the role of self-making) one learns greater self-control and develops more self-reliance and deliberative power. All of that is essential to developing free, mature, trustworthy individuals. Obviously, then, if we value individual freedom we must give people opportunities to play important social roles and nurture their development of role-responsibilities. But (as also emphasized in Chapter Five) such role-responsibility is *not* moral responsibility: the importance of individual role-responsibility does not imply the legitimacy of moral responsibility. For one is not morally responsible for whether one has had the opportunity to develop social role-responsibilities, and one is not morally responsible for receiving or not receiving the support necessary for a successful and positively reinforcing series of satisfactory role-responsibility performances, and one is not morally responsible—deserving of special praise or blame, benefits or detriments—for failure or success at developing the characteristics essential for effectively taking and discharging role-responsibilities. When people have a healthy sequence of role-responsibilities, at which they work successfully (from feeding the goldfish to doing their homework to completing their seminar papers to arguing a case or designing a building), then they are nurtured into responsible, self-controlled, deliberative behavior. But it is quite a different claim to suggest that such fortunate people are morally responsible for their very desirable development. Role-responsibilities are worthwhile; it does not follow that moral responsibility is either possible or desirable.

THE FIRST ARGUMENT against pragmatic moral responsibility was that it is unfair. But the real struggle turns on the second objection. The champions of pragmatic moral responsibility take their stand on the practical benefits of the practices of moral responsibility; and the second argument against pragmatic moral responsibility is that it is impractical.

Dennett claims that ascribing responsibility *is* useful:

> But whatever responsibility is, considered as a metaphysical state, unless we can tie it to some recognizable social desideratum, it will have no rational claim on our esteem. . . .
>
> Why then do we want to hold people—ourselves included—responsible? [As Gomberg states,] "By holding someone responsible and acting accordingly, we may cause him to shed an undesirable trait, and this is useful regardless of whether the trait is of his making. (1984, pp. 163–164)

But in fact pragmatic moral responsibility is *not* an effective means of shaping "responsible" behavior. It is not a useful guide to developing better character, and it is not an institution that can be justified pragmatically. To the contrary, moral responsibility is an impediment to the most effective—and fairest—means of shaping better human behavior.

Holding people responsible is not "the best game in town." With only a crude understanding of why people behave as they do and only the crudest means of shaping behavior, then "holding people responsible" (and rewarding or punishing accordingly) was perhaps the *only* game in town. In those circumstances, the maintenance of social order required treating people as if they were responsible, and similar measures were advocated whether moral responsibility was regarded as fact or as fiction. No one deserves punishment, but we must protect society from criminals, and thus offenders may have to be isolated from society (imprisoned) and (regretfully) perhaps punished to improve them and deter others; and no one deserves reward, but reward is an effective motivator, so those who work hard and deliver the goods must continue to be rewarded. The policies proposed by those who denied moral responsibility were practically indistinguishable from the policies advocated by those (compatibilists and libertarians) who championed moral responsibility. But responsibility is no longer the only game in town, and it is certainly not the best one.

When behavioral science (with its improved account of how behavior is shaped by patterns of contingencies and schedules of reinforcement) is wedded to no-fault naturalism (with its elimination of moral responsibility) they beget new possibilities for shaping and controlling behavior, possibilities quite different from—and better than—the responsibility-based practices of rewarding virtue and punishing vice. (It has already been argued that moral resonsibility practices are unfair; the point now is that they are also inefficient.) When moral responsibility guides rewards, those who perform good acts receive (deserve) greater reward than those who act lethargically or badly. But the contemporary behavioral no-fault naturalist— rather than acquiescing in that reward pattern, with a twinge of bad conscience—will often dispense rewards in the *opposite* manner. If an individual has been conditioned to act virtuously then very infrequent positive reinforcement (reward/praise) will suffice to sustain that behavioral pattern. In contrast, an individual who is lethargic or vicious will require quite substantial work if her behavior is to be reshaped into better patterns. The behavioral no-fault naturalist will attempt to reshape the reprobate's undesirable behavior through applying the appropriate schedules of positive reinforcement (reward), in the process frequently rewarding (positively reinforcing) the reprobate for improving behavior that still falls far short of the virtuous individual's exemplary (and minimally rewarded) behavior. As a result, the vicious individual may be more generously rewarded (positively reinforced) than the virtuous.

For a clear view of the chasm that behavioral science opens between the no-fault naturalist and the believer in moral responsibility, consider details of the way no-fault naturalists might attempt to reshape bad behavior. Early in the process, the scoundrel's behavior will be positively reinforced (rewarded) when it remotely resembles the desired good behavior. As the behavior gradually improves, positive reinforcement will be given only for closer approximations to the ideal. Thus less virtuous behavior (occurring early in the shaping process) will be rewarded more than better (later) behavior. Indeed, under a stretched interval schedule of reinforcement, the individual's good behavior may be strongly sustained by increasingly infrequent positive reinforcement/reward. As the reinforcement becomes increasingly infrequent (on the stretched interval schedule) the individual's behavior becomes more strongly entrenched: the more virtuous the individual (on this schedule), the less the reward/reinforcement.

Ultimately the desired virtuous behavior will become itself a secondary conditioned positive reinforcer. At that point the individual will (in the familiar way of speaking) do good of her own volition, will act virtuously purely from a love of virtue. Some ethical traditions (such as the Aristotelian) regard that as the highest moral attainment. On this view an individual who does good strictly for love of the good (for example, because she delights in—is positively reinforced by—the joy of others) is the paradigm of a virtuous individual. But such a paragon of virtue requires no (or minimum) external reward/reinforcement in order to sustain her virtuous behavior; and thus on the behavioral no-fault naturalist view, this most virtuous of individuals will receive the least (external) reward/ reinforcement.

This story has a moral. When no-fault naturalism is considered along with contemporary behavioral learning theory the contrast between rejecting and accepting moral responsibility is quite clear: those who deny moral responsibility will often assign praise/reward/ positive reinforcement in a manner that is exactly opposite the way reward is assigned by proponents of moral responsibility. Behavioral no-fault naturalism rejects just deserts claims, and the schedule of rewards (positive reinforcement) it proposes is fundamentally *in*compatible with those based on desert/responsibility.

The no-fault naturalist may indeed believe that positive reinforcement (reward) and perhaps even aversive conditioning (punishment) are sometimes justified. But it does not follow that no-fault naturalists must therefore admit moral responsibility and moral desert. Not only will the no-fault naturalist *practices* of positive/aversive reinforcement commonly be the opposite of the responsibility-based practices of reward/punishment (as described above); also, the no-fault naturalist *justification* of positive and aversive conditioning will be the opposite of the justification given for reward/punishment by believers in moral responsibility. Advocates of moral responsibility justify reward/punishment on the grounds that the person's actions deserve reward or punishment, that giving such reward/punishment is right in those circumstances and that withholding it would be at least *prima facie* unjust. The no-fault naturalist approaches the question from the opposite perspective. Everyone is exactly equal in deserts (or, alternatively, no one ever deserves anything): the *prima facie* right result is always exactly egalitarian. But no-fault naturalists might—depending on what *other* value beliefs they hold—decide that on some occasions egalitarian principles should be overridden by other goods. If praise is used judiciously as a positive reinforcer it shapes good behavior, the good of which might outweigh the *prima facie* wrong of departing from strictly egalitarian treatment. But no one will be given praise because he deserves it; instead, praise (and all positive reinforcement) will be dispensed *despite* the fact that no one deserves it, on the grounds that such praise will promote some other good.

MORAL RESPONSIBILITY CLAIMS are not only an impediment to the most effective and humane treatment of malefactors and the most effective shaping of self-motivated virtuous individuals; they also distort our view of larger social and cultural issues. Part of the charm of Dennett's position is that it seems so open and egalitarian: you are judged on the basis of what you do now, not on your background. It matters not who your parents were, what your social and economic background was, what side of the tracks you were born on, whether you went to an elite prep school or a poorly funded public school: each individual is judged on his acts and merits, background be damned. I have no doubt that the motivation behind this is genuinely good-hearted. But, under careful scrutiny, its unfairness is painfully obvious. It's like pairing two milers against one another, one of whom has had top coaching and superb training facilities and careful nutritional supervision and the best of equipment, while the other has struggled with inferior coaching and faulty equipment and poor nutrition. If we now insist that the officials be scrupulously fair, and that no one be allowed to jump the gun or race in a superior lane, that will still *not* make it a fair contest. The winner may "deserve" (act-deserve) the prize, in the sense that the race was won in accordance with the rules of that game; but justly deserving the prize is another matter. And in fact *if* we focus narrowly on the running of the race, and the immediate conditions of competition, that myopic focus will prevent us from understanding some very important factors in the race. If, for example, we concentrate exclusively on the running of the race—ignoring the runners' backgrounds—we shall say that the winner paced herself better and ultimately had greater endurance. But this short-sighted view will prevent us from examining the conditions that caused the loser to have less endurance and that prevented the loser from learning effective pacing in distance races.

We need not worry overmuch about who wins the mile; but the race is, after all, only a metaphor—a metaphor for the way humans live and behave. And if we focus too narrowly on the fact that this individual will not work diligently for sustained periods—and we simply hold the person morally responsible for that immediate behavior, and punish (or withhold benefits) accordingly—then we ignore the causal factors that resulted in this individual's indolence and that are even now shaping other indolent individuals. It is true, as Moritz Schlick insists, that we cannot exert pressures on "the great-grandparents of the man"; but we can examine the environment that shaped the individual and consider how it should be revised to prevent further lethargic (or criminal) behavior by this or other individuals. In short, holding people morally responsible not only blocks the most effective means of shaping individuals as they are now, but also obscures the causes that shaped their current characters and behavior, and thus prevents effective programs that could change the large-scale social conditions that cause weak or undesirable characters. "Holding people responsible" is not a good game on either the individual or institutional level: it is unfair and impractical.

CHAPTER ELEVEN

The Radical Denial of Moral Responsibility

THE CENTRAL CONTENTION of this book is that individual freedom is worthwhile and defensible (within the naturalist-determinist context), but just deserts and moral responsibility must be rejected: no one is ever, under any circumstances, morally responsible. A number of arguments in favor of compatibilist moral responsibility have been examined and found wanting. But, in addition to attacking compatibilist arguments for moral responsibility, the no-fault naturalist must also deal with counterattacks.

A frequent, important, and troubling criticism of the no-fault naturalist denial of moral responsibility is that it is of no practical significance (and thus is trivial, or perhaps even meaningless): those who deny moral responsibility seem to derive some satisfaction from mouthing that denial, but it has no effect on their actual practices. In practical circumstances the denial of moral responsibility makes no difference.

Initially the denial of moral responsibility seems distinctive and full-blooded: no one deserves blame, credit, special treatment; punishment and reward are basically unfair, since one's character and behavior result from forces beyond one's control. Such strong assertions herald a radically new approach to problems of reward and punishment and just distribution. But gradually the radical edge is dulled down by social policy considerations: no one deserves punishment, but we must imprison to protect society and punish to reform malefactors; and no one deserves reward, but reward is required in order to motivate and sustain those who perform the many tasks vital to a well-ordered society. Thus the practices of those who deny moral responsibility merge with those of the believers. The fervent denial of moral responsibility apparently degenerates into petulant insistence on a difference that makes no difference.

But, as argued in the previous chapter, the denial of moral responsibility *is* a significant moral assertion, with important practical implications. Its significance has been blunted by inadequate knowledge of the causes and control of human behavior. The no-fault naturalist denial of moral responsibility is a case of ethical insight ("all are equal in deserts") outstripping scientific development, of ethical advances awaiting improvements in psychology. No matter what view is held of moral responsibility and the desert of punishment and reward, so long as rewarding virtue and punishing vice are the most effective means of shaping behavior then such practices remain in effect. Those who regard moral responsibility as genuine and those who think it a necessary fiction wind up advocating similar measures. But the development of a science of behavior brings both the moral and practical significance of denying moral responsibility fully to bear. In the contemporary scientific context, the complete denial of moral responsibility does make a practical difference.

There is, however, another line of attack (against those who deny moral responsibility) that takes a slightly different approach to asserting the insignificance of the no-fault naturalist denial of moral responsibility. Rather than claiming practical insignificance, these opponents object that the no-fault naturalist denial of moral responsibility is empty and *meaningless*.

This challenge to the rejection of moral responsibility may be framed in a particularly powerful manner: as a challenge to the no-fault naturalist to *make sense* of exactly what is being denied in the denial of moral responsibility. If the denial of moral responsibility is not vacuous—a mere preference for an empty verbalism—then it must be possible to state precisely the nature of that which is being denied. That is, what would you *count* as moral responsibility? And if *nothing* would count as morally responsible behavior, then (by the principle of vacuous contrast) the *denial* of moral responsibility is meaningless. If you cannot specify some behavior somewhere that would count as morally responsible behavior, then the claim that there is no moral responsibility is an empty claim, vacuous because there is nothing substantial with which to contrast it.[1]

In answering this objection, the contrast drawn earlier (Chapter Two) between compatibilist (naturalist) and transcendent autonomy will be crucial. The rejection of moral responsibility is based on rejection of the overall system that supports transcendent free will. This section will show why that rejection is significant and meaningful.

A child is abused at an early age, grows up in a violent home, lives in a crime-ravaged area, and suffers one bad influence after another until emerging a hardened criminal. Such cases are grist for the no-fault naturalist mill: how can you say that such an unfortunate *deserves* blame for his vicious character and criminal acts? But that is a standard opening, with standard counterattacks: what about the child from a similar environment, with an equally disadvantageous family life and the same constant exposure to crime and poverty, who perseveres and triumphs and becomes (pick your favorite) a banker or barrister or priest? And the book response is parried with the standard answer: the cases may appear similar, but in fact they are crucially different. The individual who escaped the cycle of crime and poverty had an extra measure of intelligence or special drive or fortunate positive influence (the proverbial kindly priest or sensitive teacher or dedicated coach) that the other individual lacked. But the criminal is surely not to be blamed for having less intelligence (whether that is genetic or the result of early environmental influences such as malnutrition or inferior education) nor for having less drive (due to an unfortunate early schedule of reinforcement) nor for failing to encounter an opportune good influence. Neither deserves credit or blame for good or bad fortune.

But the champion of moral responsibility may now counter with the accusation of meaninglessness: very well, the slum-child-turned-banker may be only lucky rather than morally responsible. But if you refuse to count that individual as morally responsible, whom would you count? You no-fault naturalists bandy about claims that individuals are *not* morally responsible; so you apparently think that the notion of moral responsibility makes sense (it is not like denying that an individual is frumious). By the principle of vacuous contrast a term is meaningful only if one can specify contrasting cases in which it does and does not apply. Thus if it is meaningful to claim that an individual is *not* morally responsible, it must be possible to specify at least some (contrasting) case in which an individual *is* morally responsible. Or failing that, one must admit the no-fault naturalist enthusiasm for general absolution is gibberish.

Now that sort of attack wedges the no-fault naturalist between a rock and a hard place. No-fault naturalists are rightly reluctant to abandon the principle of vacuous contrast, but any admission of moral responsibility abandons no-fault naturalism. Admitting the bare possibility of intelligible transcendent "contracausal free will" leaves sufficient space for sophisticated libertarians (like C. A. Campbell) to fashion enough moral responsibility to satisfy the most guilt-ridden soul; and to allow that an individual may be responsible for completely determined behavior is to give up the game to soft determinists (compatibilists).

The answer to this formidable dilemma will show how broad is the gulf that divides no-fault naturalists from their opponents. What would a no-fault naturalist count as morally responsible behavior?

Nothing. But that is not an admission that the no-fault naturalist is guilty of violating the principle of vacuous contrast, because the principle of vacuous contrast is an intrasystematic principle. It does not apply across competing systems of thought, and the no-fault naturalist regards moral responsibility as an element of an alien framework.

When operating *within* a naturalistic system it is required—by the principle of vacuous contrast—that we be able to specify what would count against the existence of some subatomic particle we are proposing; and if we deny the existence of positrons we must know what positrons are and how to recognize one should we unexpectedly stumble over it. I do not believe that the Loch Ness monster exists; but if reputable biologists should capture a thirty-foot slinky sea creature from Loch Ness and place it on public exhibit in an aquarium then I would acknowledge the existence of Nessie. The notion of a creature thought to be extinct but surviving in Loch Ness is certainly meaningful to me, even though I think it very unlikely.

But in contrast to subatomic particles and Nessie and other items that can fit within the naturalist ontology, *nothing* could convince me of the existence of a gorgon. Should someone report the existence of a woman whose scalp grows snakes instead of hair (leave aside the bit about turning all who behold her to stone) I would attribute the report to a hyperactive imagination. Were the observer a usually reliable friend I would suspect drugs or drink or overwork. If I myself saw the gorgon I would believe it an elaborate hoax or see a psychotherapist or perhaps become a teetotaler. I know that there are people who invest enormous resources and energy in perpetrating hoaxes (a circus recently toured the United States with a "unicorn"), and I can also imagine that I might go a bit batty and begin to "see" all manner of strange creatures; but nothing could convince me of the existence of a genuine gorgon. Belief in such a creature is in direct conflict with my system of basic beliefs. Adding a gorgon to my taxonomy is not like adding Nessie. There is a niche for Nessie, however unlikely it is to be occupied. But the gorgon would shatter the system. To acknowledge the existence of a gorgon would require giving up my beliefs about biology, destroy my confidence in scientific inquiry, breach my distinction between myth and reality, undermine all my assumptions concerning what is reasonable and what is preposterous. In short, belief in gorgons is part of a system of thought and belief that I reject. I can understand at least some of the elements of such a system, but nothing—or nothing short of shattering my current way of thinking—could convince me to accept one of those alien beliefs.

This is a common phenomenon. What would a noncognitivist count as an intuition of objective values? What would a modern physician count as demon possession? What would an atheist count as a miracle? Nothing, nothing, and nothing. The "evidence" cannot even begin to get a purchase, since it will be interpreted in terms of an opposing system. Thus the noncognitivist A. J. Ayer believes that "the experiences which some philosophers want to describe as intuitions, or as quasi-sensory apprehensions, of good are not significantly different from those that I want to describe as feelings of approval" (Ayer, 1954); the patient's impassioned reports of demon possession are interpreted as part of his illness; the miraculous cure is the natural remission of the disease.

Demon possession and gorgons and miracles are not meaningless, but instead are elements of alien systems of thought. Belief in miracles would require a complete restructuring of my thought processes—literally a conversion experience. I cannot say under what circumstances my entire belief system would crumble, but my inability to state what I would acknowledge as the occurrence of a miracle does not entail that my rejection of miracles is vacuous.[2]

Moral responsibility is part of the miraculous belief system, and no-fault naturalists therefore reject it. As an indication of the vast differences between the systems of thought, consider the position of Roderick Chisholm on free will and moral responsibility. Chisholm maintains that moral responsibility requires that one have the power to do or refrain from doing some act; and that implies:

> If we are responsible . . . then we have a prerogative which some would attribute only to God: each of us, when we really act, is a prime mover unmoved. In doing what we do, we cause certain events to happen, and nothing and no one, except we ourselves, causes us to cause those events to happen. (1975, p. 395)

So this particular view of moral responsibility is at home in a system of Western religious thought that countenances a God and/or human souls with extraordinary powers. It is not surprising that Martin Luther (and many other theologians) ascribe such powers only to God. Nor is it surprising that those (such as Nietzsche and Sartre) who want to reclaim God as "man's best creation" emphasize such radical autonomous choice as an essential human characteristic. But both the Christian and the existentialist views are fundamentally different from the no-fault naturalist system. As Chisholm notes, if one adopts his position, then "This means that, in one very strict sense of the terms, there can be no complete science of man (1975, p. 396)." In stark contrast the no-fault naturalist view assumes that humans, like all other natural phenomena, are appropriate subjects for science and that there are no inherent limits on the power of science to deal with such a subject matter.

And this brings us to the moral of the story. Obviously no-fault naturalists reject the compatibilist account of moral responsibility: that is what makes them *no-fault* naturalists (similar in that respect to *hard* determinists). But it does not follow that their denials of moral responsibility are vacuous. Rather, no-fault naturalists are claiming that moral responsibility is part of an obsolete system of thought—a system that can accommodate spirits, deities, self-moved movers, and moral responsibility. Among the miracles moral responsibility is quite appropriate. It may be that moral responsibility can be attributed only to God—as Luther argued; or it may be that moral responsibility can be attributed to humans who have taken on the attributes once reserved for God—as Chisholm, Nietzsche, and Sartre maintain; but in either case, moral responsibility fits snugly into that system.[3] And no-fault naturalists maintain that notions of moral responsibility are vestiges of such systems, vestiges that can no more fit into the naturalist world view than gargoyles can be harmoniously added to Bauhaus architecture. The proper response to the compatibilist claim that *some* sense must be made of moral responsibility is that *no* variety of moral responsibility can be accommodated within the determinist-naturalist system. In short, the no-fault naturalist denial of the possibility of moral responsibility is just as meaningful and significant as is the contemporary physician's refusal to consider the possibility of demon possession when making a diagnosis.

As noted in the previous chapter, Daniel Dennett claims that those who deny moral responsibility are misled by absolutism:

Skepticism about the very possibility of culpability arises from a misplaced reverence for an absolutist ideal: the concept of total, before-the-eyes-of-God Guilt. The fact that *that* condition is never to be met in this world should not mislead us into skepticism about the integrity of our institution of moral responsibility. (1984, p. 165)

Perhaps some skepticism about moral responsibility arises from "misplaced reverence" about "absolutist ideals" (that might, for example, have influenced Martin Luther's denial of moral responsibility). But the contemporary naturalist-determinist-behaviorist "skepticism about the very possibility of culpability" certainly has little "reverence" for such ideals. To the contrary, the contemporary no-fault naturalist rejection of moral responsibility is based (as noted above) on the rejection of such absolutist ideals, and particularly on the rejection of the transcendent free will that is the cornerstone of that absolutism. The difference is that Dennett strives to breathe pragmatic life into the moribund notion of moral responsibility, while no-fault naturalists prefer to leave moral responsibility in the only place in which it is appropriate—among the ruins of the metaphysical system of gods and miracles and absolutes. Neither that metaphysical system (with its transcendent free will) nor the moral responsibility that it supports holds any charms for the contemporary naturalist-determinist who rejects moral responsibility.[4] It may be a historically interesting place to visit, but I have no wish to live there.

Finally, then, no-fault naturalists should not be intimidated by the demand that they must recognize *some* sort of moral responsibility, that they must specify what they would *count* as moral responsibility. The no-fault naturalist answer is that we have no need of that hypothesis, nor any room for it.

This chapter—in combination with the previous one—answers some criticisms of the no-fault naturalist denial of moral responsibility. The next chapter will defend the denial of moral responsibility against a more formidable attack, along a different front. The issue to be joined is whether (as some advocates of moral responsibility claim) the denial of moral responsibility also entails the denial of all genuine morality. Indeed, since those who deny moral responsibility usually continue to make moral judgments and assertions, some proponents of moral responsibility purport to have a difficult time "taking seriously" the arguments against moral responsibility. This chapter should make clear that the no-fault naturalist does indeed thoroughly and categorically deny all moral responsibility. While that unconditional denial of moral responsibility is still echoing, it is time to move on to the question of what follows from that denial.

CHAPTER TWELVE

Morality Without Moral Responsibility

IT IS COMMONLY BELIEVED that denial of moral responsibility entails the denial of all genuine morality.[1] That mistaken belief has made life miserable for those who deny moral responsibility: they are accused of lacking moral principles and moral sentiments; and then when they champion moral principles they are reviled as hypocrites. For example, Peter van Inwagen states:

> I have listened to philosophers who deny the existence of moral responsibility. I cannot take them seriously. I know a philosopher who has written a paper in which he denies the reality of moral responsibility. And yet this same philosopher, when certain of his books were stolen, said, "That was a *shoddy* thing to do!" But no one can consistently say that a certain act was a shoddy thing to do *and* say that its agent was not morally responsible when he performed it. (1983, p. 207)

It is not surprising that van Inwagen should draw such a conclusion, for the logic is impeccable: If there is no moral responsibility, then there are no genuine moral judgments; but there are genuine moral judgments; therefore, by *modus tollens,* moral responsibility must exist; and thus no-fault naturalism is refuted. The problem with that deduction is that the first premise is false. Moral principles and moral judgments can survive and prosper without moral responsibility. No one justly *deserves* special treatment (praise or blame, reward or punishment) for acting morally or immorally or amorally. But that does not mean the denial of morality, and it does not diminish the importance of moral principles. This chapter will discuss the sources of no-morality-without-responsibility, critically examine arguments for that claim, and explain how morality can flourish as moral responsibility withers.

IT IS NOT DIFFICULT to construct examples that challenge the widespread belief that there can be no morality without moral responsibility. For example, if you are convinced of the truth of utilitarianism, then you can believe in it just as confidently while also believing that you deserve no praise for your enlightened moral beliefs and that benighted deontologists deserve no blame. Again, you may fervently follow the moral principle of "love your neighbor" while believing you deserve no credit for the excellent moral education that shaped your character and that those with less fortunate moral training should not be blamed for their moral limitations. Indeed, someone might consistently believe that knowledge of the Morally True is given directly by God, that God gives such knowledge purely from grace and that no one deserves such grace, and that therefore no one is morally responsible for having (or not having) knowledge of the Morally True, but nonetheless some people do have such wondrous knowledge. On a more mundane level, I can believe in my own moral principles, and strive diligently to follow them, and still believe that I deserve no credit for the strength or the substance of my moral beliefs. Such obvious counterexamples to no-morality-without-moral-responsibility prompt the first question for this chapter: why is it

so commonly believed that moral responsibility is a necessary condition for moral beliefs and moral principles and moral judgments
and moral behavior?

PERHAPS THE BELIEF that denial of moral responsibility undermines
morality stems from the Judaeo-Christian emphasis on sin and guilt
and atonement. On such a view if there is no moral responsibility
(no deserving of punishment) then there is no sin; and since sin is the
major moral concern, the denial of moral responsibility is regarded
as denial of all morality. Vestiges of that religious outlook remain
(in ordinary usage we continue to use "blameworthy" almost as a
synonym for "bad").

Whatever its origins, the most important contemporary source of
no-morality-without-responsibility is a fundamental misunderstanding of the real reasons for rejecting *all* moral responsibility. For
believers in moral responsibility the usual reason for denying moral
responsibility (in an exceptional case) is some defect in the excused
individual: the agent who is not morally responsible is insane, is too
young to control emotions, is in the grip of passion, is drugged. On
this view moral responsibility is denied only when an individual is
severely defective or is overwhelmed by debilitating circumstances,
a fit object for treatment or pity but not for full human interaction.
Seen from that perspective the no-fault naturalist universal denial of
moral responsibility is mistakenly perceived as a claim of universal
human infirmity:[2] humans lack reasoning capacities or are driven by
uncontrollable passions or are manipulated by diabolical forces. But
that is a fatally flawed view of why no-fault naturalists deny moral
responsibility.

The no-fault naturalist believes that no one is ever morally responsible, but not because everyone is defective. People are (ordinarily)
capable of reasoning, of reflective deliberation, of making choices,
of controlling their desires. However, those impressive capacities are

not sufficient for moral responsibility; they do not justify praise or blame or reward or punishment. If there were some sort of miraculous contracausal free will by which humans could "make themselves" then no-fault naturalists might acknowledge moral responsibility. But there is no soul (insulated from environmental forces) that originates choices and is the final source for responsible acts, no contracausal free will that transcends conditioning. As noted in the previous chapter, such notions are regarded by no-fault naturalists as unintelligible or part of an implausible world view. And no-fault naturalists consider anything short of such *ab initio* miraculous self-making inadequate for moral responsibility. Of course my current character is substantially the product of my own earlier choices (as compatibilists note); but those choices are ultimately the product of fortuitous circumstances for which the individual is obviously not morally responsible (as has already been argued). In any case, the immediate point is that the no-fault naturalist does not deny moral responsibility on the basis of individual defects; rather, moral responsibility is eliminated entirely from the naturalist-determinist world view.

IF THE NO-FAULT NATURALIST DENIAL of moral responsibility were based on denial that humans can act from reasons and purposes and principles, then no-fault naturalism would indeed leave little room for morality: it would be impossible to distinguish between Joe's wicked act of purposefully and maliciously stabbing Jim, and Bill's accidental and innocent act of stabbing Bert (when Bill was carrying a sharp knife and tripped over the linoleum). Nor would there remain any distinction between Jill's generous act of feeding the hungry and Joan's apparently similar act of providing food in the hope of perpetuating a docile source of cheap labor. Since almost any behavior may be done for good or bad motives, being unable to draw such distinctions would undermine moral claims. But since no-fault naturalists do not deny that people reason and form intentions and act purposefully, this reason for believing that no-fault naturalism destroys morality turns out to be groundless.[3] No-fault naturalists will certainly be interested in whether the stabbing was purposeful or accidental, but not in order to affix blame or assign punishment. If deliberate, we shall have to take steps (including moral instruction) to prevent the stabber from performing other such vicious—and morally wrong—acts. If accidental, we shall be careful to instruct the stabber in the proper handling of dangerous household items, but that will require a quite different sort of instruction. The former individual is vicious, is morally bad; the latter is accident prone. Nothing in the denial of moral responsibility precludes such moral judgments. The no-fault naturalist will not believe that either deserves blame or punishment (the wicked intentional stabber is not morally responsible for his morally bad character nor for his morally bad behavior); but that does not prevent the no-fault naturalist from judging the intentional stabber a vicious and morally bad person and distinguishing him from a good-willed blunderer.

Thus no-fault naturalists do not deny that there is a difference between intentionally malicious acts and nonintentional injuries; rather, the no-fault naturalist denies that the difference turns on moral responsibility. Van Inwagen is certainly correct that "few people if any will react to an act of gratuitous injury deliberately done them by a human being in the way that they would react if that same injury were caused by a bolt of lightning or a bough broken by the wind" (1983, p. 206). But it does not require belief in human moral responsibility to account for such differences in reactions. The no-fault naturalist will react differently to the deliberate human act because it involves purposive behavior, intended to cause harm. The lightning bolt had no such intentions. No-fault naturalists do not deny intentional behavior; rather, they deny that anyone is morally responsible for intentional acts. We shall do very different things to prevent injuries from lightning bolts and injuries from deliberate human acts, but that does not imply that the difference turns on the belief that one is and the other is not morally responsible.

The deliberately inflicted injury is also different in another important way. When I am deliberately shoved aside by someone walking along the same path, the injury is not only to my shoulder but also to my psyche. The act of the intentional shover manifests an insulting and demeaning attitude toward me: I am of no value and can be shoved aside for no reason. That is a different sort of injury from the one inflicted by the broken bough, and it is not surprising that we react differently to it. But the judgment that the intentional shover is a mean-spirited and deliberately insulting person—a thoroughly unpleasant sort—does not require that we judge that individual morally responsible for her bad character and bad behavior. (Of course it does not follow that we must meekly accept insulting mistreatment: we may struggle against it, attempt to prevent it, seek ways of preventing its recurrence. There may even be an obligation to struggle against such wrongs and wrong-doers. The fact that the wrong-doer does not deserve blame or punishment does not imply that victims or potential victims must passively accept mistreatment.)

In short, those who deny moral responsibility can distinguish intentional from inadvertent and rational from irrational behavior; furthermore, the denial of moral responsibility is consistent with recognizing the difference between raw desiring and reflective valuing.[4] No-fault naturalists do not regard everyone as "wantons" (in Frankfurt's [1971] sense); people commonly are capable of reflecting on their first-order desires. What the no-fault naturalist denies is that such rational and reflective capacities are sufficient for moral responsibility. Since compatibilists generally describe such capacities in order to use them as a basis for attributing or claiming moral responsibility, it is natural that compatibilists might conclude that those who deny moral responsibility are therefore denying the (supposed) sufficient conditions for moral responsibility. Natural or not, that conclusion is mistaken.

Someone might object that no-fault naturalists cannot consistently acknowledge rationality, and thus cannot admit the use of value principles—that the naturalist-determinist basis of the no-fault naturalist denial of moral responsibility also undermines all claims of reason and deliberation, and thus precludes any use of or appeal to principles (moral or otherwise). That attack has a much larger target than the no-fault naturalist denial of moral responsibility. It challenges the entire naturalist-determinist viewpoint and is directed as much against compatibilists as against no-fault naturalists. And it is not merely an attack on the possibility of no-fault naturalists using moral principles and making moral evaluations; it is the much larger attack against the possibility of any naturalist-determinist (including compatibilists like Hume, Dennett, Frankfurt) being able to use any principles or carry out any deliberation (whether about ethics or any other subject). Since this book is concerned with a narrower issue— specifically, why moral responsibility should be rejected within the naturalist-determinist framework—I shall avoid this much broader challenge to naturalist rationality, except to say that I think this sort of attack on the possibility of reason (and morality) within a naturalist-determinist system has been quite adequately answered (by arguments from both compatibilists and incompatibilists).[5]

There is nothing in the no-fault naturalist denial of moral responsibility that precludes teaching, believing, and following moral principles (or scientific or logical principles either, for that matter). Whether someone does (or does not) receive a good moral education/training, and whether someone has (or has not) learned to respond to the complex contingencies of value systems and moral principles (and logical reasoning and scientific method and chess-playing and map-reading) is a matter of good or bad fortune, and not something for which anyone is morally responsible. But given the right conditions, value principles can be and are important in formulating our ethics and our purposes and our system of moral education, and important in deciding what behavior to reinforce positively and what behavior to discourage, and important in selecting bedtime stories and mottoes and religious practices. Those things do influence behavior. Of course the no-fault naturalist believes that *given* Sam's *complete* causal-environmental-conditioning history, Sam cannot do otherwise than what he does (and thus is not morally responsible). Nonetheless, it may still be useful—as one causal element of Sam's individual's environment—to admonish him that "stealing is wrong," since such verbal contingencies may be an important causal-environmental influence in shaping him not to steal.[6] Thus without moral responsibility moral language continues to be meaningful and functional, and can still play important educational and persuasive and institutional and ritual roles—*except* in statements of credit or blame (which certainly do not comprise the whole of moral discourse).

No-fault naturalists do not deny rationality and intentionality and higher-order reflection; and it is a mistake to suppose that such a denial is the basis of the no-fault naturalist rejection of moral responsibility. However, that basic mistake is subtle and pervasive. To examine it in one of its most sophisticated and influential manifestations, consider the arguments of P. F. Strawson's rightly famous "Freedom and Resentment." Strawson argues *not* that denial of moral responsibility logically entails the denial of morality but that many basic and valuable human attitudes and emotions are so closely linked to belief in moral responsibility that to deny moral responsibility would eviscerate human emotional life. The human emotions of love, hate, and resentment would dry up, along with the human activity of rational discussion and the human belief in morality. All of these are held together in a close weave of what Strawson calls reactive attitudes, such that pulling out the strand of moral responsibility would unravel the pattern of human reactive attitudes, leaving only the emotionally impoverished objective attitudes. Denying moral responsibility would require that we give up "the range of participation with others in inter-personal human relationships," that we disallow such attitudes as "resentment, gratitude, forgiveness, anger, or the sort of love which two adults can sometimes be said to feel reciprocally, for each other." No-fault naturalists are confined to the objective attitude:

> To adopt the objective attitude to another human being is to see him, perhaps, as an object of social policy; as a subject for what, in a wide range of sense, might be called treatment; as something certainly to be taken account, perhaps precautionary account, of; to be managed or handled or cured or trained. . . . If your attitude towards someone is wholly objective, then though you may fight him, you cannot quarrel with him, and though you may talk to him, even negotiate with him, you cannot reason with him. You can at most pretend to quarrel, or to reason, with him.
>
> Seeing someone, then, as warped or deranged or compulsive in behaviour or peculiarly unfortunate in his formative circumstances—seeing someone so tends, at least to some extent, to set him apart from normal participant reactive attitudes on the part of one who so sees him, tends to promote, at least in the civilized, objective attitudes. (1974, p. 9)

But nothing in Strawson's account indicates that the denial of *moral responsibility* would destroy reactive attitudes. Strawson's case concerns the effects of denying *rationality,* not moral responsibility. Strawson is probably correct that it would be impossible to enter into full human reactive attitudes and relations with a "warped" or "deranged" or nonrational individual. But the no-fault naturalist does not deny rationality, and does not regard everyone as deranged; instead, the no-fault naturalist believes that no one is ever morally responsible, including the most rational, balanced, serene persons. If rationality were pulled out of the weave of reactive attitudes, then very likely the whole fabric would unravel. However, no-fault naturalists leave the rationality strand intact, and there is nothing to indicate that removing the strand of moral responsibility would have such disastrous consequences for the reactive attitudes.

Jonathan Bennett dramatically elucidates Strawson's position, but without making it any more convincing:

> The most basic way in which our willingness that a man should suffer is connected with our belief that he has offended is through their roles in adverse reactive attitudes. If I resent some attitude of yours towards me, my resentment must involve some measure of willingness that some unpleasantness should befall you. An adverse reactive attitude essentially involves some disposition to hit back or to be pleased if God or Nature does it for one. To divorce judging someone to be an offender from willingness that he should suffer, therefore, we should have to strip ourselves of all adverse reactive attitudes; and that is unthinkable or unacceptable. So the connection between 'He offended' and 'It is all right to make him suffer' is forged by an aspect of human nature which is ineliminable and undisgraceful; and that aspect of our natures is what is expressed in our judgment that guilt but not innocence justifies the infliction of suffering. (1980*b*, p. 48)

Bennett's comment goes to the crux of the matter. A negative moral judgment (an "adverse reactive attitude") is psychologically linked to "willingness that he [the offender] should suffer" in such a way that to deny the latter "we should have to strip ourselves of all adverse reactive attitudes," and that would leave us in a psychologically impoverished condition. Judgments of moral responsibility are an essential element of the reactive attitudes, which are "a valuable aspect of human nature" (1980*b*, p. 48). It might be logically possible to retain moral judgments while deleting moral responsibility, but (given our psychological nature and the nature of reactive attitudes) it is not psychologically possible. Thus the denial of moral responsibility does undermine reactive attitudes and moral judgments.

The Strawson-Bennett focus on psychological (rather than logical/ philosophical) implications of denying moral responsibility wafts a fresh breeze into a musty philosophical corner. Freshness notwithstanding, it fails to establish that loss of moral responsibility renders moral judgments psychologically impossible. First, Strawson and Bennett confuse "reactive attitudes" with considered judgments. It is one thing to have a reactive attitude toward something; quite another to conclude that one ought to act in accordance with that reactive attitude. The denial of moral responsibility does not entail the denial of reactive attitudes of distaste for an offender, nor does it deny the reactive attitude of being disposed to "hit back or to be pleased if God or Nature does it for one." What it does deny is that anyone *deserves* such treatment. That is, one who denies moral responsibility will consider such reactive attitudes a poor moral guide to behavior. But that certainly does not imply the elimination of adverse reactive attitudes, much less the elimination of the full range of reactive attitudes. Obviously one can have all manner of emotional responses and desires that one (frequently) judges it best to restrain, without thereby eliminating or even lessening those emotional responses and desires (concupiscence leaps to mind). So *if* one concluded that the elimination of adverse reactive attitudes would also undermine a large pattern of desirable reactive attitudes (a conclusion that I shall soon argue is mistaken), one would still have nothing to fear from the denial of moral responsibility. The denial of moral responsibility would not eliminate such reactive attitudes, but would instead counsel that one ought not act on them.[7]

Second, even if it were true that denial of moral responsibility would lead to the elimination of the "hitback" adverse reactive attitudes, it does not follow that it would result in eliminating *all* adverse reactive attitudes—much less the entire range of reactive attitudes.[8] In fact, such empirical evidence as can be brought to bear on the question counts against the Strawson-Bennett claim. There are apparently people who judge behavior wrong (and who have "adverse reactive attitudes" toward that behavior) and yet do not believe (and perhaps do not even feel) that the transgressor deserves punishment or censure. (Such people may express their attitude with the saying, "To know all is to forgive all"; they do not deny that there is a wrong act to forgive.) It also seems possible to admire an individual's good behavior and her strong rational resolve to behave well, while believing that she does not deserve reward for that upstanding behavior.

Additional empirical support (for the claim that denial of moral responsibility does *not* eliminate reactive attitudes) can be drawn from the modern evolution of notions of moral responsibility. At one time no distinction was made between harms done unintentionally—by accident—and harms inflicted purposefully: in both cases the victim feels wronged and the victim feels an immediate strikeback reactive attitude (and it is easy to imagine why natural selection would have favored an immediate counterattack over a delay to ascertain motives). But gradually we have come to distinguish such cases, and most people now believe that it is inappropriate to strike back in cases when one is harmed by the nonnegligent accidental behavior of others. People do not deserve blame for such accidental behavior; they are not morally responsible for it.[9] However, the reactive strikeback attitude still occurs in such situations (as probably all of us can attest from personal reactive experience) even though we do not believe that we should act on it. Furthermore, the narrowing of our sense of when an adverse reactive attitude is appropriate toward other people (it is not appropriate in response to accidental injuries) does *not* seem to be accompanied by any corresponding general narrowing of our reactive attitudes. Of course this is not a case of total elimination of belief in moral responsibility (as is proposed by the no-fault naturalist); but it is a case of revising our assessment of what adverse reactive attitudes we should act on, and in this case the general withering of reactive attitudes (feared by Strawson and Bennett) does not occur. That is at least some empirical evidence for the claim that lessening or eliminating moral responsibility does not threaten important reactive attitudes. Thus the Strawson-Bennett claim that eliminating moral responsibility would eviscerate our reactive emotional life is shown to be a doubtful one. The empirical evidence on the subject may be inconclusive, but what evidence there is indicates that moral responsibility could be eliminated while our reactive attitudes prosper.

There is a third point to be made against the Strawson-Bennett claim that denying responsibility weakens the weave of reactive attitudes: should it prove difficult to discover clear cases in which people preserve positive or negative reactive attitudes while denying moral responsibility, that would not prove it impossible. It is hardly surprising that in our culture reactive attitudes are often tied to attributions of moral responsibility. The Western tradition closely links the reactive attitudes of moral approval/disapproval to reward/punishment (moral responsibility). Furthermore, rewards do promote good behavior and punishment often stops (at least briefly) bad behavior; so the use of reward and punishment has been positively reinforced for those employing the reward and punishment (rewarding the desired behavior causes more of it). Naturally, then, reactive attitudes (such as moral approval/disapproval) have become associated with feelings about moral responsibility (desert, blame, praise, reward). But that proves nothing. No-fault naturalists are pushing for *reform* of common practice. The question at issue is not whether moral responsibility is *now* closely linked to the reactive attitudes of moral judgment, but whether moral responsibility *could* be deleted while the reactive attitudes are preserved. The reasons given for supposing that impossible are based on bad *a priori* psychologizing (or perhaps bad *a priori* sociobiologizing). Whether it is possible for humans to continue to feel strongly the reactive attitudes of moral approval/disapproval while no longer feeling inclined to reward or punish is not a question that can be settled by philosophical speculation. Once again, *if* no-fault naturalists were denying rationality and intentionality, that might well undermine many valuable reactive attitudes. But Strawson and Bennett offer no reasons to suppose that the denial of moral responsibility would diminish worthwhile reactive attitudes, much less that such denial would invalidate all value beliefs.[10]

IN THE PREVIOUS SECTION it was argued—contra Strawson and Bennett—that valuable reactive attitudes can survive the demise of moral responsibility. But the reactive attitudes of penance and guilt require further discussion: first, because it is unclear how valuable they are, and whether they are worth retaining; and, second, because it is not at all obvious that they could be retained in the absence of moral responsibility.

Certainly for many people the loss of all sense of guilt would be a great loss—and I am not speaking of those who revel in guilt, which they explore obsessively, like a hypochondriac telling in glorious detail each symptom of encroaching disease. Quite unobsessive people might well feel diminished if it were impossible for them to feel guilt—or at least a special sort of regret—for their bad acts. (It would prompt fears of becoming one of Frankfurt's "wantons," who have no evaluative concern for their own desires and acts.)[11]

Obviously we cannot take such attitudes as a perfectly reliable guide. It has already been argued that many such attitudes are vestiges of common but discredited notions of moral responsibility. However, guilt seems to pose special challenges. For imagine that someone were to say, after committing a particularly cruel and heinous act: "Well, I don't feel bad about that; after all, I'm not morally responsible for my behavior; others should not blame me, and obviously neither should I blame myself." Certainly that would seem despicable and self-serving rather than an admirable recognition of reality.

Is our negative reaction to the malefactor's self-excusing claim justified (assuming the rejection of moral responsibility)? Obviously not, at least in a certain sense. The thesis of this book is that no one "deserves blame" for bad acts, nor credit for good ones. How then can it make sense to say that one *should* feel deep regret over one's own willful bad acts, that one should "feel guilty" about them?

It makes sense in this way. One who can perform vicious acts with little or no regret is a profoundly vicious person. If an individual does a particularly bad act, it is important that that individual feel the full significance of that bad act, be deeply disturbed that such motivation exists within his character, examine the sources of the act, and resolve to take steps—perhaps difficult steps—to change. That is hard work, and one who flippantly denies that any of that is his concern is not likely to undertake the strenuous effort of character reform. (The individual is not *morally responsible* for the bad act, and not morally responsible for wishing or not wishing to change. That does not imply that there is *no* moral difference between the vicious individual who glories in brutal behavior and the vicious individual who is struggling to reform.)

Also, it is reasonable for one who denies moral responsibility to feel profound sorrow and regret for an act. If in a fit of anger I strike a friend, I shall be appalled at my behavior, and profoundly distressed that I have in me the capacity for such behavior. If the act occurs under minimum provocation, and with an opportunity for some brief reflection before the assault, then I shall be even more disturbed and disappointed by my behavior: I find in myself the capacity for a vicious and despicable act, and the act emerges more from my own character than from the immediate stimuli (thus it may be more likely to recur in many different settings), and my capacity to control such vicious behavior is demonstrably inadequate. Certainly I shall have good reason to regret my character—its capacity for vicious acts and its lack of capacity to control anger. I do not deserve blame; I may (or may not) even be able to trace my vicious desires and lack of self-control to early training or childhood abuse. Be that as it may, I still regret my behavior and those elements of my own character. Those aspects of my character are my own, even though they may not be as deeply my own as my higher-order wish that I were of a less volatile and aggressive nature. (They will not be as profoundly my own, certainly, as they would be were I delighted by my quick temper—as some people do take pride in such a low flash point.)

So there is no inconsistency in regretting my character flaws while denying my moral responsibility for them. I regret, after all, my weak backhand, even though I certainly do not think myself morally responsible for it (my lousy high school coach—lousy, not blame-worthy—instilled bad tennis habits I cannot now overcome); when the problem is more important and more closely linked to how I regard myself—aggressive volatility, for example—then I have greater reason for regret. But is there any reason to preserve that regret, or should those who deny moral responsibility strive to eliminate such emotions? That is a tougher question. There is no doubt that regret and guilt can be destructive emotions. However, there may be a legitimate role for at least some degree of regret and penance for past behavior. Even though regret is probably not a very effective motivator of change it may be important and ineliminable as a concomitant of some kinds of change. Obviously the mere presence of deep regret and guilt is not sufficient for changing character and behavior. If it were, the individual who oscillates between episodic violent anger and deep guilt and regret for such behavior would change for the better; and, on a more mundane level, if regret prompted change then those of us who repeatedly succumb to junk food temptations and then regret our weak-willed characters would actually follow our repeated resolutions to diet scrupulously. Instead, what often happens is quite the reverse: my guilt over violating my diet triggers a binge of shame and chocolate. Nonetheless, it may well be that regret over my character/behavior is necessary in order to carry out the process of changing my behavior: after all, if I do not regret the behavior—if I think my volatile striking of a friend in a fit of anger a good act, one I happily identify with—then I am certainly not likely to take any steps to try to change it.

In short, while regret is certainly not sufficient, and there is reason to doubt that it is even an effective tool in changing behavior, it may still be the case that regret is an ineliminable concomitant of efforts to change behavior. Thus one who denies moral responsibility need not strive to eliminate all regret (or even "guilt").

Why, then, will we be disturbed by an individual who shows little or no regret for his despicable behavior? Why, for example, should one who denies moral responsibility be upset if an individual who has just engaged in a vicious hot-tempered assault glibly asserts that "that's just the way I am, I'm not morally responsible for that vicious act"? There are several possible reasons. First, lack of concern may be evidence that the attacker does not really regard the vicious behavior as bad, as undesirable. Imagine a person who, while driving safely and carefully, strikes and kills a small child who has darted under the wheels of the car and could not be avoided. The driver may well insist that it was not his fault; but we should certainly regard it as appallingly cold-blooded if the driver showed no regret, no remorse. It would indicate belief that killing a child is not such a bad thing. Or, second, perhaps the glib denial of guilt indicates that the actor has no intention of changing and intends to repeat such vicious acts. Or, third, possibly it indicates a particularly weak-willed and spineless individual, who makes no efforts of any kind. All such people may well be cruel and dangerous sorts, and unlikely to change—at least unlikely to change of their own efforts, and probably very difficult to change in any case. That may quite reasonably disturb us. It does not mean, however, that we must regard the individual as morally responsible. The individual is not morally responsible for the vicious act; nor is the individual morally responsible for approving of that act, or for lacking the effort-making capacity to change. But nothing in that precludes regarding the vicious person who glibly acquiesces in his vicious acts as more profoundly bad— and perhaps more dangerous and more likely to repeat such acts— than one who commits the acts but then despises and regrets them and resolves to change.

Finally, what of the person who does a vicious act and then really does reform and becomes a better and kinder person? Does it make any sense—when moral responsibility is universally denied—for that individual to reflect with special regret on her past behavior? Of course. It makes sense to regret any bad and harmful act, and particularly any bad act done intentionally and deliberately. And if the act is one that I did in the past, from my own past motivations and character, then I have a special connection with that vicious behavior, and thus have special grounds for regretting it. I may recognize that I was not morally responsible, and I need not blame myself (any more than I can claim credit for my reformed good character); but that does not imply that I should not profoundly and personally regret those past acts. Indeed, one might well feel a special desire to requite the wrongs done, to "set things right" to the greatest degree possible. Of course one should feel a desire to see all wrongs righted, whether the wrongs were done by one's self or by others; but the special intimacy with past wrongs perpetrated by one's self should provide special motivation.

In sum, regret can be accommodated and even put to good service in the absence of moral responsibility. Indeed, when the blame and guilt are set aside, and the obsession with moral responsibility is eliminated, regret may be more effectively and rationally deployed to make genuine changes. In the absence of moral responsibility, there will be less tendency to regard regret and penance as an end in itself and a greater tendency to examine how the behavior can be effectively modified.

BEFORE DETOURING to examine penance, it had been argued that no-fault naturalists deny moral responsibility, not rationality. The mistaken assumption that no-fault naturalists deny rationality is at the core of the belief that denial of moral responsibility entails denial of all morality, and the discussion to this point in the chapter (with the exception of the remarks on penance) has focused on that mistaken assumption and the mistakes following from it. But there is another important error behind the view that no-fault naturalism entails denial of moral responsibility: confusion over what *sort* of responsibility is denied. "Responsible" is often used of people who deliberate, who think carefully about what they are doing, who "take responsibility" and are "responsible members of society." A responsible person in this sense is one whom you trust with serious affairs. Moral considerations would have little if any significance in a society devoid of such responsibility: "responsible" people are precisely the ones who take moral considerations seriously.[12] But the no-fault naturalist is not denying the existence of responsibility in that sense. There *are* people who are responsible, who are trustworthy, on whom we can depend: they are good candidates for important *role*-responsibilities (as noted in Chapter Five). But, as discussed in that chapter, what the no-fault naturalist denies is that anyone is *morally responsible* (deserves praise or blame) for being (or failing to be) reliably role-responsible. That a person acts responsibly (in the role-responsibility sense), deliberates carefully, and takes moral principles seriously is a result of good upbringing or other fortunate environmental contingencies. If the person became "responsible" through long and diligent practice, still the encouragement to carry out that practice, the occasional positive reinforcement that prevented the extinction of such effort, was a matter of good fortune and not something for which anyone is morally responsible.

THIS CHAPTER HAS EXAMINED the basic confusion behind the widespread belief that the denial of moral responsibility entails the general rejection of morality. There is one last confusion to be considered, perhaps the trickiest and most revealing. The slide from "morally good/bad" to "morally responsible" is greased by ordinary usage; and ordinary usage stems from a tradition of moral responsibility. As suggested earlier, the Judaeo-Christian emphasis on guilt and atonement links wrong acts (sins) so closely with the desert of punishment that "blameworthy" is used as a synonym for "bad" and "praiseworthy" as synonymous with "acting virtuously." That close connection leads to the mistaken supposition that denial of all moral responsibility is also the denial of all moral judgments and moral principles; and correcting that mistake has been the major task of this chapter.

The same basic confusion also cuts the other way. That is, confusing "bad" with "blameworthy" (and "virtuous" with "praiseworthy") makes it almost impossible to resist the apparently easy (and linguistically natural) step from "bad/good behavior" to "morally responsible." Thus it is sometimes argued that an individual must have genuine moral responsibility since the individual's behavior is acknowledged to be nefarious or exemplary. One example of this mistake is van Inwagen's claim—quoted at the beginning of this chapter—that if someone's behavior is characterized as "shoddy" then the behaver must be regarded as morally responsible. In a similar manner, Susan Wolf offers a case of an individual exhibiting paradigmatically generous behavior, and concludes that though the behavior is determined it is still certainly good ("praiseworthy") behavior—and then draws the natural (but mistaken) conclusion that the individual is therefore morally responsible ("deserves praise") for his good behavior. In Wolf's example of a generous man:

> He does not *decide* to feel an independent pleasure in performing acts of generosity, or decide that such acts will make it easier for him to make friends. He discovers that these are consequences of a generous nature—and if he is observant and perceptive, he cannot help but discover this. . . . He cannot help but have these experiences—they are beyond his control. So it seems that what reasons he *has* for being generous depends on what reasons there *are*.
>
> If the man's character is determined in this way, however, it seems absurd to say that it is not under his control. His character is determined on the basis of his reasons, and his reasons are determined by what reasons there are. What is not under his control, then, is that generosity be a virtue, and it is only because he realizes this that he remains a generous man. But one cannot say for *this* reason that his generosity is not praiseworthy. This is the best reason for being generous that a person could have.
>
> So it seems that an agent can be morally praiseworthy even though he is determined to perform the action he performs. . . . Determination, then, is compatible with an agent's responsibility for a good action. (1986, pp. 231–232)

But here the ambiguity of "praiseworthy" is the source of confusion. Wolf starts with the sense of "praiseworthy" as simply "morally good": the individual is generous, and is generous for all the right reasons—and certainly that is a good and virtuous thing to be. But in the final paragraph comes the erroneous slide into the quite different moral responsibility sense of "praiseworthy": the individual is "praiseworthy" in the sense of deserving praise for his acts, being morally responsible for his good character. And that does not follow. Even if it were true (which it is not), it could not be assumed without argument—unless one is running together the two senses of "praiseworthy." For there is a question of whether the splendidly good and generous individual deserves praise (deserves special treatment) for his good character and behavior, or is instead merely lucky enough to have been in an environment that shaped such virtuous character. Of course one may still claim that a lucky generous individual deserves praise (praise that the unlucky selfish individual does not deserve). However, noting the difference between being virtuous ("praiseworthy(1)") and being deserving of special credit/reward for one's virtue ("praiseworthy(2)") makes it obvious that the step from the former to the latter requires substantive argument: argument that those who fail to recognize the ambiguity of "praiseworthy" do not provide.

The same confusion can be observed in moves from "blameworthy" to "deserves blame." Dennett offers this case, and falls into the same ambiguous confusion:

> But suppose that what you see when you contemplate your own biography is that whatever else may be true, you have been, are, and no doubt will continue to be one of the villains. For the rest of your life you will be in trouble—vilified, condemned, punished, shunned. There are such people. They make the grade as responsible agents, but are so thoroughly mean-spirited, so untouched by human warmth that, in a word, we despise them. Isn't it unfair that we should treat them so? The retort suggests itself: who more deserves to be despised than someone utterly despicable. (1984, p. 167)

But this is just the flip side of the ambiguity that misled Wolf. It may seem obvious that one who is "despicable" therefore "deserves to be despised," just as it may seem obvious that the "praiseworthy" character therefore deserves praise. But it seems obvious only if one fails to recognize the difference between *being* bad-wicked-mean and *deserving blame* for being bad (the difference between "blameworthy(1)" and "blameworthy(2)"). Again, even if one supposes that anyone who is bad therefore deserves blame (a very doubtful supposition indeed) simply to recognize that distinction is to recognize that the move from the first claim to the latter requires justification—justification that will be difficult to provide. Only the fallacy of ambiguity makes the step seem simple and immediate.

This wide gap between being bad (acting badly, being of bad character) and *deserving* blame for being bad must be marked as a dangerous chasm: it is a much broader and more doubtful leap than is generally supposed. A famous example might serve as a warning sign. In Charles Dickens' "Christmas Carol" (1967) Ebeneezer Scrooge (pre-ghosts) is the paradigm for a "thoroughly mean-spirited" individual who is "untouched by human warmth" and is "utterly despicable." Furthermore, Scrooge is a man of sharp intelligence who can weigh alternatives and make his own choices; and he is a man of iron self-control, who resolutely follows his miserly pattern of life. So Scrooge is utterly despicable, and his miserly character is thoroughly his own. But it does not follow that he "deserves to be despised," for it is something quite different to say that Scrooge is morally responsible, that he deserves blame. Dickens shows us how Scrooge's early poverty marked him with a terrible fear of the cruel treatment the world metes out to the impoverished—"there is nothing on which it [the world] is so hard as poverty," he asserts— and his early love, Belle, describes his resulting character accurately: "You fear the world too much. . . . All your other hopes have merged into the hope of being beyond the chance of its sordid reproach. I have seen your nobler aspirations fall off one by one, until the master passion, Gain, engrosses you." But miserliness is a characteristic that Scrooge considers and approves: " 'What then?' he retorted. 'Even if I have grown so much wiser, what then?' " Scrooge is a thoroughly sordid and greedy character. But when Dickens lets us glimpse the grinding poverty that shaped him we feel less confident that he deserves blame: moral responsibility is made—at least—doubtful.[13] Certainly Scrooge has moral faults (such as miserliness) and they are his own moral flaws; but it does not follow that he is morally responsible for his moral faults.

The moral of this story is a simple one: it is one thing to consider a person bad, mean-spirited, greedy, wicked (or their opposites); it is quite another to suppose that the individual deserves blame (or praise) for that character.[14] Justifying moral judgments does not justify moral responsibility, and denying moral responsibility is not the denial of moral judgments.[15]

THE KEY POINT of this chapter is that when we acknowledge that praise, blame, punishment, reward are never deserved—when we eliminate moral responsibility—concern with moral principles remains. The no-fault naturalist does not reject moral principles and moral judgments, but instead champions the basic moral principle of fairness and rejects claims that anyone deserves reward, privilege, or punishment. In the interest of fairness, moral responsibility *ought* to be eliminated: morality without moral responsibility is a better *moral* system.

CHAPTER THIRTEEN

Rejecting Responsibility, Preserving Freedom

THE PREVIOUS CHAPTER claims that the no-fault naturalist denial of moral responsibility can be a central part of an attractive moral system—a freer, fairer, and more humane moral system than one that includes moral responsibility and just deserts. But in order to make room for a positive account of how no-fault naturalism promotes individual freedom, it is first necessary to clear away the mistakes underlying a common but erroneous belief—the belief that denial of moral responsibility destroys individual freedom. The first of those mistakes has already been critiqued (in Chapters Three and Four)—the assumption that, since individual freedom and moral responsibility are inseparable, denying the latter entails rejecting the former. But that mistake cuts both ways: compatibilists argue for the compatibility of individual freedom with moral responsibility and then assume that such arguments establish moral responsibility; and, from the opposite direction, hard determinists deny moral responsibility and conclude that they must also challenge individual freedom. (That error is especially vexing, since the hard determinist rejection of both moral responsibility and individual free will entrenches the assumption that the two are united.) An example of this sort of confusion—from rejecting moral responsibility to denying individual free will—can be seen in some of B. F. Skinner's work.

Skinner's occasional intemperate remarks against "freedom" (such as 1976a, pp. 241–242) are prompted by his strong aversion to moral responsibility and transcendent freedom, not by real opposition to naturalist-compatibilist freedom. His actual target can be seen clearly in the final chapter of *Beyond Freedom and Dignity*. There he asserts that the abolition of "autonomous man" (possessed of transcendent free will) is "long overdue":

> Autonomous man is a device used to explain what we cannot explain in any other way. He has been constructed from our ignorance and as our understanding increases, the very stuff of which he is composed vanishes. Science does not dehumanize man, it dehomunculizes him. . . . Only by dispossessing him [autonomous man] can we turn to the real causes of human behavior. Only then can we turn from the inferred to the observed, from the miraculous to the natural, from the inaccessible to the manipulable. (Skinner, 1971, pp. 200–201)

And part of what Skinner explicitly rejects—part of what "autonomous man" holds in place—is the notion that an individual "may be held responsible for his action and justly rewarded or punished for its consequences" (Skinner, 1971, p. 211). But that is not a rejection of naturalist individual freedom; instead, Skinner rejects transcendent freedom because belief in such miracle-working free will stifles efforts to study and enhance genuine naturalist freedom. As Skinner notes in a later essay:

> In spite of our lip service to freedom, we do very little to further the development of the individual. How many Americans can say that they are doing the kinds of things they are best qualified to do and most enjoy doing? What opportunities have they had to

choose fields related to their talents or to the interests and skills they acquired in early life? . . .

And once one is lucky enough to be doing what one likes, what are the chances of being successful? How easily can artists, composers, and writers bring their work to the attention of those who will enjoy it and whose reactions will shape behavior in creative ways? Those who know the importance of contingencies of reinforcement know how people can be led to discover the things they do best and the things from which they will get the greatest satisfaction. (Skinner, 1976b, pp. xii–xiii)

Thus what Skinner wants is not just lip service to individual freedom, but programs and policies that would actually nourish such (compatibilist-naturalist) freedom—programs to develop individual talents, to give people control over their work and their activities, to enhance the ability of individuals to make things happen, to shape energetic and effective efforts. That is the crux of real individual freedom (as philosophers like Dennett and psychologists like Seligman have helped to make clear). And those (like Skinner) who oppose moral responsibility and transcendent free will are particularly likely to seek and discover effective measures for enhancing naturalist individual freedom.

The naturalist opponent of moral responsibility is not a threat to individual freedom, but is likely instead to be vigilant against subtle threats to freedom. For example, Skinner is deeply troubled by the danger of "the happy slave"—the individual who is exploited in ways that are immediately pleasant (positive incentives are used to motivate the individual, rather than chains or whips, which might generate escape behavior) but that are deleterious in the long run:

In the incentive system known as piece-work pay, the worker is paid a given amount for each unit of work performed. The system seems to guarantee a balance between the goods produced and the money received. The schedule is attractive to management, which can calculate labor costs in advance, and also to the worker, who can control the amount he earns. This so-called "fixed-ratio" schedule of reinforcement can, however, be used to generate a great deal of behavior for very little return. It induces the worker to work fast, and the ratio can then be "stretched"—that is, more work can be demanded for each unit of pay without running the risk that the worker will stop working. His ultimate condition— hard work with very little pay—may be acutely aversive. (1971, pp. 34–35)

And Skinner makes clear the danger of being conditioned to ac- quiesce in exploitative circumstances that will ultimately undermine one's genuine freedom:

It is said that even though behavior is completely determined, it is better that a man "feel free" or "believe that he is free." If this means that it is better to be controlled in ways which have no aver- sive consequences, we may agree, but if it means that it is better to be controlled in ways against which no one revolts, it fails to take account of the possibility of deferred aversive consequences. A second comment seems more appropriate: "It is better to be a conscious slave than a happy one." The word "slave" clarifies the nature of the ultimate consequences being considered: they are exploitative and hence aversive. What the slave is to be conscious of is his misery; and a system of slavery so well designed that it does not breed revolt is the real threat. The literature of freedom has been designed to make men "conscious" of aversive control, but in its choice of methods it has failed to rescue the happy slave. (1971, pp. 39–40)

So there is nothing in the rejection of moral responsibility and tran- scendent free will that requires rejection of compatibilist individual

freedom; to the contrary, those who deny the transcendent freedom that moral responsibility requires are likely to be alert against
insidious dangers to real individual freedom.

So much for the first of the errors behind the belief that denial of
moral responsibility entails denial of individual freedom. Moral responsibility is not inseparably linked with individual freedom; thus
those who deny moral responsibility may (and do) promote and protect individual freedom. The second error is rooted in the assumption
(discussed in the previous chapter) that universal denial of moral
responsibility is based on claims of universal human infirmity. As a
result of that erroneous assumption, denial of moral responsibility
(and "just deserts" and retributive punishment) conjures up fears
of a dangerous and demeaning therapy system: if everyone is ex-
empted from moral responsibility, then everyone must be considered
defective; and if everyone is defective, then everyone is incompetent
to choose or refuse treatment; and it follows that everyone is subject to coercive therapeutic intervention, and individual freedom is
trampled. Indeed, for many retributivists the main value of retribution is as a bulwark against abusive imposition of "therapy." Herbert
Morris claims:

> The primary reason for preferring the system of punishment as
> against the system of therapy might have been expressed in terms
> of the one system treating one as a person and the other not . . . .
> When we talk of not treating a human being as a person or
> "showing no respect for one as a person" what we imply by our
> words is a contrast between the manner in which one acceptably
> responds to human beings and the manner in which one accept-
> ably responds to animals and inanimate objects. When we treat a
> human being merely as an animal or some inanimate object our
> responses to the human being are determined, not by his choices,
> but ours in disregard of or with indifference to his. And when we

"look upon" a person as less than a person or not a person, we consider the person as incapable of a rational choice. (1985, p. 34)

Morris' appeal for retributive punishment is based on a false dilemma—that the only alternative to retributive punishment is demeaning and dehumanizing "therapy."[1] And that false dilemma is generated by two closely connected, commonly made, and egregiously false assumptions. First is the assumption that ordinarily everyone is morally responsible, and denial of individual moral responsibility requires special circumstances (such as insanity). The second mistake follows naturally from the first: when it is mistakenly assumed that moral responsibility is normally operative and is denied only for incompetent individuals, then it seems obvious that the no-fault naturalist universal denial of moral responsibility is based on universal denial of human competence. On that misinterpretation of no-fault naturalism, offenders are excused from moral responsibility because they are sick and irrational (and obviously not acting freely); thus they should be treated (rather than punished). But the no-fault naturalist denial of moral responsibility is not based on defect. There is no invidious comparison between "normal, rational, responsible law-abiders" and "abnormal, irrational, nonresponsible scofflaws." Rather, no-fault naturalists reject the miraculous uncaused-cause metaphysics that moral responsibility requires. No one, whether a menace to society or a pillar of same, is ever morally responsible. There are no "persons" in Morris' sense of transcendently autonomous morally responsible beings; but that does not mean that everyone is irrational or otherwise defective and thus fit only for treatment, nor does it deny that individuals may act freely. So the no-fault naturalist denial that anyone deserves punishment does not establish a class of subjugated subhumans fit only for therapy, set in piteous contrast to morally responsible "persons."

Willard Gaylin raises the spectre of the behavioral no-fault naturalist's denying moral responsibility and individual competence, and thus planning the most brutal and degrading programs of "treatment" for prisoners:

> While conditioning is a less dramatic form of behavior modification than, for example, psychosurgery, it should concern us no less, especially when the federal government is preparing programs designed along Skinnerian lines. Inevitably these experiments are to be undertaken in the prisons, those unfailing institutions of failure, where each new indignity is traditionally presented as an act of grace. (1973, p. 48)

Abusive "therapy" (in the form of psychosurgery and drugs and extreme or coercive forms of "behavior modification") is now an ever-present danger (and it should be noted that Skinner has raised many of those concerns himself).[2] But belief in retribution and just deserts is certainly no safeguard against it. As Gaylin notes, such coercive "therapy" methods *are* usually proposed for prisons,[3] which are institutions of retribution and just deserts and moral responsibility. The question is: under what conditions are such methods likely to be employed, and under what conditions is such "therapy"[4] more likely to be held in check?

The no-fault naturalist denial of moral responsibility will not encourage brutally repressive "therapeutic" measures; it is more likely to undergird than undermine respect for individual freedom. Consider under what conditions demeaning and debilitating methods of shaping/coercing behavior are most likely to be adopted. Such brutal means seem justified when those on whom they are imposed are cast as inferior or flawed, or as so fundamentally different from us that extreme measures must be employed and "ordinary" restrictions are felt not to apply. But it is not those who deny moral responsibility who are most likely to regard miscreants in that manner. Contrary to popular retributivist opinion, it is more probable that those who believe in moral responsibility will consider violators "sick" or "different" or even "monstrous."

As discussed in Chapter Three, ascriptions of moral responsibility require restrictions on inquiries into the "responsible" individual's history (to prevent discovery of environmental influences that undercut claims of moral responsibility). Thus when the miscreant acts in a vicious manner, quite different from the way we act—*and* ascription of moral responsibility obscures the causal background—then the most likely conclusion is that the criminal just *is* is very different from us—so different that our human sympathies are suppressed. And the alienation produced by the sense of radical difference is exacerbated by increased fear. We are more likely to fear what we cannot understand, and when claims of moral responsibility make causal understanding of criminal behavior less likely they make fear of criminals more probable. Criminal behavior may be frightening in the best of circumstances; when insistence on criminal moral responsibility limits causal inquiries and makes the criminal seem strange and capricious and mysterious, then criminal behavior becomes terrifying. It is hard to imagine that we would tolerate the well-known horror of our prisons without the belief that the (morally responsible and deserving of punishment) prisoners are radically different from ourselves. Such fear of the alien criminal is fertile ground for "experiments" with coercive "therapy."

Contrast that with the perspective of the no-fault naturalist. The individual who violates laws and principles is not some monster devoid of our human capacities, nor someone who inexplicably and mysteriously chooses evil. Instead, the miscreant is simply one shaped by somewhat different social-environmental contingencies, most likely involving very small initial differences that were magnified through cumulative reinforcement processes (as discussed in Chapter Nine). Thus the no-fault naturalist is more likely to discover what sorts of influences shaped such behavior, and that increased knowledge reduces strangeness and relieves fear. Also, the no-fault naturalist will be drawn to the conclusion that fundamentally there is little difference between the vicious and the virtuous: "There but for a few differences in fortuitous environmental contingencies go I." It is not difficult to judge which perspective is more likely to enhance respect and concern for individuals.

THE CLAIM HERE is that the no-fault naturalist denial of all moral responsibility supports individual freedom and makes it more likely that malefactors (and everyone else) will be respected as human individuals and as full members of our society, and not ostracized and certainly not subjected to coercive and demeaning "therapy." In opposition to such claims, retributivists sometimes argue that moral responsibility and retributive punishment practices are essential for making individuals feel like full members of the moral community.[5] For example, Oldenquist argues:

> In general, membership in a moral community is revealed by who is affronted by insults to it, who enlists, or puts in time and contributes money, by who is blamed and criticized for not behaving in these ways, or feels shame and guilt. It follows that a powerful way to tell young delinquents they still belong and are members of a moral community is to hold them personally accountable and punish them, whereas not holding them accountable is to alienate them more than they already are, to cast them out emotionally. (1988, p. 467)

Thus those who would try to find means other than retributive punishment for dealing with delinquents in fact treat such persons with special cruelty.

The same false but common notion that "punishment preserves dignity" (because to be a full member of the human community implies being morally responsible, which in turn implies eligibility for retributive punishment) is probably the reason many condemned criminals make death-watch claims of complete moral responsibility. Dennett makes note of this phenomenon in his brief for moral responsibility: "Many a murderer has no doubt of his own culpability" (1984, p. 65). And certainly many murderers do insist on such moral responsibility. After describing the brutalizing childhood of executed murderer Robert Harris (he was hated by his mother, abused by his alcoholic father, teased at school for a speech defect, and at age fourteen was raped repeatedly in a federal detention center), Gary Watson then states that "it is noteworthy that Harris himself seems to accept responsibility for his life," quoting someone with whom Harris talked: "He told me he had his chance, he took the road to hell and there's nothing more to say" (Watson, 1987b, p. 281n.). John Spenkelink (the first person executed in Florida after the resumption of capital punishment in that state) at age eleven found the body of the father he idolized (a suicide victim), and began a series of petty crimes that finally led to the murder of a fellow drifter. Shortly before his execution Spenkelink asserted: "Man is what he chooses to be. He chooses that for himself." Thus those most brutally shaped for failure are often most insistent on their own moral responsibility. But that is hardly surprising. They have been taught that moral responsibility distinguishes humans from subhumans, that moral responsibility is the condition for membership in the human community. So miscreants most severely damaged by their conditioning histories (deprived of any freedom or human dignity, and brutally excluded from the social community) are pitifully eager to claim full moral responsibility (as symbolized by retributive punishment). After a life of abuse and indignity and exclusion, they clutch at a spurious straw of human dignity and human community before they drown in the dehumanizing processes of incarceration and methodical execution.

The condemned prisoners' claims of moral responsibility and Oldenquist's claims—that only through liability for retributive punishment can an individual be a full member of the moral community—are both based on the assumption that retributive punishment is and must be the standard social practice. *If* retributive punishment (moral responsibility) is the norm of a society, and people are excused from retributive punishment only when they are considered insane or otherwise defective, then denying eligibility for retributive punishment denies full membership in the moral community. But the real question is whether individuals could be—and could be made to feel—full members of the moral community if *all* moral responsibility and retributive punishment were denied. Since in that case no member of the moral community would deserve punishment, denying an individual's desert of retributive punishment would not mark that individual as an inadequate or substandard outsider.[6] When we put aside the question-begging assumption that moral responsibility and retributive punishment *must* be generally present, then the focus can turn to a real and interesting issue: how can individuals (including criminals) *best* be included in the moral community? It is no challenge to find better means than retributive punishment.

The best way of demonstrating that an individual is a valued member of the moral community is through vigorous efforts to ensure that the individual has the opportunity and means and incentives for living a rich human moral life within that community. That requires access to a good education (which includes motivating the student to learn), opportunities to perform important and challenging and satisfying work in the society, a full and equal voice in the community's political and governmental decisions, and significant control over her vocational and social and governmental environment. An individual who suffers inferior health care, terrible early education, no worthwhile employment opportunities, and political disenfranchisement can not be welcomed into the moral community through attribution of responsibility and application of retributive punishment.

In the comparatively rare cases in which the delinquent has already enjoyed such benefits, then concern can be manifested through diligent efforts to understand why the individual is violating the community's principles. Such efforts can demonstrate a genuine concern for saving that individual for the moral community—and it is necessarily an individualized concern, which scrutinizes the individual's history and development and present environment. That seems a likely way to demonstrate the moral community's desire to have that particular individual as a member; certainly it is preferable to treating the delinquent as a nondescript pawn in retribution rituals.

Moral responsibility, "just deserts," and retributive punishment are not the best means of preserving individual freedom and dignity; instead, the no-fault naturalist denial of moral responsibility is more likely to promote and protect genuine individual freedom. In particular, the notion of no-fault naturalist's opposing freedom and imposing narrow "mind control" on anyone who deviates is a grossly mistaken one. Nothing in determinism-naturalism or in the no-fault naturalist denial of moral responsibility implies such repressiveness, and in fact (as will be argued in the final chapter) no-fault naturalism is more naturally supportive of the broadest and deepest individual freedom. (Some theological opponents of moral responsibility have indeed championed authoritarian intolerance; however, those authoritarian and absolutist views stem from the religion—as in "one true" religion—and not from the denial of moral responsibility. That type of Absolutism is indeed a threat to tolerance and openness and individuality. But such absolutist intolerance is more likely to be found in a system of moral responsibility and just deserts and retribution; it is not likely to flourish in an environment of no-fault *naturalism*.)

IT WAS ARGUED ABOVE that the no-fault naturalist rejection of moral responsibility does not lead to wholesale "therapy", but of course it does undercut any claims of just deserts and retribution. So another question now arises: if not retribution, then what? How would a no-fault naturalist society deal with transgressors? And a closely related question also must be considered: how would a no-fault naturalist society express its value principles without "just deserts" and retributive punishment? Those challenging issues are posed by Oldenquist (a retributivist advocate of moral responsibility) in the following passage:

> A society that never held its members personally accountable for good or evil, never expressed its collective will through praise and censure, would have a weak conception of the difference between members and nonmembers; and, what may amount to the same thing, it would have a weak or diffuse conception of a common good worth defending. It is doubtful we could possess common values and a common way of life if we were totally lacking in indignation at affronts to them. Serious crimes, when they go unpunished, diminish the value we place on our social identities, and hence our valuation of ourselves. (1988, p. 467)

There are two basic errors: one, that a society that denies moral responsibility will lack a strong sense of moral values; second, that punitive measures are the only adequate response to serious violations of community values. The errors are not unrelated.

As discussed in the previous chapter, an individual can certainly hold strong value beliefs without believing in moral responsibility; and that holds true for communities as well. The question of whether an act is dreadfully wrong is different from the question of whether the actor deserves to be punished. But Oldenquist raises the issue from another angle: how can the community (or the individual) properly *express* abhorrence of wrong acts if no one deserves punishment?[7]

Oldenquist obscures the question with the penultimate sentence of the paragraph quoted above: "It is doubtful we could possess

187

common values and a common way of life if we were totally lacking in indignation at affronts to them." But that is not the issue.
It is one thing to feel indignation at affronts to our values, quite
another to decide how we should act and what sort of response
such indignation calls for. One can feel indignation while denying
that the transgressor deserves blame or retributive punishment.[8] The
real question posed by Oldenquist is: how can the seriousness of
and respect for the moral community's values be properly asserted
and acclaimed and acculturated without punishing those who violate
those values?[9]

David A. Hoekema—a proponent of legal punishment—suggests
some possibilities:

> A society which does not employ legal punishment might employ
> any of a number of other means of influencing individuals to com-
> ply with the law. Perhaps wide-ranging and pervasive means of
> persuasion and suggestion might be employed—posters on every
> street corner and broadcast messages over every radio station.
> (Hoekema, 1986, p. 134)

What Hoekema's suggestion best indicates is the degree to which
belief in moral responsibility and retributive punishment stifles the
capacity to consider alternatives. Papering over social problems with
banners and bumper stickers is not the best the no-fault naturalist
can offer. The choice is not between legal punishment and slogan-
izing. Perhaps it is not so surprising that Hoekema would suggest
posters and slogans. Such ineffectual measures seem a natural accompaniment to belief in moral responsibility and retributive punishment. Slogans may seem sufficient when directed at possessors
of transcendent free will: if they are merely reminded of what to
do, then by transcendent contracausal willing they can overcome
all detrimental social-environmental influences and seek the good
and obey the law and follow the slogan. (And if they do not, they

deserve punishment.) It is no coincidence that the inane "just say no" anti-drug campaign (complete with posters and jingles) was accompanied by harsh retributive punishment for offenders and severe cuts in funding for the drug treatment facilities, early education, housing, job training, and college loan programs that might have effectively changed the environmental factors encouraging drug abuse. (I am not suggesting that all believers in moral responsibility—compatibilists or libertarians—favor such insipid programs as "just say no"; nor is it suggested that they lack concern for the real social-environmental factors that can enrich or destroy individual freedom and opportunity. However, I do suggest that belief in moral responsibility is likely to weaken or limit such concern.)

How a society that rejects retributive punishment could express its values is an important question; only a long history of narrow focus on punishment and blame and just deserts makes it seem difficult. When we slip the blinkers of retributive punishment it is obvious how a moral community might strictly deny punitive measures (because of a denial of moral responsibility) and still strongly affirm and celebrate and teach its values. The most important method is by serious efforts to find the *causes* of violations and diligent work at correcting those causes. Obviously we must deal with vicious individuals: stop their vicious acts, protect society from their behavior, reform them if we can. But a key problem with focusing retributive punishment on a vicious individual is that it encourages us to regard the individual (or the individual's will) as an independent iniquitous source, and thus to neglect the continuing environment that shaped that individual. (As noted in Chapter Three, even compatibilist claims of retributivist moral responsibility require that inquiries into the individual's causal/environmental history be blocked or ignored.) We execute Eichmann, and are appalled to find neo-Nazism and anti-Semitism growing from the same neglected roots. Eichmann was profoundly evil; but that is all the more reason to study the environment that shaped him and may remain to shape others.

If an egregious violation of our moral principles occurs—a brutal rape, a callous murder—then the best way of showing that the moral community takes such violations seriously is strenuous and immediate and committed effort to find the causes of that crime, genuinely reform the perpetrator, and change the conditions that caused such behavior. That will show a deeper commitment to the violated principles than does a policy that perpetuates the known causes of violations and employs obviously failed measures to reform those who commit violations. When the only means of preventing serious violations of our basic values was the use of punishment (inadequate though it obviously was) then such punishment might indeed have been the best means of demonstrating commitment to violated values; but when the community continues such practices despite their known inadequacy, and does not make the effort to find the best possible means of preventing violation of values, then the punitive practices show commitment to the moral community's professed values to the same degree that the modern physician would manifest commitment to good health by treating tuberculosis with leeches.

When we affirm that even the most heinous, deliberate, intentional criminal is *not* morally responsible (does not deserve punishment) that does not suggest a meek acceptance of that individual's harmful behavior. And certainly it does not imply that we can make no moral judgments, and that we can have no strong feelings that the individual and the individual's behavior are egregiously bad. The choice between enervated acquiescence and hitback retribution is a false dilemma. There are many things we can do to stop wrongs, prevent their recurrence, seek out and destroy their causal roots. And the responses supported by rejection of moral responsibility and retribution are more effective, and ultimately more satisfactory.

There remain some genuine quandaries for a no-fault naturalist society that must deal with dangerous and destructive criminal behavior. I have argued that rejection of moral responsibility focuses attention on the vital causal factors that shape vicious (and virtuous) behavior, and so encourages more effective long-term means of promoting good citizenship and preventing crime. (At the most obvious level, a program to improve housing and education and job opportunities will do more to prevent crime than the currently popular retributive "solution" of building more prisons.) But what do we do *today* with the dangerous criminal who threatens the safety of all around her? Planning a better early environment for those like her is the best long-term policy; but what do we do with her, here and now? She does not deserve punishment, and coercive "therapy" has been rejected. The no-fault naturalist who values individual freedom must also value her freedom; and (by no-fault naturalist lights) she no more justly deserves to have her freedom curtailed than does the most upstanding citizen. So what do we do with her?

That is a troublesome question—perhaps the most troublesome that a no-fault naturalist must face. It is little comfort to note that ascribing moral responsibility only exacerbates the problem. After all, under retributivist policies she is likely to do "life on the installment plan," harming many members of society in the process—while others are growing up in the same environment that shaped her. And while the short-term, short-sighted policy of "locking her up" to protect society may provide temporary relief, it should be remembered that *saying* she is morally responsible (and justly deserves punitive incarceration) does not *make* her so. She is not morally responsible (as has already been argued as best I can argue it), and so a society that locks her up on the basis of her "just deserts" does not solve this problem: it merely adds error to injustice. Still, what shall we do with her?

No-fault naturalists will not give up on her. She did not inexplicably "choose" crime; rather, she is the product of an environment that shaped her into criminal patterns of behavior, and, difficult as it may be, new and different and socially productive behavioral patterns can be shaped. Not, of course, by coercive drug treatments

or brainwashing: good and sufficient reasons for avoiding such programs have already been noted. But that does not mean there is nothing we can do. Offering genuine educational opportunities, vocational programs that are patterned to promote success rather than
failure, group support, professional counseling: such things can be
done without coercion and without violating individual freedom (indeed they would enhance the individual's freedom and autonomy).
It would not be difficult for a society that focused on reform rather
than retribution to devise effective programs to help her and most
of those like her.

But that still does not completely solve the problem. There are,
after all, some criminals who have been profoundly shaped for criminal behavior, and who cannot be persuaded to participate voluntarily
in any of the programs described above. Even the most "hardened"
criminal is not incorrigible: since there are no limits on improving our scientific understanding of how criminal behavior is shaped,
there are also no limits on improving our methods of reforming
criminal behavior; and with continued research, we may find effective noncoercive measures for reforming those who are now the
most intractably vicious. The no-fault naturalist rejection of moral
responsibility would expedite such research. But that is a confident
hope for the no-fault naturalist future, and the problem posed is immediate: what do we do, now, to protect society from the (currently
incorrigible) criminal?

When that question is pressed, it forces the no-fault naturalist to
bite an unpalatable bullet. If an individual engages in criminal behavior, then energy and ingenuity should be exerted to reform her
behavior; but there may be occasions when the protection of society
requires that the criminal be isolated—to put it bluntly, locked up—
not because she deserves it (she does not, no matter how vile her
behavior) but because the protection of society requires it. That is
a conclusion with which I am hardly comfortable. However, I think
the position is defensible—and it is still significantly different, and

significantly better, than the policies propped up by mistaken belief in moral responsibility.

It is important that such "isolation" (imprisonment, if one insists) of criminals is *not* being proposed as a socially desirable policy: it is instead a desperate measure for desperate circumstances. When all else fails, and a convicted criminal poses a clear and present danger of continuing to commit vicious acts against members of society, then the criminal must—undeservedly—be isolated for the protection of society. But that is obviously not an endorsement of punishment. There is no claim that the criminal *deserves* such treatment, and that has two important advantages.

First, it will mean that society places such individuals under coercive isolation only with the greatest regret and reluctance, and thus only with elaborate safeguards and in the worst cases. Rather than feeling satisfied that the criminal has "received her just deserts," we shall feel disappointment at the failure of our society and the inadequacy of our reform processes. The isolation of the individual will not be considered a finished accomplishment, but a constant and disturbing reminder of failure (and efforts will continue to correct that failure by reforming and releasing the criminal). Instead of the criminal's being imprisoned and otherwise ignored, the involuntarily isolated criminal in a no-fault naturalist society will be a constant spur to developing better ways of reforming criminals and improving the social environment to prevent others from winding up in this situation.

There is a second advantage to the no-fault naturalist recognition that the involuntarily isolated criminal does not deserve such isolation. In such circumstances, the conditions of isolation are likely to be very different from those that prevail in societies that believe in moral responsibility and just deserts. The appalling conditions in almost all our prisons are the natural result of their punitive role in our society. But if instead the criminal is isolated not because she deserves it, but strictly as a sacrifice required of her for the protection of society, then the situation is vastly different. Instead of the smirking attitude that "prison is not supposed to be fun," there will be the sense that the isolation from society that is being imposed on the criminal should be as free of discomfort as circumstances permit. (Thus to speak of "isolating" the individual rather than "imprisoning" her is not an exercise in euphemistic double-speak. The isolation imposed—while it would involve deprivation of some important freedoms, and would be a very serious and disturbing matter—would be quite different in setting and circumstances from punitive imprisonment.) [10]

The problems precipitated by criminal behavior (joined with the legitimate desire to protect the freedom and welfare of all citizens) pose a constant threat to the freedom of any society, including the no-fault naturalist. But that threat is not exacerbated by the denial of moral responsibility. Instead, no-fault naturalists are more likely to protect the individual freedom of both criminals and their potential victims, by focusing attention on the sources of criminal (as well as productive) behavior and combining that with effective concern for individual freedom. Individual freedom—and how it is enhanced by the no-fault naturalist denial of moral responsibility—is the topic of the final chapter.

CHAPTER FOURTEEN

No-Fault Naturalist Freedom

THE NO-FAULT NATURALIST DENIAL of moral responsibility is consistent with valuing and preserving individual freedom. In particular, denying moral responsibility does not license assaults on individual freedom under the guise of "therapy." But the claim to be argued in this chapter is stronger: individual freedom is not threatened by no-fault naturalism; to the contrary, the no-fault naturalist denial of moral responsibility establishes optimum conditions for preserving, broadening, and strengthening individual freedom.

As already noted, no-fault naturalism is not fatalism. On the naturalist-determinist-mechanist view, there is no deity guiding events to a pre-planned tragic or beatific end. If we are to increase knowledge, improve social conditions, expand freedom, extend life —all such accomplishments will require the diligent and intelligent efforts of human beings. (Whether any particular human being has been shaped to advance such enterprises is not something for which the individual is morally responsible; that does not change the fact that intelligent efforts can and do have significant effects.) Thus the acknowledgment of no-fault naturalism is perfectly compatible with striving to achieve greater knowledge and better social conditions. Indeed, the no-fault naturalist has better reason to be concerned with preserving freedom and diversity of ideas than does the libertarian:

the libertarian can hope for sparks of creative inspiration from transcendent free will, no matter how narrow and stultifying the social environment; but the determinist-naturalist must depend entirely on a fruitful environment for original ideas and discoveries and artistry. And a fruitful environment is one in which new ideas are welcomed, challenges to the status quo are tolerated, variety and experiment are encouraged, and widely varying environmental stimuli (including competing views) abound. (Thus—to reinforce the arguments of the previous chapter—the no-fault naturalist who values individual freedom and autonomy will promote conditions favoring careful and informed and effective individual deliberation, and will vigorously oppose any "therapy" process that subverts deliberative capacities.)

The no-fault *naturalist* is likely to be more concerned with promoting individual freedom than is the libertarian champion of transcendent free will. But the main contention of this chapter is that the *no-fault* naturalist's denial of moral responsibility also nurtures individual freedom. Focusing strictly on the denial of moral responsibility reveals several important reasons for thinking that no-fault naturalism will strengthen—rather than stunt—individual freedom.

The first advantage to individual freedom (from the denial of moral responsibility) stems from increased knowledge of the causal conditions that enhance (or inhibit) free individual behavior. It was argued in Chapter Three that claims and ascriptions of moral responsibility choke causal inquiry. That is most obvious in the libertarian case, in which causal inquiry into empirical conditions reaches an abrupt halt at the point of transcendent free willing; but even for the compatibilist (soft determinist), causal inquiries are subtly discouraged. The compatibilist who is intent on preserving moral responsibility cannot look too hard or deeply into an individual's environmental-conditioning history, since tenacious pursuit of such causal inquiries reveals factors that undercut moral responsibility. Thus, when the compatibilist discovers the "free choices" that supposedly justify claims or ascriptions of moral responsibility, the prudent course for preserving moral responsibility is to inquire no further. But in contrast the no-fault naturalist insists on probing deeper, without limit, in the belief that differences in behavior must be due to differences in environmental contingencies that shaped the individuals (and for which the individuals are not morally responsible). Such unrestricted research will best promote discovery of and concern for social-environmental factors—those environmental influences that insidiously undermine the exercise of individual freedom, as well as those that enhance individual autonomy.

The problems posed for moral responsibility by unlimited causal inquiries can be seen in Dennett's attempt to justify responsibility:

> Instead of investigating, endlessly, in an effort to *discover* whether or not a particular trait is of someone's making—instead of trying to assay exactly to what degree a particular self is self-made—we simply *hold* people responsible for their conduct (within limits we take care not to examine too closely). And we are rewarded for adopting this strategy by the higher proportion of "responsible" behavior we thereby inculcate. (1984, p. 164)

It has already been argued that "holding responsible" is not the best strategy for shaping "responsible" behavior (Chapter Ten). The point here is Dennett's wonderfully honest account of what is involved in holding people morally responsible: it requires that we place a limit on the investigation of how individual characters and traits were formed. And such limits are placed at precisely the points we must thoroughly scrutinize in order to understand the causes of individual behavior and discover the best means of shaping self-reliant, independent, autonomous character.

Why does the bright young woman lethargically settle for a stultifying dead-end job? The compatibilist believer in moral responsibility finds that she really does favor such a job: she prefers not to have the added responsibility and challenge of more stimulating work. She could have set higher goals and sought another job had she wished; she was not coerced; it was her own deliberate choice. "She chose to take that job (or stay in that marriage, or join that religion); it's her own fault; she has no one to blame but herself." Such assertions discourage—or disallow—inquiries into the environment that shaped her character and her choices.[1] Thus she has moral responsibility, and deserves full credit or blame, and no further questions are asked (further questioning of her environmental history would raise disturbing doubts about her moral responsibility for her choices).

Indeed, much of her character certainly is of "her own making," in the sense that she chose many of the tasks and commitments and environments (a dead-end job, a stultifying marriage, a narrow, small-town social environment) that subsequently shaped her. But the no-fault naturalist will find such causal explanations—true as they may be, so far as they go—intolerably shallow. *Why* did she choose such deadening and unchallenging work? Why did she not wish to exercise and stretch her talents? Why did she marry a dolt, and remain in her insular home town environment? Further causal inquiry soon reveals sexist conditioning—it is unfeminine to think too hard, women are not suited for positions of responsibility, it is selfish for a woman to strive for her own development, a woman should not be out on her own—that stifled the woman's ambitions and interests. The no-fault naturalist's deeper probes discover social factors that undermine the full exercise of talents and abilities and choices and opportunities. In short, the no-fault naturalist insistence on deeper causal inquiry uncovers obstacles to exercise of full freedom and promotes social reforms that will broaden freedom.

When empirical investigations of the conditions that shape behavior are pursued relentlessly, then moral responsibility withers away as environmental factors are discovered that account for the various behavioral patterns—virtuous and vicious, resolute and indecisive, independent and conventional. Thus is undermined any claim that the vicious product of her environment is deserving of punishment while the virtuous product of a different environment deserves reward. And it is those unrestricted inquiries—which undermine moral responsibility—that are essential for discovering the subtle but crucial environmental factors that shape individuals into effective, deliberative, independent, perspicacious, autonomous adults (or the opposite).

Not only does eliminating moral responsibility open the way to more effective inquiries into the causal factors that strengthen (or stifle) free, informed, self-controlled, individual behavior; furthermore, by eliminating moral responsibility more effective—as well as more freedom-preserving and freedom-enhancing—means of shaping effective self-reliant individual behavior can be developed. When we think of the "morally responsible" person receiving his "just deserts," that typically conjures up pictures of punitive measures. Certainly questions of "who is responsible for this?" sound more like threats than promises of reward. Punitive policies are prominent features of social policies founded on moral responsibility. And, indeed, a policy founded on belief that transgressions justly deserve punishment—to at least the same extent as good acts justly deserve reward—can hardly dispense with punitive measures.

But punishment has two disadvantages: first, it is not very effective; second, it typically involves some limitation or deprivation of freedom. (Contemporary retributivists insist on both points: that retributive punishment is right even though it probably does little to reform the punished, and that the punitive deprivation of liberties is justified by the acts of the individual punished.) Punishment may temporarily stop the punished behavior, but often the same behavior—or an undesirable substitute—reappears. And punishment is especially unhelpful when it tempts us to suppose that the punitive process has "solved the problem" or "settled the score," and nothing else need be done. In such cases the environmental influences that shaped the original criminal behavior continue in force, to shape successive behavior of the criminal who returns to that environment (and the behavior of others in the same environment). And even if the threat of punishment is sometimes temporarily effective in preventing undesirable behavior, it is hardly the optimum solution for those who value freedom: living and acting under the constant threat of punishment, and refraining from desired behavior only because one fears the punishment that might result from it, is not living freely.

When moral responsibility is denied, the fundamental justification for punishment is undermined: no one will ever deserve it. And from the other direction, effective alternatives to punishment are opened up. Rather than relying heavily on punishment (because it is "justly deserved"), a more effective alternative is to encourage behavioral patterns that are incompatible with the undesirable behavior. The student who refrains from plagiarism from fear of punishment is not acting freely; the student who is not tempted to plagiarism because she has learned to enjoy the intellectual stimulation of researching and writing and thinking for herself—and because she values the spirit of intellectual community that plagiarism betrays—not only acts freely, but is also less likely to engage in plagiarism than is the student who refrains from fear of punishment. But (as noted in Chapter Ten) optimal use of nonpunitive measures requires abandoning the traditional conception of just deserts. If we are trying to shape good behavior (behavior incompatible with the behavior to be discouraged), then the individual who behaves detrimentally or lethargically may receive special treatment—more benefits (through a pattern of stretched interval reinforcement, for example) than are accorded the individual who behaves well. Such a "violation" of "just deserts" cannot be used effectively so long as the myth of moral responsibility remains. Without moral responsibility, there is greater scope for more positive and freer (noncoercive and nonpunitive) methods to shape free and "responsible" behavior—behavior performed because the person wants to do it, behavior that ultimately is sustained and strengthened by natural sources of positive reinforcement.

The freedom-enhancing advantages of positive over punitive practices are substantial. The uninspired student may be coerced into studying her chemistry book by threats of poor grades, suspension of privileges, and cuts in allowance; but she will certainly—and quite rightly—feel that she is acting under duress, that she is not freely pursuing her science education. If instead the student is offered participation in a science fair, and (at appropriate intervals) is positively reinforced for successful progress on her project, and perhaps is awarded a small scholarship[2] for her work, then that student feels that she is working freely, as indeed she is. And in the latter case, it is quite likely that the student will reach the point at which natural (rather than socially contrived) contingencies of reinforcement sustain her interest in science. She will continue to pursue her own interests in science, because such work results in naturally reinforcing gains in knowledge and ability: a successful experiment, a hard-won insight, a new connection, a better way of making things happen, greater control over her environment. That is the best—and freest— of all possible worlds: a program of freedom-enhancing positive reinforcement with ultimate results that increase individual freedom and self-control. Unfortunately, positive reinforcement can be turned to iniquitous ends, as shown by Skinner's example of the "happy slave" (Chapter Thirteen), who is positively shaped to willingly work in ways that are ultimately disadvantageous. But of course punishment can also be used for such ends: one need look no further than the *un*happy slave for an example.

Positive reinforcement programs are not a guarantee of individual freedom. There are no such guarantees. Protecting individual freedom requires constant vigilance, and use of positive reinforcement rather than punitive methods does not change that. Nonetheless, positive programs of reinforcement—encouraged by the absence of moral responsibility—still offer substantial advantages: they are effective, they are noncoercive and nonaversive and they leave individuals free to operate from their own (learned) desires, and, ideally, they may shape free, effective, genuinely advantageous behavior that is sustained by its own natural success.

FINALLY, THE NO-FAULT NATURALIST DENIAL of moral responsibility is likely to enhance individual freedom by encouraging a more egalitarian society. Careful focus on the full details of our environmental histories eliminates moral responsibility and thus offers solid, worldly grounds for equality: exact equality of just deserts. That brings the principle of equality down from the transcendent realms of "all created equal" or a Kantian "kingdom of ends" and anchors it in the gritty environments that shaped us and were—at critical points—not of our own choosing or making.[3] And, if everyone is precisely equal in just deserts, then the vast differences in wealth and power among individuals in our society are unjust. Recognizing the injustice of that distribution is the first step toward righting that distributive balance and lifting the severe practical restraints on individual freedom imposed by such inequities.[4]

Ways in which an inegalitarian society stifles freedom are easily observed. In such a society some members have inadequate access to the goods that are fundamental for living freely. Freedom involves more than absence of prison walls; it requires the opportunity to exercise one's abilities, to develop one's skills, to learn to think carefully and critically, to have an influence on events and society. For those who suffer from inadequate housing, poor education, inferior health care, and the other debilitating factors that are associated with poverty, living in "freedom" is a cruel reminder of opportunities open only to others.

Even if one escapes the freedom-stifling effects of poverty to live in solid middle-class comfort in a "free" (but inegalitarian) society, there remain severe practical limitations on one's actual freedom. Part of our cultural democratic myth is that anyone—black or white, male or female, rich or poor—can hold elective office. And certainly a genuinely free democratic society cannot make access to great wealth a precondition of holding national elective office. But that is so far from being the fact that it is embarrassingly inane to state it. It is all but impossible to mount an effective campaign (at even the level of U.S. Congress) without access to the vast financial resources controlled by the very wealthy. So such inegalitarian distribution of wealth places real restraints on individual freedom: not only does it restrict who can run for office, but also it limits voters' choices to candidates "approved" by a substantial segment of the monied elite. (The effects of this process on "equality of access" to "our elected representatives" are obvious.) Claims of just deserts and moral responsibility help prop up this inegalitarian and freedom-restricting distribution of wealth; denial of moral responsibility—and recognition of equality of just deserts—is an important step toward real democratic equality and the freedom it fosters.

THE ORIGINAL CLAIM was that moral responsibility must be distinguished from individual freedom: the no-fault naturalist denial of moral responsibility does not entail denial of individual freedom, and evidence of (naturalist-compatibilist) individual freedom does not count in favor of moral responsibility. This chapter has brought the argument full circle: instead of mutual support between moral responsibility and individual freedom, there is conflict. Moral responsibility wanes as effective freedom-enhancing inquiry into causes of behavior waxes. And from the other direction, claims of moral responsibility impede the most effective steps for enhancing individual freedom: belief in moral responsibility blocks deeper inquiries into the conditions that shape (both autonomous and heteronomous) behavior, promotes punitive rather than positive social programs, and encourages inegalitarian social policies. Without the hobbles of spurious moral responsibility, individual freedom is more likely to flourish. A culture in which moral responsibility is denied is the optimum environment for individual freedom.

NOTES

CHAPTER TWO

1. Kavanau (1967) offers an intriguing account of how captive white mice strive to shape/control/modify their environments.

2. See J. S. Watson, 1967; J. S. Watson, 1971; and Watson and Ramey, 1972.

3. For more on the problems of rewards received without effort, see Seligman, 1975, pp. 34–36, 96–99.

4. From the play *Sheppey*, by W. Somerset Maugham. I discovered this story in Salmon, 1970.

5. For an enlightening discussion of the psychological importance of doing things that have effects in the natural world, see Seligman, 1975.

CHAPTER THREE

1. That is what Thomas Nagel (1986, p. 110) suggests should happen if we take seriously the naturalist-determinist view.

2. Thomas Nagel (1979) suggests that recent research on the "divided brain" offers the possibility that each of those we currently regard as a distinct individual might also be regarded as multiple distinct individuals—a move in the opposite direction from the one suggested by Spinoza.

3. Others have suggested the separation of free will from moral responsibility. For example, Raymond Smullyan (1977) offers a Taoist perspective that supports free will while opposing moral responsibility. And it seems to me that a similar position—in favor of free will but opposed to moral responsibility—can be found in Samuel Butler's *Erewhon* (1872), especially chap. 19. Bernard Berofsky (1983, 1987) also notes the importance of distinguishing autonomy from moral responsibility. However, his view of moral

responsibility is quite different from the one presented here; Berofsky states: "To judge a person morally responsible for an action A is, I believe, to regard it as proper to include certain of A's features as relevant in drawing up a moral estimation of the agent" (1983, p. 307). But as noted in this chapter—and as will be discussed at length in Chapter Twelve—that is not the view of moral responsibility taken in this book. (I believe an action may be relevant to the moral estimation of the agent without the agent's being morally responsible for that action.) Furthermore, Berofsky wishes to preserve both freedom and moral responsibility, and the main reason I distinguish between them is in order to save the former while eliminating the latter.

Susan Wolf (1981, p. 386) notes the possibility of separating the issues when she suggests that it would be possible to deny free will while still justifying the practices of blame and punishment and praise. However, she subsequently treats freedom and responsibility as a unit (pp. 392, 397). Also, her account of moral responsibility is similar to Befofsky's: according to Wolf (p. 394) if an individual's act "may fairly enter into an assessment of what kind of person he is" then the individual is responsible for that act.

Also, Kai Nielsen (1985) notes that "an acknowledgment of autonomy, a prizing of it, and an ability to achieve it, might be quite in place even for someone who had jettisoned the concept of desert or for whom it played no part in his moral universe" (p. 124). Nielsen's work on this issue is particularly insightful; however, while he recognizes that autonomy can be distinguished from moral responsibility and desert, he still—due I think to confusion of moral responsibility with role-responsibility (discussed in Chapter Three)—regards situations of enhanced autonomy as conducive to establishment of just deserts. (Also, Nielsen regards the notion of just deserts as much more useful to society than I believe it to be.)

Finally, Galen Strawson (1986) notes quite perspicuously that the compatibilist account of freedom "does nothing to establish that we are truly responsible for our actions, nor, in particular, to establish that we are *morally* responsible for our actions, in the ordinary, strong, desert-entailing sense" (p. 109). However, he also believes (as I do not) that the stronger self-originating sense of freedom is essential to us, and that such freedom (as well as belief in moral responsibility) is essential for regarding ourselves as fully human beings toward whom (and in whom) the reactive attitudes are appropriate.

4. No doubt there are exceptions. But that is not a problem: all that is required for the notion to be convenient is that there generally be a match, in ordinary circumstances, between individual freedom and the degree to which the behavior is a product of long-term learning-conditioning.

5. Harry Frankfurt's appeal to decisive identifications—which establish a commitment that " 'resounds' throughout the potentially endless array of higher orders" (1971, p. 16)—is obviously an effort to block regress criticisms. That is, decisive identifications are supposed to preclude questions about whether one must identify with a third-order volition that approves one's second-order volition, and then must identify with a fourth-order volition to legitimize the third-order, and so on. In commenting specifically on Frankfurt's "decisive identifications," Gary Watson (1975, pp. 217–219) cogently argues that Frankfurt's hierarchical position "does not do the work that Frankfurt wants it to do. It does not tell us why or how a particular want can have, among all of a person's 'desires,' the special property of being peculiarly his 'own.' " But if the burden on Frankfurt's decisive identification is eased—so that it need not support moral responsibility, but only clarify one's sense that a particular desire is deeply and without reservation one's own—then it seems more likely that decisive identification can carry that weight.

6. Some may suppose that the denial of moral responsibility precludes all judgments of moral disapproval; that claim will be considered—and rejected—in Chapter Twelve.

7. Honderich (1988) maintains that it is "an extraordinary claim" to suggest that some sort of error or confusion could explain the long persistence of the compatibilist belief that voluntariness (rather than self-origination) is all that is required for moral responsibility (p. 485). Honderich believes that any attempt to "explain away" compatibilism as based on error is implausible, since surely no error would have escaped the attention of so many astute compatibilists for such a long time. But there are some strong reasons why such an error has been difficult to detect. First, the compatibilists have been quite successful in showing the compatibility of individual freedom with naturalism-determinism, and since the focus has usually been on issues

of freedom (with moral responsibility traditionally assumed to be so closely linked with freedom that a sighting of the latter is regarded as sufficient evidence of the former), it has been easy to ignore the loss of an adequate foundation for moral responsibility. Furthermore, so long as the best available practices for shaping behavior and sustaining social order consisted in rewarding and punishing and praising and blaming in accordance with the demands of moral responsibility, the assumption of moral responsibility was held in place by strong social practices; and in that situation, there seemed little reason to challenge the underlying assumption of moral responsibility. That situation has now changed (as is discussed in Chapter Ten), and now closer scrutiny of compatibilist moral responsibility is demanded by the possibility of new and different social conditioning practices that are in conflict with the principles of moral responsibility. Thus it is not so surprising that a compatibilist error might persist, nor is it surprising that it should be detected now.

CHAPTER FOUR

1. That is, such rationality-based freedom will not support moral responsibility under a naturalist-determinist-mechanist interpretation of rationality, of the sort both hard and soft determinists—for example, Dennett (1984, p. 49)—favor; whether the more exalted Kantian rationality will support moral responsibility is another question.

2. See Seligman, 1975, pp. 23–44; and Hirototo, 1974.

3. Frankfurt's hierarchical account does clarify the notion of free individual behavior, and it is doubtful that the hierarchical features of his account can be easily eliminated. Irving Thalberg (1978) argues that hierarchical analyses of *un*willing addicts are not necessary, because "an 'unwilling' addict does not merely elect to be rid of his desire for narcotics. What does he care about the craving *per se*? . . . He is mainly opposed to the actions he performs, and their long-term effects, when he succumbs to his craving" (p. 221). But not all who struggle with unwanted desires (obsessions, cravings) object exclusively to the actions performed as a result of the desire; one may genuinely abhor the desire itself, and be disgusted that one harbors a first-order desire that one regards as depraved or (in milder cases) simply in bad taste. In fact, one can have such unwanted desires even if one holds

them in check and never acts upon them. (See Frankfurt, 1976, p. 246; also Berofsky, 1983, p. 305; Berofsky, 1987, p. 169; and Penelhum, 1971.)

4. Such restrictions are discussed in Chapter Thirteen.

5. If one identifies with and favors a desire, that may be the strongest way of making it "authentically" one's own; but favoring it may not be *necessary,* as Frankfurt notes (1976, pp. 245–247).

6. It is clear from a number of his essays that Frankfurt believes his compatibilist freedom supports the *deserving* of praise or blame (moral responsibility). See Frankfurt, 1969, p. 837; Frankfurt, 1973, p. 75; Frankfurt, 1975, p. 115; and Frankfurt, 1983, p. 331.

7. As Bernard Williams has noted, "It is precisely a mark of extreme exploitation or degradation that those who suffer it do *not* see themselves differently from the way they are seen by the exploiters; either they do not see themselves as anything at all, or they acquiesce passively in the role for which they have been cast" (1973*a*, p. 237).

8. I am here suggesting that when cases like that of Saul and Paul are set out clearly, and the appropriate distinctions are drawn between freedom and moral responsibility, then we will (almost) all agree that it is unfair to blame Paul and credit Saul. I believe that when we reach the fundamental level of value beliefs, then no further argument is possible; that at that point we can only appeal to what we really feel, what we value; and that most of us do share the basic value that it is unfair to blame Paul and credit Saul when the difference between them turns on purely accidental differences. That is, I believe that at that most basic level the issues are noncognitive (although intuitionists could make similar claims, and insist that they are recognizing the most basic indisputable truths). However, it does not follow that these fundamental noncognitively established value beliefs are simply attitudes and thus without truth value (as Honderich, 1988, p. 478ff., suggests). They cannot be cognitively justified, but they are propositions and they do make truth claims and they can thus be compatible and/or incompatible with other claims (such as claims about what offenders and heroes deserve). (The question of how our most basic value beliefs are—or are not—justified is obviously related to the issues raised in this book, but not in a way that requires resolving basic metaethical issues.) But in this context the important point is that, when all the confusions are stripped away, most people who examine moral responsibility claims will reject them as unfair;

the grounds they have for that final value judgment—whether cognitive or noncognitive—need not be examined here. (My own metaethical views [Waller, 1986] are a revised version of noncognitivism, and draw heavily on the work of Herbert Feigl [1950, 1952].)

CHAPTER FIVE

1. The term "role-responsibility" is from H. L. A. Hart (1968*b*, pp. 212–213); his splendid discussion of the concept obviously influences this chapter. Judith Andre (1983, p. 205) suggests a somewhat similar distinction between two senses of "responsible." Also, the distinction between role-responsibility and moral responsibility is somewhat analogous to the difference (in discussions of philosophy of law) between crimes for which one is morally culpable and crimes in which one is responsible for the acts of others (under the doctrine of *respondeat superior*). For a discussion of that last distinction, see Kleinig, 1973, pp. 106–108; and Sayre, 1929–1930.

2. This notion of role-responsibility is also behind our desire (noted by David Zimmerman, 1981, p. 364) to be free to "make our own mistakes." We would rather not turn our lives over to the control of anyone else: we shall make our own decisions, including our own mistakes. Zimmerman insists that this desire "must be accommodated by any theory of freedom and responsibility"; however, it is also essential to note that the sort of responsibility that is required is role-responsibility, not moral responsibility.

3. Lawrence Haworth (1986) seems to have role-responsibility in mind when he moves from his interesting account of autonomy to its applications to responsibility. He states: "An individual is said to be a 'responsible person,' meaning that he can be trusted to meet his commitments. Another 'assumes responsibility': he takes it upon himself to ensure that things get done" (p. 47). And his later comments (p. 184) fit role-responsibility, not moral responsibility. Indeed, Haworth (p. 49) regards "accountability" (which he connects with reward and punishment) as a pragmatic question, distinct from questions about "responsibility" (that is, role-responsibility). Therefore when Haworth remarks that "given autonomy, responsibility follows" he is making a claim about the relation of autonomy to role-responsibility. Thus that claim is not (as I understand Haworth) the claim that autonomy automatically establishes moral responsibility (the claim that

is strongly rejected in Chapter Three of this book). Whether Haworth is correct about the relation between autonomy and role-responsibility is an interesting question in its own right; but since it is quite different from questions concerning the relation between autonomy (and/or free will) and moral responsibility, it is not an issue that must be resolved here.

4. A superb discussion of the advantages of controlling (being role-responsible for) one's own life is found in Mill, 1859, chap. 3.

CHAPTER SIX

1. Michael J. Zimmerman (1987) draws a distinction between "given character" and character "as so far formed," and then argues that the latter supports moral responsibility. Zimmerman's distinction is useful in bringing these issues into clearer focus; however, this chapter argues that one is not morally responsible even for the dispositions "to which one has contributed by virtue of one's own actions" (Zimmerman, 1987, p. 380). That is, in contrast to Zimmerman the position taken here is that one is not ever morally responsible—obviously not for one's "given character," and also not for one's "character as so far formed."

CHAPTER SEVEN

1. As George Sher states, "Of all the bases of desert, perhaps the most familiar and compelling is diligent, sustained effort. Whatever else we think, most of us agree that persons deserve things for sheer hard work" (1987, p. 53).

2. Secord does not concur with that claim; see Secord, 1985.

3. See Seligman, 1975, pp. 153–159.

4. For experimental substantiation of that claim (if any is wanted), see Carder and Berkowitz (1970); Neuringer (1969); Seligman (1975, p. 98); and Singh (1970).

CHAPTER EIGHT

1. This is perhaps the closest sense of "deserves" to "entitlement." However, the focus here is on deserts rather than entitlements, and no at-

tempt is made to draw precise connections and distinctions between deserts and entitlements. For an excellent discussion of the relation of deserts to entitlements, see Steven Sverdlik (1983*b*). Sverdlik distinguishes rights-entitlements from desert; I think entitlement might better be thought of as one type of desert (a type quite distinct from just deserts), but that will not be discussed here. In any case, I agree with Sverdlik that rights and entitlement-based claims "do not exhaust the conceptual terrain of justice"; and in particular, I would insist that what is here called "justice-deserving" is quite different from act-deserving and entitlements. Feinberg (1970*b*, p. 65) is the classical source for distinguishing act-deserving (which he prefers to call "entitlements") from other sorts of desert; and Pincoffs (1977, p. 80) also elucidates the distinction. While there is certainly an important distinction to be drawn between entitlements (in the sense of act-deserts) and justice-deserving, I am very skeptical of entitlement theory (of the sort that Nozick [1974] champions). For excellent arguments challenging entitlement theory see Nielsen (1985) and Cohen (1978).

2. The difference between act-deserving and talent-deserving is noted by Joel Feinberg: "There are several possible grounds for maintaining that the person who deserves the prize is not the person who deserved to win it. The latter may have had bad luck or an off day, or the victory conditions written into the rules might themselves have been ill chosen, not truly gauging excellence at the skill which is the ostensible basis for the competition" (Feinberg, 1970*b*, p. 65).

Feinberg (1970*b*) makes a number of important points concerning the various categories under which one may act-deserve praise, blame, a prize, a grade, and so on. Feinberg distinguishes various types of deserving within the act-deserving level; the present chapter distinguishes several senses of deserving in *addition* to act-deserving.

3. I am here adopting Michael Slote's term (1973). However, our conclusions about the implications of (what Slote calls) "desert for effort" are quite different. Slote maintains that "desert for effort" can support claims that I believe would require "justice-deserving."

4. "Justice-deserving" is the sort of deserving that would be noted from what Elizabeth L. Beardsley (1960) calls "the perspective of ultimate moral equality."

I do not claim that this is an exhaustive taxonomy of senses of "deserves." I only wish to note several important senses of "deserves" that have often been mistakenly identified as justice-deserving, in the hope that when these senses of "deserves" are distinguished the sorts of deserving that could only be supported by justice-deserving claims will not be spuriously supported by claims of act- or talent- or effort-deserving.

5. Steven Sverdlik (1983a) notes that it may be contrary to deserts to harm or reward someone who has *no* deserts, and that category of wrong is distinct from wrongs done through failure to recognize actual deserts.

6. See, for example, Alan Zaitchik, 1977, pp. 373–374.

7. The dangers are clearly described in Kai Nielsen (1978).

CHAPTER NINE

1. Wright Neely (1974) shows quite clearly that determinism-naturalism does not imply that we are the helpless pawns of our desires (not even of our highest-level desires). What we rightly fear is being controlled by desires that we find repulsive; but, as Neely notes, when we want to change our desires we can often do so: "The degree to which we are free to alter our own desires, like the degree to which we are free to do anything else, depends on our knowledge, our circumstances, and our skills—and on our other desires which determine the price we shall have to pay. There are no more logical or metaphysical obstacles to success in making ourselves to be the kind of people we wish to be than there are to our success in making the world the kind of place in which we wish to live" (p. 52).

CHAPTER ELEVEN

1. For example, Dennett (1984, esp. chap. 7) and Hook (1961).

2. Among the many interesting discussions of competing systems of beliefs are Hare (1955), Quine (1969), and Wittgenstein (1969).

3. Jonathan Bennett (1980a) perspicuously describes why notions of transcendent free will should grow out of efforts to reconcile moral responsibility with Christian metaphysics. Bennett (explicitly agreeing with the views of Williams [1973b] then rejects such accounts of transcendent free will as

"logically impossible." And indeed such accounts are logically incoherent in the naturalist system in which Bennett (and Williams) are working; but they fit comfortably into the world of miracles.

4. Mackie (1977) suggests that hard determinists (anyone who rejects moral responsibility) are stuck with a Kantian "noumenal or metaphysical self" that is "an idle spectator of a causal order in which it cannot intervene" (p. 223). Mackie then asserts: "But here there is an important difference among incompatibilists between hard determinists and voluntarists. The latter can consistently suppose that there is such a metaphysical self, since they give it work to do. Allowing that it sometimes in fact initiates action, they can say that *if* determinism held, it *would be* idle. But hard determinists have to say that this metaphysical self always *is* idle; it is then unclear what reason they can have for postulating its existence" (1977, p. 223). But no-fault naturalists (and hard determinists) do not deny moral responsibility on the grounds of an *idle* metaphysical self; rather, that self is part of a miraculous system, and the entire system is rejected. (A similar misinterpretation can be found in Gregory Rich's critique [1985, p. 83] of Paul Edwards [1961].) No-fault naturalists do not put the metaphysical self out of work; rather, they put it out of existence. (Mackie also rejects such a metaphysical self, but on the grounds that it is yoked with an implausible Kantian ethics.)

CHAPTER TWELVE

1. There are abundant examples of the belief that denial of moral responsibility entails denial of any genuine morality. C. A. Campbell (1957) argues that "if one has to give up freedom in the traditional elective sense" then no one can be morally blameworthy nor morally praiseworthy; and he equates that to "giving up . . . , quite simply, the reality of the moral life." F. C. Copleston (1948, p. 488) asserts that, if humans could be "conditioned" to behave well or ill, then there would be no moral responsibility and "there would be no objective moral distinction between the emperor Nero and St. Francis of Assisi." John Hospers (1961) argues against all ascriptions of moral responsibility and then, in the final section of his paper, asserts it as an obvious truth that at the level at which moral responsibility is denied " 'Right' and 'Wrong' . . . have no meaning here either." Howard

Hintz (1961) states of Hospers' view: "I do not see how he can escape the conclusion that this thesis destroys the foundations of all prescriptive ethics except on the arbitrary-power level."

More recently, Joseph F. Rychlak (1979) asserted that if responsibility is denied on the grounds that "we are what our biology and our social environments have shaped us into being" then morality is rendered alien as "morality becomes something imposed on people by others." Susan Wolf (1981, p. 4) claims that denying desert and moral responsibility would require that we "stop thinking in terms of what ought and ought not to be. We would have to stop thinking in terms that would allow the possibility that some lives and projects are better than others." Jeffrie Murphy (1988, p. 400) asserts that if one goes "too far" with natural lottery arguments they "would spell the end of moral responsibility and the moral significance of human beings that is founded upon such responsibility—would, indeed, spell the end of one's own moral significance" (p. 102). And Peter van Inwagen's contemptuous dismissal of the denial of moral responsibility assumes the linkage of moral responsibility with moral evaluation: "No one can consistently say that a certain act was a shoddy thing to do *and* say that its agent was not morally responsible when he performed it" (1983, p. 207).

In contrast, Frankfurt (1973, p. 79) recognizes that judgments of moral distaste or even of moral contempt can be made without believing that the object of those evaluations is morally responsible; Blum (1980, p. 189) makes a similar point; and John Stuart Mill (1979, p. 456) insists that "the highest and strongest sense of the worth of goodness, and the odiousness of its opposite," can be sustained when moral responsibility (desert of punishment) is denied. And Honderich (1988) notes the possibility of moral disapproval that does not carry a belief that the agent is the ultimate origination of a wrongful idea, but instead "has in it, in so far as ideas as to the initiation of action are concerned, only beliefs as to voluntariness, and does not include retributive desires" (p. 592). Also, Bennett (1980*a*) is particularly clear on this issue. Bennett notes that even if we deny *all* reactive feelings (including all claims of praise or blame), such rejection would *not* pose "the slightest threat to the value-system according to which we judge some actions to be good or right or successful and others to be bad or wrong or failures. Without having any tendency to remorse or guilt, I may resolve not to exhibit contempt towards other people, and when I do contemn someone I may regret this very much, and be concerned to find out what went wrong . . . and correct it" (p. 31).

2. Daniel Dennett (1984, p. 157) notes that, when people think of the general denial of moral responsibility, they are most likely to think that perhaps "no one ever really deserves the punishment society metes out—since all miscreants are *ipso facto* deluded, deranged, or radically ignorant in one way or another." P. F. Strawson (1974) notes two situations in which moral responsibility is ordinarily not ascribed. One involves a temporary exception: a person is under severe duress, so we excuse her from moral responsibility in these specific circumstances. In the other type of case, an individual is so severely damaged—by early environment, mental abnormalities, insanity—that the person is regarded as never morally responsible.

3. It is sometimes maintained that determinism undermines not only morality but also rationality and indeed all truth claims. Such assertions can be found in Colson (1982); Eccles (1976, p. 101); Flew (1986); Hinman (1979a); Hinman (1979b, pp. 294–295); Llewelyn (1966); MacIntyre (1957); and Wolf (1981, pp. 397–399). That issue cannot be addressed here: it would require at least another volume, and I think satisfactory answers to that line of argument have already been developed. For refutation of such claims see Churchland (1981); Dennett (1984, chap. 2); Toulmin (1970); Skinner (1969, chaps. 6 and 8); Skinner (1974, chaps. 7, 8, and 9); Waller (1985); and Waller (1982).

4. Such as in Gary Watson (1975).

5. For references to such arguments, see note 3 above.

6. Eugene Schlossberger (1986) makes a similar point on p. 47.

7. Along somewhat similar lines, Jeffrie Murphy (who sympathizes with retributivism) writes: "Since I regard retributive hatred as in principle the natural, fitting, and proper response to certain instances of wrongdoing, I do not regard the passion itself as either immoral or irrational. (It is not the moral equivalent of a phobia.) I do, however, believe that it is generally both irrational and immoral to be *led,* to use Spinoza's phrase, by this dangerous and often blind passion. I have called the case against hatred a set of cautions; taken together these cautions constitute a body of reasons so profound that instances where it is acceptable to proceed in spite of them are, in my judgment, rare. Thus rational and moral beings would, I think, want not a world utterly free of retributive hatred but one where this pas-

sion is *both* respected *and* seen as dangerous, as in great need of reflective restraint" (1988, p. 108).

I do not agree that retributive hatred is even in principle the fitting and proper response to wrongdoing; however, the point here is that one can believe the retributivist emotional response is healthy and appropriate without thinking that one should (always, or even ordinarily) act on it.

8. A point noted by Glover (1970, pp. 64, 67). Also, Galen Strawson (1986) parenthetically notes that "one possibility not allowed for by this all-or-nothing view of our commitment to the reactive attitudes is that of local erosions, within the general framework of human life, of certain facets of this commitment" (p. 90). However, he does not pursue that possibility.

9. This point is noted in Richard Burgh's excellent critique of attempts to justify punishment (1982, p. 196).

10. In an essay that develops the implications of Strawson's work on the loss of reactive attitudes, Wolf effectively demonstrates that the loss of such reactive attitudes would result in a bleak world indeed. As she states, "A world without reactive attitudes would be a tragic world of human isolation" (1981, pp. 400–401). And no doubt it would be. But again, there is no reason to conclude that the denial of moral responsibility entails the elimination of all reactive attitudes. (For comments on why determinism would not destroy all reactive attitudes, see Honderich, 1988, p. 521.)

11. There may be other, less defensible, grounds for concern over the loss of guilt. Elaine Pagels (1988, p. 146) suggests that Augustine's bizarre doctrine of original sin (all later humans are infected with the guilt of Adam's sin) survived as Christian dogma because "people often would rather feel guilty than helpless." But, as argued earlier, belief in free will (and in the power to have an effect and avoid "fate" and helplessness) is quite consistent with denial of blame, desert, moral responsibility. There may be good reasons for preserving some sense of guilt; but combatting helplessness is not one of them.

12. This is the type of responsibility discussed by Stephen Cohen (1982).

13. Jonathan Bennett (1980a) recognizes that there is a tension between praise/blame judgments (reactive responses of praise/blame) and inquiries into the individual's causal history. As he states, "Reactive attitudes must be especially associated with praise- and blame-related responses, and must stand in contrast—I do not say conflict—with an objectively inquiring atti-

tude" (p. 32). But Bennett underestimates the fundamental incompatibility between praise/blame judgments and causal inquiries. There is not only contrast, but also conflict—as was noted in Chapter Three.

14. A similar answer might be given to Robert M. Adams' statement: "To me it seems strange to say that I do not blame someone though I think poorly of him, believing that his motives are thoroughly selfish" (Adams, 1985, p. 21).

It should also be clear that (contrary to Glover, 1970, pp. 63ff.) it is *not* true that the no-fault naturalist "could dislike actions but not disapprove of people." The no-fault naturalist can consistently consider an individual morally repugnant—but would not *blame* the individual for being so.

15. This is important to note, since confusion on this point has often led philosophers to the conclusion that the importance of preserving moral principles and moral ideals justifies preserving moral responsibility. Such reasoning is evident in the following passage by Milo: "Viewing things from the perspective of moral responsibility retains its importance for us even if we admit the truth of determinism. For we cannot do without ideals of what human beings should be like, any more than we can do without principles to guide our particular actions. This means that it is necessary for us to evaluate human behavior not only as right or wrong but also as good or bad, admirable or reprehensible. It means, also, that the perspective of moral responsibility is not wholly undermined or invalidated by the perspective of determinism" (1984, p. 232). However, what Milo wants to preserve is not moral responsibility, but moral principles and ideals. When it is recognized that the latter do not require the former, then moral responsibility can be happily discarded.

The same confusion bedevils Elizabeth Beardsley's admirable "Determinism and Moral Perspectives" (1960). Beardsley insists on the legitimacy of a "level of moral credit" (at which judgments of desert and moral responsibility are appropriate) even though she believes that from a higher (or deeper) perspective of "ultimate moral equality" no one deserves praise or blame. And her reason for wanting to preserve the level of moral credit is this: "We value in a special way those whose acts meet the standards of moral worth and moral credit, and this is something that we cannot change. . . . The idea of a man who performs a right act voluntarily, knowingly, and from a good desire, and the idea of a man who, when confronted by odds, can still do these things—these *are* the models we have formed. Conformity to these patterns is what we regard as worthy of praise. . . . We cannot feel about persons who thus conform or deviate as we do about animals or inanimate objects which measure up or fail to measure up to certain standards. All this being so, judgments of praise and blame based on moral worth and moral credit are not only legitimate but vitally necessary parts of moral discourse" (p. 14).

As noted earlier in this chapter, nothing about the denial of moral responsibility entails that we must "feel about persons" who perform nobly "as we do about animals or inanimate objects"; and once again, moral responsibility—being deserving of praise or blame—is not a necessary condition for ideals of virtue and goodness. It is certainly important that we have ideals of a virtuous person, and it is a wonderful thing when an individual's behavior approximates such ideals; but it does not follow that the individual deserves praise.

CHAPTER THIRTEEN

1. The same kind of mistaken belief—that denial of moral responsibility is based on human defects, and thus those who deny all human moral responsibility must believe that such defective humans should be subject to the whims or designs of therapists—can be found in other retributivists. C. S. Lewis makes an impassioned plea for retributive punishment on the grounds that "treating" criminals is inherently dehumanizing: "To be 'cured' against one's will and cured of states which we may not regard as disease is to be put on a level with those who have not yet reached the age of reason or those who never will; to be classed with infants, imbeciles, and domestic animals. But to be punished, however severely, because we 'ought to have known better,' is to be treated as a human person made in God's image" (1970). Oldenquist (1988, p. 467) makes a similar claim. Even that most reasonable and naturalistic of retributivists, Jeffrie Murphy, draws the same contrast: "Indeed, if the alternative is having our personalities involuntarily restructured by some state psychiatrist, we might well want to claim the 'right to be punished' that Hegel spoke of" (1979, pp. 109–110). And Bernard Williams (1985, p. 194) tolerates "blame" (which he acknowledges requires an incoherent transcendent freedom) because the moral system "leaves us, as the

only contrast to rational blame, forms of persuasion it refuses to distinguish in spirit from force and constraint."

2. See Skinner (1971, p. 171); Skinner (1974, p. 191); Skinner (1972b, p. 11); Skinner (1978b, pp. 9–13).

3. See the disturbing account by Weiner (1972). For a report on more recent efforts to use the U.S. prison system for coercive conditioning of dissidents, see Reuben and Norman (1987).

4. Gerald Dworkin (1976, pp. 27–28) proposes excellent guidelines for therapy programs that respect and enhance individual freedom; but they certainly do not require any notion of moral responsibility, much less any claims of transcendent free will.

5. Oldenquist (1988) insists that retributive punishment is "a powerful way to tell young delinquents they still belong and are members of a moral community." But there is an obvious exception that Oldenquist cannot ignore: "Retributive punishment (excepting execution and its analog in tribal societies, banishment) aims at a criminal's contrition and reintegration into the society" (p. 470). Oldenquist apparently does not think that capital punishment is an important problem for his view that retributive punishment is a means of welcoming people into a moral community (it is merely an "exception"). However, it seems to me a serious challenge to a "retribution-as-welcome" position. But perhaps Oldenquist is thinking of capital punishment as offering the special sort of welcome we afford to overnight guests: we want them to feel welcome, so long as they do not stay too long.

6. This is also the answer to the eloquent argument by Moore (1987, pp. 215–216) to the effect that, if we "excuse" as not morally responsible those who commit criminal acts, then, "far from evincing fellow feeling and the allowing of others to participate in our moral life, it excludes them as less than persons."

7. Here Oldenquist is adding a twist of the expressive theory to his basic retributivism. More detailed accounts of the expressive theory of punishment can be found in Duff (1986, chap. 9) and Feinberg (1970a).

8. Another claim that Oldenquist makes for retributive punishment—institutionalized revenge—is that feelings of revenge cannot be eliminated, or at least that they cannot be eliminated if we are to retain strong moral beliefs and strong community values: "There is no doubt that retribution is

revenge, both historically and conceptually. I do not believe that the logic of this chain can be broken—from moral community, to accountability, to retribution, to revenge" (1988, p. 473). That issue is discussed in the previous chapter, in response to the arguments of Strawson and Bennett.

9. Morris (1988, p. 69) asserts that "determinations of guilt and the infliction of punishment upon the guilty, vividly communicate, in a way no other social practice can, the community's values." But like Oldenquist, he offers no support for that claim and ignores alternatives for "vividly communicating" values.

10. One closely related question is likely to be asked: will the no-fault naturalist society use preventive detention? It might seem that if a no-fault naturalist society were willing to make some use of coercive isolation in order to protect society from criminal acts, then preventive detention would also be allowed to at least the same degree. After all, the person who is subjected to coercive isolation does not (according to the no-fault naturalist denial of moral responsibility) justly deserve such treatment; then why not also coercively isolate those who are judged *likely* to commit a crime, but have not actually done so? The two are exactly equal in just deserts (that is, neither justly deserves such deprivation of liberty); so if the justification for coercively isolating the criminal is to prevent harm to society, then it would seem that exactly the same case could be made for treating the potential criminal in the same manner. But in fact preventive detention does not so easily follow from no-fault naturalism. As noted before, the no-fault naturalist society will (or at least is likely to) place great value on individual freedom; so every effort would be made to avoid any sort of freedom deprivation (especially since it would be recognized by the society as an undeserved deprivation). So such involuntary isolation would be used only in the direst circumstances, when no other means of preventing harm could be imagined and the harm to be prevented greatly outweighed the wrong of undeserved coercive detention. Involuntary isolation would only occur when the society was very confident that such isolation would prevent a severe and eminent harm. And one indication of such danger would be a severe criminal act that it is judged quite likely the criminal would soon repeat. By contrast, preventive detention would involve a great deal less certainty: there would have to be a prediction that the individual was about to do something she had not done before. In such a case, there would not be the

same degree of confidence that the individual in question really was about to commit a severely harmful act; and thus the conditions required to outweigh the wrong of undeserved liberty deprivation (confidence that the individual was about to commit a severe crime, with no other means of prevention or reform possible) would be absent. If the predictive powers of psychology and sociology reached the point that we could be extremely confident that someone—who had not recently committed a crime—would later do so, then at that (hypothetical) point the social and behavioral sciences would no doubt also be able to offer much better guidance to altering the individual's environment and reforming the individual, and thus preventive detention would not be required.

CHAPTER FOURTEEN

1. One qualification: if some have chosen to stay in a deadening job or situation, then there are good reasons not to coerce those individuals into something else (even though we know that their choices are not liberty-enhancing). Compulsory programs would probably be worse—would pose a greater threat to individual freedom—than the problems they are designed to solve. But (consistent with respect for individual freedom) we can and should continue to offer good and accessible opportunities to move into freer environs; and we should encourage individuals to use their abilities on small projects in which they are likely to succeed, so that they experience success and make greater efforts and eventually overcome the conditioned restraints that limit their opportunities and their freedom. And, above all, we shall not be tempted to add blame to the injurious environment that shaped their unfreedom.

2. Such "awards" and other positive reinforcers would be scheduled to optimize the student's efforts and satisfaction; and (as noted in Chapter Ten) that would be very unlikely to match the schedule dictated by "just deserts." (In short, no moral responsibility or just deserts are being smuggled in through this proposal.)

3. Beardsley (1960, p. 416) is eloquent on this point.

4. Nozick (1974) would not agree. I think Nielsen (1985) and Cohen (1978) quite adequately answer Nozick's claims, but that is obviously a vexed question.

BIBLIOGRAPHY

Adams, R. M. 1985. "Involuntary Sin." *Philosophical Review* 44: 3–31.
Andre, Judith. 1983. "Nagel, Williams, and Moral Luck." *Analysis* 43: 202–207.
Aristotle. 1955. *The Nicomachean Ethics*, trans. J. A. K. Thomson. Harmondsworth, Eng.: Penguin Books.
Ayer, A. J. 1954. "On the Analysis of Moral Judgements." In Ayer, *Philosophical Essays*. London: Macmillan. 231–249.
Barrett, William. 1961. "Determinism and Novelty." In Sidney Hook (ed.), *Determinism and Freedom in the Age of Modern Science*. New York: Collier Books. Orig. pub. 1958. 46–54.
Beardsley, Elizabeth L. 1960. "Determinism and Moral Perspectives." *Philosophy and Phenomenological Research* 21: 1–20.
Bennett, Jonathan. 1980a. "Accountability." In Zak van Straaten (ed.), *Philosophical Subjects*. Oxford, Eng.: Clarendon Press. 14–47.
———. 1980b. "Towards a Theory of Punishment." *Philosophic Exchange* 3: 43–54.
Berofsky, Bernard. 1983. "Autonomy." In L. S. Cauman, Issac Levi, Charles Parsons, and Robert Schwartz (eds.), *How Many Questions?* Indianapolis, Ind.: Hackett. 301–320.
———. 1987. *Freedom from Necessity: The Metaphysical Basis of Responsibility*. New York: Routledge & Kegan Paul.
Blum, Lawrence A. 1980. *Friendship, Altruism, and Morality*. London: Routledge & Kegan Paul.
Burgh, Richard W. 1982. "Do the Guilty Deserve Punishment?" *Journal of Philosophy* 79: 193–210.
Butler, Samuel. 1872. *Erewhon*, 2nd ed. London: Trübner.
Campbell, C. A. 1957. *On Selfhood and Godhood*. London: George Allen & Unwin, and New York: Macmillan.

Carder, Brooks, and Kenneth Berkowitz. 1970. "Rats' Preference for Earned in Comparison with Free Food." *Science* 167: 1273–1274.

Chisholm, Roderick. 1975 (1964). "Human Freedom and the Self." In Joel Feinberg, ed., *Reason and Responsibility*, 3rd ed. Encino, Cal.: Wadsworth. 391–397.

Churchland, Patricia. 1981. "Is Determinism Self-Refuting?" *Mind* 40: 99–101.

Cohen, G. A. 1978. "Robert Nozick and Wilt Chamberlain: How Patterns Preserve Liberty." In John Arthur and William H. Shaw (eds.), *Justice and Economic Distribution*. Englewood Cliffs, N.J.: Prentice-Hall. 246–262.

Cohen, Stephen. 1982. "Rationality and Responsibility: A Central Thesis." *Pacific Philosophical Quarterly* 63: 75–85.

Colson, Darrel D. 1982. "The Transcendental Argument Against Determinism: A Challenge Yet Unmet." *Southern Journal of Philosophy* 20: 15–24.

Copleston, F. C. 1965. "The Existence of God: A Debate." In Paul Edwards and Arthur Pap (eds.), *A Modern Introduction to Philosophy*, rev. ed. New York: Free Press, 1965. 473–490. Orig. broadcast 1948.

Dennett, D. C. 1978. "On Giving Libertarians What They Say They Want." In Dennett, *Brainstorms*. Montgomery, Vt.: Bradford Books. 286–299.

———. 1984. *Elbow Room*. Cambridge, Mass.: MIT Press.

Dewey, John. 1922. *Human Nature and Conduct*. New York: Henry Holt and Company.

Dickens, Charles. 1967 (1843). *A Christmas Carol*. New York: James H. Heineman.

Dostoyevsky, Fyodor. 1961. (1864). *Notes from Underground*, trans. Andrew R. MacAndrew. New York: New American Library.

Duff, R. A. 1986. *Trials and Punishments*. Cambridge, Eng.: Cambridge University Press.

Dworkin, Gerald. 1976. "Autonomy and Behavior Control." *Hastings Center Report* 6: 23–28.

Eccles, John C. 1976. "Brain and Free Will." In Gordon Globus, Grover Maxwell, and Irwin Savodnik (eds.), *Consciousness and the Brain: A Scientific and Philosophical Inquiry*. New York: Plenum Press. 101–121.

Edwards, Paul. 1961 (1958). "Hard and Soft Determinism." In Sidney Hook (ed.), *Determinism and Freedom in the Age of Modern Science*. New York: Collier Books. 117–125.

Feigl, Herbert. 1950. "De Principiis Non Disputandum . . . ? On the Meaning and the Limits of Justification." In Max Black (ed.), *Philosophical Analysis*. Ithaca, N.Y.: Cornell University Press. 119–156.

———. 1952. "Validation and Vindication." In Wilfrid Sellars and John Hospers (eds.), *Readings in Ethical Theory*. New York: Appleton-Century-Crofts. 667–680.

Feinberg, Joel. 1970a (1965). "The Expressive Theory of Punishment." In Feinberg, *Doing and Deserving*. Princeton, N.J.: Princeton University Press. 95–118.

———. 1970b. "Justice and Personal Desert." In Feinberg, *Doing and Deserving*. Princeton, N.J.: Princeton University Press. 55–94.

Flew, Antony. 1986. "Rationality and Unnecessitated Choice." In Newton Garver and Peter H. Hare (eds.), *Naturalism and Rationality*. Buffalo, N.Y.: Prometheus Books. 41–51.

Frankfurt, Harry G. 1969. "Alternate Possibilities and Moral Agency." *Journal of Philosophy* 66: 828–839.

———. 1971. "Freedom of the Will and the Concept of a Person." *Journal of Philosophy* 68: 5–20.

———. 1973. "Coercion and Moral Responsibility." In Ted Honderich (ed.), *Essays on Freedom of Action*. London: Routledge & Kegan Paul. 65–86.

———. 1975. "Three Concepts of Free Action, II." *Aristotelian Society Proceedings* suppl. Vol. 49: 113–125.

———. 1976. "Identification and Externality." In A. O. Rorty (ed.), *The Identities of Persons*. Berkeley: University of California Press. 239–251.

———. 1983. "What We Are Morally Responsible For." In L. S. Cauman, Isaac Levi, Charles Parsons, and Robert Schwartz (eds.), *How Many Questions?* Indianapolis, Ind.: Hackett. 321–335.

Gaylin, Willard. 1973. "Skinner Redux." *Harper's Magazine*, Oct.: 48–56.

———. 1983 (1982). *The Killing of Bonnie Garland*. Harmondsworth, Eng.: Penguin Books.

Geach, Peter. 1977. *The Virtues.* Cambridge, Eng.: Cambridge University Press.

Glover, Jonathan. 1970. *Responsibility.* New York: Humanities Press.

Hampshire, Stuart. 1967 (1959). *Thought and Action.* New York: Viking Press.

Hare, R. M. 1955. "Theology and Falsification." In Antony Flew and Alasdair MacIntyre (eds.), *New Essays in Philosophical Theology.* New York: Macmillan. 99–103.

Hart, H. L. A. 1968a (1959). "Prolegomenon to the Principles of Punishment." In Hart, *Punishment and Responsibility.* Oxford, Eng.: Clarendon Press. 1–27.

———. 1968b. "Postscript: Responsibility and Retribution." In Hart, *Punishment and Responsibility.* Oxford, Eng.: Clarendon Press. 210–237.

Haworth, Lawrence. 1986. *Autonomy: An Essay in Philosophical Psychology and Ethics.* New Haven, Conn.: Yale University Press.

Hinman, Lawrence M. 1979a. "Can Skinner Tell a Lie? Notes on the Epistemological Nihilism of B. F. Skinner." *Southern Journal of Philosophy* 17: 47–60.

———. 1979b. "How Not to Naturalize Ethics: The Untenability of a Skinnerian Naturalistic Ethic." *Ethics* 89: 292–297.

Hintz, Howard. 1961 (1958). "Some Further Reflections on Moral Responsibility." In S. Hook (ed.), *Determinism and Freedom in the Age of Modern Science.* New York: Collier Books. 176–179.

Hirototo, D. S. 1974. "Locus of Control and Learned Helplessness." *Journal of Experimental Psychology* 102: 187–193.

Hoekema, David A. 1986. *Rights and Wrongs: Coercion, Punishment, and the State.* Selinsgrove, Pa.: Susquehanna University Press.

Holborow, Les. 1975. "Desert, Equality and Injustice." *Philosophy* 50: 157–168.

Honderich, Ted. 1988. *A Theory of Determinism.* Oxford, Eng.: Clarendon Press.

Hook, S. 1961 (1958). "Necessity, Indeterminism, and Sentimentalism." In Hook (ed.), *Determinism and Freedom in the Age of Modern Science.* New York: Collier Books. 180–192.

Hospers, John. 1961 (1958). "What Means This Freedom?" In S. Hook (ed.),

Determinism and Freedom in the Age of Modern Science. New York: Collier Books. 126–142.

Hume, David. 1902 (1748). "Of Liberty and Necessity." In Hume, *An Enquiry Concerning Human Understanding.* Oxford, Eng.: Clarendon Press.

Kane, Robert. 1985. *Free Will and Values.* Albany, N.Y.: State University of New York Press.

Kavanau, J. Lee. 1967. "Behavior of Captive White-Footed Mice." *Science* 155: 1623–1639.

Kenny, Anthony. 1978. *Freewill and Responsibility.* London: Routledge & Kegan Paul.

Kleinig, John. 1973. *Punishment and Desert.* The Hague: Martinus Nijhoff.

Levin, Michael. 1979. *Metaphysics and the Mind-Body Problem.* Oxford, Eng.: Clarendon Press.

Lewis, C. S. 1970 (1949). "The Humanitarian Theory of Punishment." In Lewis, *Undeceptions.* London: Curtis Brown. 238–249.

Llewelyn, J. E. 1966. "The Inconceivability of Pessimistic Determinism." *Analysis* 27: 39–44.

MacIntyre, Alasdair. 1957. "Determinism." *Mind* 66: 28–41.

Mackie, J. L. 1977. *Ethics: Inventing Right and Wrong.* Harmondsworth, Eng.: Penguin Books.

———. 1982. "Morality and the Retributive Emotions." *Criminal Justice Ethics* 1: 3–10.

Madden, Edward H. 1973 (1962). *Philosophical Problems of Psychology.* New York: Greenwood Press.

Maugham, W. Somerset. 1933. *Sheppey.* London: William Heinemann, and New York: Doubleday & Co.

Mill, John Stuart. 1979 (1865). "On Freedom of the Will." In Mill, *An Examination of Sir William Hamilton's Philosophy.* Vol. 9 of *The Collected Works of John Stuart Mill.* Toronto: University of Toronto Press. 437–469.

———. 1859. *On Liberty.* London: J. W. Parker and Son.

Mills, John A. 1982. "Some Observations on Skinner's Moral Theory." *Journal for the Theory of Social Behaviour* 12: 141–160.

———. 1984. "Purpose and Conditioning: A Reply to Waller." *Journal for the Theory of Social Behaviour* 14: 363–367.

Milo, Ronald D. 1984. *Immorality*. Princeton, N.J.: Princeton University Press.

Moore, Michael S. 1987. "The Moral Worth of Retribution." In Ferdinand Schoeman (ed.), *Responsibility, Character, and the Emotions*. Cambridge, Eng.: Cambridge University Press. 179–219.

Morris, Herbert. 1985 (1968). "Persons and Punishment." Reprinted in Jeffrie G. Murphy (ed.), *Punishment and Rehabilitation*, 2nd ed. Belmont, Calif.: Wadsworth. 24–41.

———. 1988. "The Decline of Guilt." *Ethics* 99: 62–76.

Murphy, Jeffrie G. 1979 (1973). "Marxism and Retribution." In Murphy, *Retribution, Justice, and Therapy*. Dordrecht, Holland: D. Reidel. 93–115.

———. 1988. "Hatred: A Qualified Defense." In Murphy and Jean Hampton, *Forgiveness and Mercy*. Cambridge, Eng.: Cambridge University Press. 88–110.

Nagel, Thomas. 1979 (1971). "Brain Bisection and the Unity of Consciousness." In Nagel, *Mortal Questions*. Cambridge, Eng.: Cambridge University Press. 147–164.

———. 1986. *The View from Nowhere*. Oxford, Eng.: Oxford University Press.

Neely, Wright. 1974. "Freedom and Desire." *Philosophical Review* 83: 32–54.

Neuringer, Allen. 1969. "Animals Respond for Food in the Presence of Free Food." *Science* 166: 399–401.

Nielsen, Kai. 1978. "Class and Justice." In John Arthur and William H. Shaw (eds.), *Justice and Economic Distribution*. Englewood Cliffs, N.J.: Prentice-Hall. 225–245.

———. 1985. *Equality and Liberty*. Totowa, N.J.: Rowman & Allanheld.

Nozick, Robert. 1974. *Anarchy, State, and Utopia*. New York: Basic Books.

———. 1981. *Philosophical Explanations*. Cambridge, Mass.: Belknap Press of Harvard University Press.

Oldenquist, Andrew. 1988. "An Explanation of Retribution." *Journal of Philosophy* 85: 464–478.

Pagels, Elaine. 1988. *Adam, Eve, and the Serpent*. New York: Random House.

Penelhum, Terence. 1971. "The Importance of Self-Identity." *Journal of Philosophy* 68: 667–678.

Peters, R. S. 1958. *The Concept of Motivation.* London: Routledge & Kegan Paul.

Pincoffs, Edmund L. 1977. "Are Questions of Desert Decidable?" In J. B. Cederblom and William L. Blizek (eds.), *Justice and Punishment.* Cambridge, Mass.: Ballinger. 75–88.

Quine, W. V. 1969. "Ontological Relativity." In *Ontological Relativity and Other Essays.* New York: Columbia University Press. 26–68.

Rachels, James. 1978. "What People Deserve." In John Arthur and William H. Shaw (eds.), *Justice and Economic Distribution.* Englewood Cliffs, N.J.: Prentice-Hall. 150–163.

Rawls, John. 1955. "Two Concepts of Rules." *Philosophical Review* 64: 3–32.

———. 1971. *A Theory of Justice.* Cambridge, Mass.: Belknap Press of Harvard University Press.

Reuben, William A., and Carlos Norman. 1987. "The Women of Lexington Prison." *The Nation,* June 27: 881–884.

Rich, Gregory. 1985. "Softening Up Hard Determinism." *Philosophia* 15: 79–84.

Rychlak, Joseph F. 1979. *Discovering Free Will and Personal Responsibility.* New York: Oxford University Press.

Salmon, Wesley C. 1970. "Determinism and Indeterminism in Modern Science." In Joel Feinberg (ed.), *Reason and Responsibility,* 5th ed. Belmont, Cal.: Wadsworth. 331–346.

Sayre, F. B. 1929–1930. "Criminal Responsibility for the Acts of Another." *Harvard Law Review* 43: 689–723.

Schlick, Moritz. 1939. "When Is a Man Responsible?" In Schlick, *Problems of Ethics,* trans. David Rynin. New York: Prentice-Hall.

Schlossberger, Eugene. 1986. "Why We Are Responsible for Our Emotions." *Mind* 95: 37–56.

Secord, Paul F. 1984. "Determinism, Free Will, and Self-Intervention: A Psychological Perspective." *New Ideas in Psychology* 2: 25–33.

———. 1985. "The Limitations of Radical Behaviorism: A Reply to Waller." *New Ideas in Psychology* 3: 27–32.

Seligman, Martin E. P. 1975. *Helplessness: On Depression, Development, and Death*. San Francisco: W. H. Freeman & Co.

Sher, George. 1979. "Effort, Ability, and Personal Desert." *Philosophy and Public Affairs* 8: 361–376.

———. 1987. *Desert*. Princeton, N.J.: Princeton University Press.

Singh, Devendra. 1970. "Preference for Bar Pressing to Obtain Reward over Freeloading in Rats and Children." *Journal of Comparative and Physiological Psychology* 73: 320–327.

Skinner, B. F. 1957. *Verbal Behavior*. New York: Appleton-Century-Crofts.

———. 1965 (1953). *Science and Human Behavior*. New York: Free Press.

———. 1966. "The Phylogeny and Ontogeny of Behavior." *Science* 153: 1205–1213.

———. 1969. *Contingencies of Reinforcement*. New York: Appleton-Century-Crofts.

———. 1971. *Beyond Freedom and Dignity*. New York: Alfred A. Knopf.

———. 1972a. *Cumulative Record*, 3rd ed. New York: Appleton-Century-Crofts.

———. 1972b (1955–1956). "Freedom and the Control of Men." Reprinted in Skinner, *Cumulative Record*, 3rd ed. New York: Appleton-Century-Crofts. 3–18.

———. 1972c (1971). "A Lecture on 'Having' a Poem." Lecture given to the Poetry Center in New York City on October 13, 1971. Reprinted in Skinner, *Cumulative Record*, 3rd ed. New York: Appleton-Century-Crofts. 345–355.

———. 1974. *About Behaviorism*. New York: Albert A. Knopf.

———. 1976a. *Walden Two*, paperback ed. New York: Macmillan.

———. 1976b. "Walden Two Revisited." Preface to *Walden Two*. New York: Macmillan.

———. 1977. "The Force of Coincidence." In B. C. Etzel, J. M. LeBlanc, and D. M. Baer (eds.), *New Developments in Behavioral Psychology: Theory, Method, and Application*. Hillsdale, N.J.: Lawrence Erlbaum Associates. 3–6.

———. 1978a (1975). "The Ethics of Helping People." Reprinted in Skinner, *Reflections on Behaviorism and Society*. Englewood Cliffs, N.J.: Prentice-Hall, 33–47.

———. 1978b (1977). "Human Behavior and Democracy." Presented at

American Psychological Association, Washington, D.C., September, 1976. Reprinted in Skinner, *Reflections on Behaviorism and Society*. Englewood Cliffs, N.J.: Prentice-Hall. 3–15.

——. 1978c. *Reflections on Behaviorism and Society*. Englewood Cliffs, N.J.: Prentice-Hall.

Slote, Michael. 1973. "Desert, Consent, and Justice." *Philosophy and Public Affairs* 2: 323–347.

Smullyan, Raymond. 1977. "Is God a Taoist?" In Smullyan, *The Tao is Silent*. New York: Harper & Row.

Stace, Walter T. 1952. *Religion and the Modern Mind*. Philadelphia: J. B. Lippincott.

Strawson, Galen. 1986. *Freedom and Belief*. Oxford, Eng.: Clarendon Press.

Strawson, P. F. 1974 (1962). "Freedom and Resentment." In *Freedom and Resentment and Other Essays*. London: Methuen. 1–25.

Sverdlik, Steven. 1983a. "The Logic of Desert." *Journal of Value Inquiry* 17: 317–324.

——. 1983b. "The Nature of Desert." *Southern Journal of Philosophy* 21: 585–594.

Taylor, Richard. 1974. *Metaphysics*, 2nd ed. Englewood Cliffs, N.J.: Prentice-Hall.

Thalberg, Irving. 1978. "Hierarchical Analysis of Unfree Action." *Canadian Journal of Philosophy* 8: 211–226.

Toulmin, Stephen. 1970. "Reasons and Causes." In Robert Borger and Frank Cioffi (eds.), *Explanation in the Behavioural Sciences*. Cambridge, Eng.: Cambridge University Press. 1–26.

Van Den Haag, Ernest. 1975. *Punishing Criminals*. New York: Basic Books.

Van Inwagen, Peter. 1983. *An Essay on Free Will*. Oxford, Eng.: Clarendon Press.

Waller, Bruce N. 1982. "Determinism and Behaviorist Epistemology." *Southern Journal of Philosophy* 20: 513–532.

——. 1984. "Purposes, Conditioning, and Skinner's Moral Theory." *Journal for the Theory of Social Behaviour* 14: 355–362.

——. 1985. "Deliberating About the Inevitable." *Analysis* 45: 48–52.

——. 1986. "The Virtues of Contemporary Emotivism." *Erkenntnis* 25: 61–75.

Watson, Gary. 1975. "Free Agency." *Journal of Philosophy* 72: 205–220.

———. 1987*a*. "Free Action and Free Will." *Mind* 96: 145–172.

———. 1987*b*. "Responsibility and the Limits of Evil." In Ferdinand Schoeman (ed.), *Responsibility, Character, and the Emotions*. Cambridge, Eng.: Cambridge University Press. 256–286.

Watson, J. S. 1967. "Memory and 'Contingency Analysis' in Infant Learning." *Merrill-Palmer Quarterly* 13: 55–76.

———. 1971. "Cognitive Perceptual Development in Infancy: Setting for the Seventies." *Merrill-Palmer Quarterly* 17: 139–152.

Watson, J. S., and C. G. Ramey. 1972. "Reactions to Response-Contingent Stimulation in Early Infancy." *Merrill-Palmer Quarterly* 18: 219–228.

Weiner, Bernard. 1972. "Prison Psychiatry: The Clockwork Cure." *The Nation*, April 3: 433–436.

Williams, Bernard. 1973*a* (1962). "The Idea of Equality." Reprinted in Williams, *Problems of the Self*. Cambridge, Eng.: Cambridge University Press. 230–249.

———. 1973*b* (1971). "Morality and the Emotions." Reprinted in Williams, *Problems of the Self*. Cambridge, Eng.: Cambridge University Press. 207–229.

———. 1985. *Ethics and the Limits of Philosophy*. Cambridge, Mass.: Harvard University Press.

Wittgenstein, L. W. 1969. *On Certainty*, ed. G. E. M. Anscombe and G. H. von Wright. London: Basil Blackwell.

Wolf, Susan. 1981. "The Importance of Free Will." *Mind* 90: 386–405.

———. 1986 (1980). "Asymmetrical Freedom." Reprinted in John Martin Fischer (ed.), *Moral Responsibility*. Ithaca, N.Y.: Cornell University Press. 225–240.

Zaitchik, Alan. 1977. "On Deserving to Deserve." *Philosophy and Public Affairs* 6: 370–388.

Zimmerman, David. 1981. "Hierarchical Motivation and Freedom of the Will." *Pacific Philosophical Quarterly* 62: 354–368.

Zimmerman, Michael J. 1987. "Luck and Moral Responsibility." *Ethics* 97: 374–386.

INDEX

Accountability, 72, 210, 221
Adams, Robert M., 218
Andre, Judith, 210
Aristotle, 77–79
Authenticity, compatibilist account of, 56–59, 209
Ayer, A. J., 146

Barrett, William, 8, 17–19
Beardsley, Elizabeth L., 212, 222
Behavioral psychology, 15, 29–30, 93–98, 136–138, 142, 208
Bennett, Jonathan, 160–164, 213–214, 215–216, 217–218
Berkowitz, Kenneth, 211
Berofsky, Bernard, 205–206, 209
"Blameworthy" (and "praiseworthy"), 46, 153; ambiguity of, 170–174
Blum, Lawrence A., 215
Burgh, Richard, 217
Butler, Samuel, 205

Campbell, C. A., 8, 11–13, 51, 144, 214
Capital punishment, 184, 220
Carder, Brooks, 211
Chisholm, Roderick, 7–8, 146–148
Churchland, Patricia, 216
Cohen, G. A., 212, 222
Cohen, Stephen, 217
Colson, Darrel D., 216
Control, fear of, 14, 19–22, 213
Copleston, F. C., 214

Criminals, 180–181, 183–184, 220; treatment of, in the absence of moral responsibility, 181–183, 186, 190–194, 221–222

Dennett, Daniel C., 15, 21, 42–45, 52–55, 63–64, 66, 71, 113–115, 122–126, 130–135, 148–149, 157, 172, 177, 184, 197, 213, 216
Deserving, 109–119, 129–134, 139, 211–213; act-deserving, 109–112, 114–115, 139, 211–213; effort-deserving, 112–113, 116–117, 212–213; justice-deserving, 111, 113–115, 118–119, 139, 211–213; talent-deserving, 110–112, 114, 116, 212–213
Determinism, 1–5; and freshness/novelty, 16–19, 22, 25. See also Naturalism
Dickens, Charles, 173
Dostoyevsky, F., 15, 20–21
Duff, R. A., 220
Dworkin, Gerald, 220

Eccles, John C., 216
Edwards, Paul, 214
Effort-making, 53–54, 79, 87, 89–108, 112–113, 116, 127–128, 167–168, 211, 212; causes of, 93–98, 127–128; does not establish moral responsibility, 91–106, 112–113
Eliot, T. S., 19

233

Entitlement, 211–212
Equality, 113, 116, 119, 138–139, 202–203, 212, 218
Expressive theory of punishment, 187, 220

Fatalism, and determinism/naturalism, 22–24, 127, 195
Feigl, Herbert, 210
Feinberg, Joel, 117, 212, 220
Flew, Antony, 216
Frankfurt, Harry G., 13–14, 30, 40–42, 45, 55–59, 66, 156, 157, 207, 208–209, 215
Free will, compatibilist/naturalist account of, 5–6, 9–10, 27–49, 52–61, 81–88, 92, 127–128, 176–179, 195–198; in contrast with libertarian free will, 4–10, 13–26, 35, 39, 94, 143–149, 176, 195–196, 214; inadequacy of, as grounds for moral responsibility, 27, 34–49, 54–61, 84–88; value of, 6, 33–34, 127–128, 208
Free will, libertarian (transcendent) account of, 4–5, 7–13, 17–23, 92–94, 122, 126, 213–214, 219
Freud, Sigmund, 10

Gaylin, Willard, 34–35, 180–181
Geach, Peter, 7
Glover, Jonathan, 45–48, 217, 218
Guilt, 153, 164–170, 217

Hampshire, Stuart, 81–83, 87
Hare, R. M., 213
Harris, Robert, 184
Hart, H. L. A., 64–65, 73, 210
Haworth, Lawrence, 210–211
Helplessness. See Learned helplessness

Higher-order desires, 13–14, 40–41, 45–46, 55, 166, 207, 208–209
Hinman, Lawrence M., 216
Hintz, Howard, 214–215
Hirototo, D. S., 208
Hoekema, David A., 188
Holborow, Les, 112
Honderich, Ted, 207–208, 209, 215, 217
Hook, Sidney, 213
Hospers, John, 214
Hume, David, 9–10, 32, 74, 157

Ideals, 137, 218–219
Individual freedom, 4, 27–34, 46, 207; promoted by rejection of moral responsibility, 195–203
Individuals, 28–30, 32–36, 46, 205

Kane, Robert, 19–21
Kant, Immanuel, 7
Kavanau, J. Lee, 205
Kleinig, John, 210

Learned helplessness, 95–98, 205. See also Seligman, Martin E. P.
Levin, Michael, 61
Lewis, C. S., 219
Llewelyn, J. E., 216
Luck, and moral responsibility, 52–55, 61, 75, 86, 90–91, 110, 113–114, 117, 121–128, 143–144, 172
Luther, Martin, 147–148

MacIntyre, Alasdair, 8, 216
Mackie, J. L., 214
Madden, Edward, 67
Marx, Karl, 10
Maugham, W. Somerset, 22–23, 205
Mill, John Stuart, 211, 215

Milo, Ronald D., 218
Moore, Michael S., 220
Moral-act responsibility, as distin-
guished from moral-judgment respon-
sibility, 73–76
Moral community, membership in,
183–186, 220–221
Moral judgment, in absence of moral
responsibility, 75–76, 151–158, 161–
164, 169–174, 190, 206, 207, 214–216
Morris, Herbert, 179–180, 221
Murphy, Jeffrie, 215, 216, 219

Nagel, Thomas, 4, 205
Naturalism, 4–5, 7, 9, 16–17, 23–24,
98, 126, 145–149, 154, 157, 195–196,
205, 213
Neely, Wright, 213
Neuringer, Allen, 211
Nielsen, Kai, 206, 212, 213, 222
Nietzsche, Friedrich, 147–148
No-fault naturalism, 5–6, 53, 71–72,
75–76, 111, 113, 115, 136–138, 141,
143–149, 153–158, 180–183, 195–204,
214, 218; definition of, 5–6
Norman, Carlos, 220
Nozick, Robert, 212, 222

Objective attitude. See Reactive attitudes
Oldenquist, Andrew, 183–184, 187–188,
219, 220
Omar Khayyám, 18

Pagels, Elaine, 217
Penelhum, Terence, 209
Pincoffs, Edmund L., 212
"Pragmatic" responsibility, 129–140;
impracticality of, 134–140; unfairness
of, 132–133

"Praiseworthy." See "Blameworthy"
Prediction, 17–19, 25
Prisons, 181–182, 192–194, 220

Quine, W. V., 213

Rachels, James, 89–92, 112–113
Ramey, C. G., 205
Rationality, 8, 60–61, 63, 72, 157–160,
208, 216; with determinism/natural-
ism, 153–157, 208, 216; with no-fault
naturalism, 157–160, 169
Rawls, John, 90, 121
Reactive attitudes, 158–164, 207,
215, 217; contrasted with objec-
tive attitudes, 159; without moral
responsibility, 158–164, 217
Regret, 164–169, 216
Retributivism, 34, 160–162, 179–189,
199, 216–217, 219–221
Rich, Gregory, 214
Role-responsibility, 64–72, 134–135,
169, 210–211, 217
Rychlak, Joseph F., 215

Salmon, Wesley C., 205
Sartre, Jean Paul, 147–148
Sayre, F. B., 210
Schlick, Moritz, 129–131, 140
Schlossberger, Eugene, 216
Scrooge, Ebeneezer, 173
Secord, Paul F., 98–101, 211
Self-making, 68–70, 77–88, 134,
211, 213
Seligman, Martin E. P., 96–97, 177, 205,
208, 211
Sher, George, 101–102, 122, 124–
126, 211
Singh, Devendra, 211

Skinner, B. F., 15, 22, 176–179, 201, 216, 220
Slote, Michael, 116, 212
Smullyan, Raymond, 205
Spenkelink, John, 184
Spinoza, B., 34, 205, 216
Stace, Walter, 111
Strawson, Galen, 206–207, 217
Strawson, P. F., 158–164, 216, 217
Sverdlik, Steven, 212–213

Taking responsibility, 66–70, 210; for one's self, 68–70
Taylor, Richard, 8
Thalberg, Irving, 208
Therapy, 81, 96, 159, 220; as threat to freedom, 179–183, 196, 219–220
Toulmin, Stephen, 216

Uneven starts, and just deserts, 121–126

Vacuous contrast, argument from, 143–145
Values, 157–158, 209–210; in absence of moral responsibility, 152, 170–174, 190, 215, 218–219; teaching and communication of, 158, 187–190, 221
Van Inwagen, Peter, 8, 151, 155, 170, 215

Waller, Bruce N., 210, 216
Watson, Gary, 184, 207, 216
Watson, J. S., 205
Weiner, Bernard, 220
Williams, Bernard, 209, 213–214, 219–220
Wittgenstein, L. W., 213
Wolf, Susan, 170–173, 206, 215, 216, 217

Zaitchik, Alan, 213
Zimmerman, David, 210
Zimmerman, Michael J., 211